Social Empath

SOCIAL EMPATHY

THE ART OF UNDERSTANDING OTHERS

Elizabeth A. Segal

Columbia University Press
New York

Columbia University Press
Publishers Since 1893
New York   Chichester, West Sussex
cup.columbia.edu

Library of Congress Cataloging-in-Publication Data
Names: Segal, Elizabeth A., author.
Title: Social empathy : the art of understanding others /
Elizabeth A. Segal.
Description: New York : Columbia University Press, [2018] |
Includes bibliographical references and index.
Identifiers: LCCN 2018020093 (print) | LCCN 2018022116 (e-book) |
ISBN 9780231545686 (e-book) | ISBN 9780231184809
(hardback : alk. paper)
Subjects: LCSH: Empathy—Social aspects. | Compassion.
Classification: LCC BF575.E55 (e-book) |
LCC BF575.E55 S443 2018 (print) |
DDC 152.4/1—dc23
LC record available at https://lccn.loc.gov/2018020093

Columbia University Press books are printed on permanent
and durable acid-free paper.
Printed in the United States of America

Cover design and illustration: Mary Ann Smith

For my parents, of blessed memory, my guides
to building a life with empathy, humility,
and a commitment to justice

Contents

Preface

I NEVER PLANNED to study empathy. When I trained to be a social worker more than thirty-five years ago, I quickly discovered my passion was in what we call the macro side of practice—understanding communities and public policy. Empathy was for the clinicians and micro practitioners, which I was not. I was fascinated by the how and why behind government social programs. I had a million questions. Why do one in five children grow up in poverty in the richest country in the world? Why did it take one hundred years after the Civil War to pass civil rights legislation? Why are the indigenous people of this country, the first to live here, the poorest group among us? Why do we spend more per person on health care but have levels of health that are far below countries that spend much less? I loved going to my social welfare policy course to try and answer these questions. It was a passion that shaped my professional career. I went on to study political science, public policy, and urban sociology. I even spent a year working in Washington, DC. All these efforts were to help me better understand social public policies.

I became pretty proficient in that effort. I even wrote a textbook on social welfare policies and programs, now in its fourth edition. With all that knowledge, I still hit a snag when teaching about social public policies. I have been teaching for more than thirty years, and the course I have taught most frequently is about social welfare policies and programs. I have taught that course at all levels, from introductory students taking their first college class to graduate students studying to get their doctorate. My primary goals in that course are to help students understand why public policies look the way they do and to answer all those questions that had prompted me to pursue this line of study.

What makes this course special is that we ask what role we each take in the development of these public policies and in the programs that evolve from these policies. Our role as social workers includes a professional commitment to advance human rights. We are mandated to advocate for social, economic, and environmental justice. To do so requires stepping into the shoes of others, not just individually, but also into different social groups and communities to understand their unique experiences.

As much as I taught about being an active member of our community and the importance of seeing the world as others see it, I found some students who "got it" and other students who did not. Some students embraced seeing the world as others do, including the historical experiences of different groups and where they fit in our larger society. Others could not go there. They were comfortable trying to see an individual's perspective, but they could not consider an entire group's experiences. Both types of students were kind and caring people, most of whom were interested in or already committed to a career as a social worker. Why did some of my students feel strongly about the well-being of the larger society, interested in the needs of people who they did not even know, while others stayed away from that? Something was different. That question led me to study empathy and develop the concept of social empathy.

My first public professional mention of social empathy was in 2003 as part of a panel on poverty. I was fortunate to have two colleagues on that panel, Drs. Madelaine Adelman and Keith Kilty, who provided my first professional feedback on the concept. Keith was instrumental in helping me to get the idea published in the *Journal of Poverty* that we coedited at the time. Madelaine was and continues to be a wonderful sounding board and collaborator on developing what social empathy means and how to measure it among students. I am most grateful to Madelaine and Keith for their early critiques and encouragement.

I started a research sabbatical in 2008 with the goal of writing all about social empathy. I had begun to develop more fully the idea of social empathy with several published professional articles exploring the concept, but I didn't know much about interpersonal empathy. When I dove into the literature on empathy, I discovered it was almost entirely focused on individuals, and I became overwhelmed. I was not proficient in psychology or behavioral biology, so the literature was thick and obtuse to me. Luckily, I had a friend and colleague, Dr. Karen Gerdes, who was also on a research sabbatical. We had a plan to meet once a week for breakfast to check in and help each other stay on track with our research projects. Over one of our early breakfasts I shared with Karen my distress over the volume of literature on empathy and that most of it required a better understanding of psychology than I felt I had. Karen was much more proficient in that area, so I asked her if she would be kind enough to do a little reading and help me develop a plan to tackle all that was out there. Karen is one of the most generous and kind people I have ever met, so I knew that asking her would mean a yes. I also did not want to take her off course of her own studies, but I felt at a loss and really needed her guidance. I hoped taking a week away from her studies would not be too much of a burden. Karen agreed to see what was out there and promised to report back at our breakfast the next week. Only a few days had passed when Karen called me to tell me how excited she was from her foray into empathy. She had found a whole new area of research on empathy that was coming from neuroscientists, experts at decoding the intricacies of how our brains work. It was research on empathy and brain imaging in its earliest stages. Karen had already been focused on how we learn and was intrigued by brain science, so this new research was fascinating and inviting to her. Over our next breakfast we talked all about what Karen had found, and over pancakes we both altered our research plans. We decided to forge ahead together to better understand all the aspects of empathy, from psychology, biology, and neuroscience, integrating our perspectives as social workers who study how human beings behave in the larger social environment. We had no idea where it would take us but were both excited to head off in this new direction.

My partnership with Karen grew into a research team and resulted in the most amazing collaborative work I have ever been involved in throughout my career. We were joined by Dr. Cynthia Lietz, an expert on family resilience who connected family well-being to empathy, and two doctoral students who are now professors in their own right, Dr. Alex Wagaman, who is an expert in community practice and helped shape the concepts behind social empathy, and Dr. Jen Geiger, who brought her psychology background and expertise on children and families. Our work led to the development of scales to measure empathy. That collective work is presented in our book *Assessing Empathy*, which provides the scholarship behind our development of scales to measure interpersonal and social empathy. This book on social empathy is built on that work, although I take full responsibility for the content. If there are mistakes or omissions, they are all my doing. But I am deeply indebted to my colleagues for the wisdom, work, and guidance that helped me get to the place of being able to write this book on social empathy.

Social empathy blends the individual ability to read and understand the *feelings* and *actions* of others with an understanding of history, the context within which human behavior happens, and the experiences of different societal groups. This book is designed to answer seven questions and closes with ways that social empathy can be a guide for understanding others to make the world a better place:

- What is empathy?
- Why do we need empathy?
- If it's so important, why is empathy so hard?
- Are power and politics barriers to empathy?
- What if stress, depression, and other physical health factors block empathy?
- Where is religion in empathy?
- Can we have empathy with technology?
- Social empathy—Making the world a better place.

I have tried to explain the concept of social empathy and all the related ideas and research that have guided me in my thinking over the years. The process has been a true labor of love and has given me profound insight into the world. I am deeply indebted to all those who helped me along the way. In addition to my wonderful colleagues, I would like to thank my students and friends, with whom I have shared ideas and tried out early theories. I am thankful for my family, especially my sister, who listened to my theories and helped me develop the ideas in ways that are relevant to current events. I owe my deep interest into understanding others to my parents, who laid the foundation for my thinking on social empathy. I do hope I have captured the content and spirit of all those discussions and influences.

It is my hope that you find the journey through this book as helpful and as inspiring as I found writing it. Thank you for your willingness to explore with me the concept of social empathy.

Social Empathy

CHAPTER ONE

What Is Empathy?

MY PERSONAL INTRODUCTION to the need to study empathy began back in August 2005, although I did not know that at the time. I had the TV news on constantly, watching the horror of Hurricane Katrina from thousands of miles away. The weather maps were interspersed with images of the storm and of residents trying to survive the hurricane. I watched from the very dry comfort of my Arizona home. I had never lived in a hurricane region, and after ten years of living in the desert, rain had become more of a miracle than a danger. I was glued to my TV watching sheets of rain come down in torrents, wind blowing trees horizontal to the ground, and rushing water turning roads into rivers. But what really captivated me was the human drama of survival, and I kept thinking how awful it would be to face such a sudden life-threatening danger. I immediately wondered about what I would do. I hoped I would be brave and help others show empathy and compassion and share what food and water I had. But I honestly thought "hell no, I would do anything I needed to do to survive."

Then came the reports of looting and the commentary on how lawless the people of New Orleans had become. I remember images of people grabbing groceries and bottles of water, stereos and clothing. The pundits condemned these people as ransackers and law breakers. Yet at that moment, I felt certain that I would be among them, taking anything I could. When the stories came in of people helping others, sharing what little water or canned food they had, I was heartened by this generosity and embarrassed by my own first reaction to want to grab whatever I could to survive. At the time I thought there was something wrong with this reaction, that I was not all that compassionate or concerned about the welfare of others. Over the years I have come to understand what I was experiencing. I was having an intense physiological reaction, the drive to survive, while I was watching the events in New Orleans. I later learned that this feeling can go on to be a foundation of empathy but does not guarantee it.

Luckily, I have never faced such a crisis in real life. I hope I never do. But I was enlightened to a side of myself that I had never before directly encountered. It was the realization that for survival I would be willing and able to steal. How could this be? I am a law-abiding citizen, I give to charities regularly, I volunteer my time, I help friends and family, and I am a trained social worker! How could I see myself in the post–Hurricane Katrina stories of looting and pillaging? It has taken years for me to make sense of this uncomfortable realization. I figured it out when I immersed myself in studying empathy.

Fast forward to today. We can see national and world events instantaneously. The news, with pictures and voices from catastrophic events, is available 24/7 on our TVs, smartphones, and computers. We have watched multiple shootings, such as those taking place at a nightclub in Orlando, Florida, and during an outdoor country music festival in Las Vegas. We have also watched people mowed down by a truck driving through crowds out to celebrate a national holiday in Nice, France. Sometimes events are posted on social media before the police are even on the scene. The young people hiding in classrooms at Marjorie Stoneman Douglas High School in Parkland, Florida, recorded and transmitted events live from their smartphones while shots were being fired by the gunman. We feel the horror and pain literally in real time. How do we make sense of our reactions to such events? Are we compassionate or numb? We might also wonder, what could possibly lead a person to commit such heinous crimes, to kill mercilessly? Where is their empathy? As with my struggle to understand my reactions to Hurricane Katrina, I have found studying empathy helps me better understand what may lie beneath some of these deeply disturbing behaviors that suggest a lack of empathy.

What Exactly Is Empathy?

Empathy is often thought of as putting ourselves in the place of others, the proverbial "walk in another's shoes" that requires us to try to understand what another person is thinking or feeling. We sometimes do this through role-playing, a "what if I were you" type of thinking. Yet the literature on empathy is rather diverse. The eminent social psychologist C. Daniel Batson, who has been studying empathy for over thirty years, finds that empathy can be thought of as knowing another person's thoughts and feelings, or it can be feeling the same way that another person feels.[1] The first is a cognitive, or thinking, action and the second is an emotional reaction. Empathy is also described as the physical act of mimicking or mirroring the actions or reactions of another person. This involves little conscious thought; it happens on an unconscious level. In a narrower definition, empathy is experiencing the suffering of others, that is, we share the distress of another.

Sometimes empathy is confused with related emotions, such as sympathy, compassion, pity, or concern. But as I will explain later in this chapter, these emotions might involve empathy but are not the same.

I define empathy as a broad overarching concept that includes two parts: interpersonal empathy and social empathy. Let's start with the narrower application, that of interpersonal empathy. This is the expression of empathy between individuals or in small group settings. It is the most common use of the term "empathy" in research and popular usage. This view of empathy is what you have probably encountered and used in your own life. "I feel your pain" may sound trite, but when someone else understands what you are feeling or what you are going through, you feel "heard" and validated. That is what we know as interpersonal empathy. Interpersonal empathy includes three distinct parts: mirroring the physiological actions of another, taking the other's perspective, and while doing so remembering that the experience belongs to the other and is not our own.[2] Neuroscientists who map brain activity regard interpersonal empathy as the activation of neural circuits in the brain that allow us to do these three things: share another's actions and feelings physically and mentally, process those inputs so we can understand what the other person is experiencing, and at the same time keep our own feelings under control.[3]

I have spent my professional career studying public policy. My work includes analyzing the laws and social welfare programs of our country to see what we do or do not do as a nation that supports people, neglects people, or even hurts people. Throughout my decades of study, I have been struck by the contrast in those policies. We as a nation have had laws that institutionalized treatment of people that demonstrated a lack of empathy, like slavery and segregation. We have also passed laws that have affirmed empathy through the abolition of slavery and promotion of civil rights. Over the years I have asked myself, why at times do we develop policies that seem to lack empathy, while at other times we create policies sensitive to the needs of others? My attempt to answer this question led me to develop the concept of social empathy.

Social empathy is the broader application of interpersonal empathy. It is the ability to understand people and other social groups by perceiving and experiencing their life situations. To do so involves learning about and understanding the historical context of group experiences, including the structural inequalities that have shaped communities. Going back to the example of Hurricane Katrina, using social empathy would require going beyond experiencing what people were going through in those first hours of the crisis. In the days following the hurricane, investigative reporting and continued news coverage helped us to learn about who lived in the flooded neighborhoods, how neglect in the upkeep of the levees contributed to the problem, and how this neglect impacted most severely those who lived in the areas of New Orleans that were poorest and were often not included in planning around emergencies. We also learned that those poor areas were almost entirely made up of African American communities, many of whom were the descendants of slaves and who experienced ongoing discrimination and segregation. These insights helped me to expand my feelings of interpersonal empathy to then experience social empathy, although at the time I did not have the concept of social empathy fully developed.

A full experience of social empathy would have taken me beyond those first moments of viscerally sharing the struggle for survival, and even beyond the later feelings of compassion and concern. Social empathy would have carried me to a place of deeper understanding of what happened. It would have helped me to see the historical conditions that made the immediate moments what they were. Using a socially empathic view of people's experiences can create the type of insight that makes us want to change social conditions, to move us toward building a better world.

Experiencing the impact of Hurricane Katrina secondhand, followed by learning about the social, economic, and political events that contributed to the human and physical devastation helped me to build the concept of social empathy. Social empathy is an emerging area of study that I have promoted over the past fifteen years. By developing our interpersonal empathy skills, we can gain the abilities to be empathic on a broader, social scale. But we need to direct those skills in new ways to develop social empathy. Why is this important? Because greater social empathy will, I believe, promote better social well-being. It is an ambitious goal, but given the evolution of our human capacity to empathize, I believe it is attainable. That is the premise of this book. Throughout, you will see that I use the term "empathy" for an overall description of the engagement of our ability to read others and experience their feelings. I use the terms of "interpersonal empathy" and "social empathy" when I am narrowing in on the specifics of those concepts to differentiate between them. You can assume that the overall term "empathy" applies to both concepts unless specifically noted. In addition, although empathy seems to be found universally, my focus is on interpersonal and social empathy in the United States. That is what I know best. But I hope that the ideas and lessons in this book can inform and guide people from all different cultures and walks of life, and that others will work with the concepts and apply them to those whom they know best.

The Origins of Empathy

In the early 1900s, two psychologists, Theodor Lipps of Germany and Edward Titchener of the United States, are credited with coining the term "empathy." Originally, Lipps borrowed the term *einfühlung* from the art world. At the time, *einfühlung* described the feeling one might have while viewing beautiful works of art or nature, that is, "feeling into" the art. Lipps applied it to human beings and the field of psychology to explain the feelings one has while reflecting the feelings of another person. Titchener took this German concept and developed an English word to match its meaning. He Anglicized the Greek word *empatheia*, which means "in passion" or "in suffering," to create the word "empathy." And he used empathy in the same way that Lipps had.[4]

In this way, empathy became known as the term that described the psychological experience of inner imitation of another person while seeing the actions or experiences of that other person. Once this term had a place in psychology, it was used by later psychologists such as Heinz Kohut and Carl Rogers to influence therapeutic practice. Psychotherapists began to use empathy to describe ways to understand what their clients were truly feeling. However, precise and consistent definitions of empathy were lacking. For example, during the 1970s, more than twenty different definitions of empathy could be found in counseling literature that explored how to be more empathic in therapeutic practice.[5]

Through the 1980s and 1990s, empathy was primarily discussed and researched among social and developmental psychologists. Empathy research was conducted primarily through two avenues: to observe it in people's behaviors, typically in a lab setting, or to ask people to describe their behaviors and then determine if those self-reports showed empathy. Although both methods have weaknesses (just because a person acts a certain way in a laboratory does not mean those same actions will happen out in the real world, and self-descriptions of our behaviors can be biased), a lot of helpful information was gathered about empathy between people. We know this to be the case because of major scientific breakthroughs that came in the early 2000s with the advent of cognitive neuroscience, which verified through brain scans and other modern technologies many of the earlier psychology findings. Cognitive neuroscience is the study of the neural circuits or brain activity behind psychological processes. Over the past fifteen years, cognitive neuroscientists have applied their work on mapping brain activity to learning about the physiological and psychological experiences of being empathic.

Much of the discussion in this book about empathy is built on what we now know through the contributions of cognitive neuroscience. But long before there were brain scans, there were efforts to understand what others were thinking and feeling. For example, religious references to putting ourselves in the place of others can be found across most of today's modern religions, originally dating back thousands of years. One of the famous biblical quotes admonishing us to think about others is "love thy neighbor as thyself," which can be found in both the Old and New Testaments (Leviticus 19:18; Mark 12:31; Luke 10:27). This command could involve parts of empathy, such as taking another person's perspective, but it could also be interpreted as caring and compassion for others in ways that you would like to be cared for yourself. However, such a position may not require you to actually understand what it is that the other person feels. Closer to empathy are the passages "the stranger that dwells with you shall be unto you as the homeborn among you" (Leviticus 19:34) and "do unto others what you would have them do to you" (Matthew 7:12 and in Luke 6:31) suggesting greater imagining of being in the place of another. This perspective of reciprocity in how we deal with others is often referred to as the "Golden Rule" and can be found in many religions. The prophet Muhammad taught "as you would have people do to you, do to them; and what you dislike to be done to you, don't do to them" (Kitab al-Kafi, vol. 2, p. 146). Often the Golden Rule is found in the negative, that is, to take care *not* to treat others in ways you would not like to be treated. This view is sometimes referred to as the "Silver Rule." Confucius included in his philosophical and religious writings the admonition to "never do to others what you would not like them to do to you" (The Analects of Confucius, 6:28). Hindu sacred literature includes the command "let no one do to another that which would be repugnant to oneself" (Mahabharata, bk. 5, ch. 49, v. 57). The Jewish teacher and philosopher Hillel taught "what is hateful to you do not do to others" (Talmud Shabbat 31a).

In light of these writings and teachings, it is surprising that empathic behavior has been absent in so much of human history! Thousands of years of violence across all parts of the world show us that people often treat others in ways that, given the choice, no one would choose to be treated.[6] Those who commit torture, genocide, and enslavement rarely, if ever, see themselves in the same positions as their victims. So how does the long history of religious and philosophical attunement with empathy square with the reality of people's behaviors? Maybe empathy is a goal to be attained, an ability to be worked for. While I think this is partially true, it is also much more complicated. Analyzing the biology, psychology, and social aspects of empathy can help us to understand the apparent disconnect between the Golden Rule, the Silver Rule, and the reality of human history.

Thus, this book is not only a presentation of social empathy as a tool for building a better world but also the story of the journey of human evolution to become empathic with those close to us, with those who are strangers, and even with those who we may consider our enemies. It is not an easy journey, and neither is it a straight line. But today we have more tools to understand empathy, and building on that understanding, we can enhance interpersonal and social empathy within and between people.

The Evolution of Empathy—How Do We Become Empathic?

Although the term is relatively new, "empathy" is actually a key part of human evolution. The noted primatologist Frans de Waal, who has spent decades studying social relations among primates, considers empathy the key to our survival and social living.[7] Empathic ability helps us to read others. Imagine being startled by the scream of someone shouting "fire" and seeing that person running. Even if you did not understand the word "fire," you would likely have a physical reaction to want to run yourself, not thinking about where to go, just mimicking the actions of the other. This is a completely understandable reaction and might be instrumental in saving your life. In early human life, the surrounding world was dangerous, and not heeding the warnings of others would likely have ended in death. There are also more subtle ways that empathy helps with our survival. Remember being scared as a child and having a parent or other adult "read" the fear in your face? When that person responded with soothing words and maybe a hug, the fear passed. You were lucky to have an adult in your life who understood what you were experiencing enough to respond appropriately.

The human infant is completely dependent on other human beings for survival. In fact, this dependence lasts for years, far longer than among most other species. The survival of human young relies most on the ability of caretakers to "read" their needs. Is the child crying because she is hungry? If her cries are interpreted correctly, then the child gets fed and grows. If they are not, she could starve. And that would mean that baby, and likely any other genetic offspring of the caretaker who lacked the ability to read the needs of that baby, would not survive. This relationship is the basis for the survival of so many species. As de Waal writes, "When pups, cubs, calves, or babies are cold, hungry, or in danger, their mother needs to react instantaneously. There must have been incredible selection pressure on this sensitivity: Females who failed to respond never propagated their genes."[8] Thus, the earliest need to be understood by others is part of our survival.

This selection pressure was first articulated by Charles Darwin, considered the father of the science of evolution. Because an infant cannot do anything to care for her- or himself, there is total dependence on adult humans for all things necessary to live. The most important concerns are eating and safety; an infant cannot take care of those needs without humans who are older and have access to resources. Of course, this physiological caretaking is critical for babies to survive, but besides laying the foundation for physical life, this care can be the beginning of babies' learning the emotional parts of life. We have already talked about the emotional attachment that can occur through the caretaking process. Darwin sees other emotional parts of life that emanate from our earliest survival.[9] From a physical perspective, we see two basic skills that had to be mastered for species survival: cooperation and competition.[10] Gathering and hunting are more successful when done in groups, as is protection from the elements, predators, and enemies. The demands for survival encourage such cooperation. At the same time, competition to secure enough for you, your family, and the group that you belong to emerges when there is a real or perceived shortage of those items necessary for survival.

Darwin viewed our struggles between cooperation and competition as similar to animals in a basic sense, but he viewed human beings as having additional abilities that made the survival process much more sophisticated. Darwin is most famous for his assessment of evolution as being based on "survival of the fittest," which describes the process of natural selection in which those who are most likely to reproduce and continue the species are those most likely to survive. This reflects de Waal's point that reproduction would not have happened for those caretakers who did not respond to their offspring's needs. For years I have heard the comment "survival of the fittest" as a way of explaining why some people are successful and others are not. In fact, many have tried to apply Darwin's survival of the fittest to humans to explain why some groups are interpreted to be superior to others based on the success of their lives. Success today is often measured in resources. Explaining survival of the fittest as the reason why some people are rich and others are poor may persist but ignores so many other variables (more on that later, but do think about where people start and what opportunities and advantages come with birth to the right parents—survival of those who start ahead may be more accurate). Social survival of the fittest is not an accurate application of Darwin. Darwin regarded the difference between human beings and animals as the ability to have a moral sense and conscience. Darwin considered our human capacity to develop intellectual powers as the pathway to morality. To balance our social instincts, which can include competition, with our need to be connected to others, we human beings set up rules and codes that help us survive. A society cannot exist when competition runs rampant. Cooperation requires some form of referee to be sure that groups work well enough together to ensure meeting their basic needs for survival. That referee takes the form of our moral and legal codes. For human beings, Darwin felt that our social instincts, our desire to be with others, our intellectual development, and our power of shared language combine to lead us to act for the public good. He felt human beings have an "instinctive sympathy."[11] Although urges to fulfill one's own needs competed with this instinctive sympathy, Darwin believed that "the social instincts—the prime principle of man's[12] moral constitution—with the aid of active intellectual powers and the effects of habit, naturally lead to the golden rule, 'As ye would that men should do to you, do ye to them likewise;' and this lies at the foundation of morality."[13] Finding this quote surprised me. Darwin actually believed that we are naturally empathic and he embraced the Golden Rule! Darwin helps us to see an evolutionary path from basic instinctual survival to advanced moral thinking and a built-in capacity for treating others with understanding.

This evolutionary urge for empathy is based in large part on an unconscious innate reaction called "mirroring." Mirroring is a physiological ability to mimic the actions or emotions of others. The neuroscientist Marco Iacoboni has written a great deal on mirroring and how this ability connects us to other people.[14] This ability is foundational to empathy. Most of us know what mirroring is like. How many times have you seen someone yawn and then, without any conscious thought or plan, you yawn as well? We say that yawning is "contagious," and in a sense, it is.

Mirroring describes what happens in our brain when we see an action being done by someone else and our brain activity is almost identical to what it would be if we were actually performing the action. Our brain mirrors what it is seeing. Is mirroring empathy? No. It can help us to experience what another person is experiencing, but it does not tell us what the other's actions mean or confirm exactly what the other person is feeling. Mirroring is important because it can be the first step in experiencing empathy.

Although by itself mirroring is not the full experience of empathy, it appears to be quite important to us. Think about a time when you shared your emotions with a friend—maybe you were excited and happy because you got a promotion or sad and distraught because you found out about the death of a close relative. In both cases, you would be reassured if your friend reflected back to you your same emotions—happy for you with the promotion or sad with you for your loss. These are socially appropriate forms of mirroring. In fact, research shows that mirroring enhances people's positive social behaviors, both for the giver and for the receiver of mirroring. In a study done in the Netherlands, researchers set up a situation in the center of a busy city in which they approached strangers passing by and asked for help with directions to the local train station.[15] Two different conditions were used, one in which the researchers imitated the body postures, facial expressions, and verbal instructions of the passerby and one in which the researchers simply listened without any mirroring. The results were that those who were mimicked while being randomly stopped on the street and asked for directions were more likely to help the researcher and, unprompted, actually go out of their way to accompany the researcher in the direction of the train station. This field experiment confirmed earlier studies done in laboratory situations in which participants engaged in unrelated activities were more likely to help in small tasks or give charitable donations if the researcher had mirrored the posture and movements of the participants.[16]

These findings should not surprise us. Who wants to share something important with someone else and have them not react at all or react in inappropriate ways? When I am upset and crying, I do not want a friend to laugh at me; it not only feels disconnected, it makes me feel unheard and misunderstood. Thus, mirroring meets another important human need: social connection. Think about a time in your life when you might have been happy or sad and someone you were with seemed to misunderstand how you were feeling. What did that feel like? It might have made you feel angry or upset, and it likely made you feel unimportant. Or it may have made you want to distance yourself from that person. After all, if the person could not connect with what you were really feeling, what was the point of continuing to interact? Now imagine that situation for a child with his or her adult caretakers. What happens if so much of the time when the child is happy, scared, or feeling some emotion, no one reads those feelings correctly? The child might get enough food to eat and live safely enough to survive, but doing so without the emotional connection of someone understanding what the child is feeling can leave the child without an emotional attachment. And what we know about emotional attachment is that it builds a sense of security, which is critical to connecting with others.

The link between empathy and attachment starts at birth. Perhaps the most famous early researcher on attachment among children was the British psychologist Sir John Bowlby.[17] His early life experience of being raised by nannies and separated from his parents during World War I contributed to his interest in child development, particularly how children bond with their caretakers. His work is credited with recognizing that children need connections with their caretakers beyond being fed and sheltered; they need a sense of security and safety. He argued that a child has a better chance at survival and healthy social relations if early life includes a sense of security. Others have built on this concept. The current perspective on attachment is that when we feel secure, it is easier to consider the feelings of others.[18] And when we can consider the feelings of others, we can be empathic. It is circular—without emotional attachment to caregivers at a young age, it is more difficult to do that with others as a person ages. And the cycle continues because those who are empathic are better able to respond to the needs of others, who then feel safe and secure because their needs are met. This is an important cycle to remember, as it comes up in so many examples in which empathy is either promoted or lacking. It is the cycle of "empathy begets empathy"—when we express our empathy, others feel heard and understood, and they in turn feel more inclined to hear and understand others. Consequently, for children, such empathy helps them to develop their own empathy. I do want to note, though, that it is not a guaranteed process. Being cared for and about does enhance empathic abilities, but there are so many variables that contribute to empathy that we cannot say it is a definite outcome. Later in the book you will find conditions that counter early attachment and can block empathy. But for now, it is fair to say that, in general, it is more likely that a child whose needs are met by an empathic caregiver will him- or herself grow up with empathic abilities.

The Neurobiology of Empathy

So where does empathy happen? We now know that the actions that contribute to us being empathic can be traced through brain activity. The processes of the brain can only be seen through sophisticated imagery, most commonly through functional magnetic resonance imaging (fMRI). The process uses noninvasive measures of blood flow to observe changes in brain activity. We now know that being empathic involves both an unconscious biological process that we are typically unaware of and a way of thinking that is taught or socialized. Both processes happen through the engagement of multiple regions and networks within our brains. Your doorbell rings and you open the door to see your best friend standing there crying. She had called ahead and told you that she was having a hard day, wondering if she could stop by for a few minutes. You open the door, see your friend crying, and immediately feel yourself tearing up. She tells you that she just found out that her grandmother died. You then have an image of your own grandmother, who died the year before. In that moment, you understand emotionally what your friend is feeling. To you, this is all immediate and instantaneous.

While it feels instantaneous, the unconscious and conscious parts are separate reactions. The two processes occur milliseconds apart. It is impossible for us to be aware of it in real time. Try this experiment some time. Take a hammer, and in front of another person, act as if you are going to hit your thumb. In fact, did just reading that statement make you flinch or cringe a bit? It is likely that the sight of a hammer near a finger will elicit a physical and emotional response. What is happening here is the experience of several pieces of empathic response that feel as one but really are the combination of several brain actions. There is the knowledge of what a hammer is, the memory of what happens when a hammer makes unwanted contact with a hand, and the reaction of what pain feels like. All of this can happen in our brain without anything happening other than seeing an image—or even just hearing a story that creates that image in our mind. Thanks to neuroscience research, we know more about how empathy works because we can identify specialized or additional activity that fires in brain regions when we think thoughts or perform actions that demonstrate empathy.

There is no one exact place in the brain nor one specific set of brain actions that represent empathy. Numerous brain regions and neurological actions are involved when people express empathy.[19] Maybe someday there will be research that identifies the exact brain action that is empathy, but I doubt it. After studying the neuroscience literature that has blossomed over the past fifteen years, I am convinced that interpersonal empathy is the collection of five different but overlapping abilities, and that social empathy builds on those with two additional abilities. These seven abilities, or components, are what neurologically come together to create the full scope of empathy, which includes interpersonal and social connections. These components are not fixed and exact. The strength or depth of each may vary by person or situation and fluctuate and change. But with the research we have, it is pretty convincing that combining these physiological and psychological actions can result in empathy. The following five behaviors, referred to as components, come together to help us express interpersonal empathy: affective response, affective mentalizing, self-other awareness, perspective-taking, and emotion regulation. When two other components are added, contextual understanding and macro perspective-taking, we can expand our insights to include social empathy.

The Components of Interpersonal and Social Empathy

I have sketched out the five components of interpersonal empathy in figure 1.1. All the arrows are meant to show this is a dynamic process with brain activity moving among abilities and shifting in emphasis depending on the situation. The five interpersonal empathy components (affective response, affective mentalizing, self-other awareness, perspective-taking, and emotion regulation) can vary in intensity and may be differently developed or triggered at various times. Together they give us a complete sense of interpersonal empathy. However, to this point in our knowledge about empathy, it is difficult to say how much of or how deeply each component is triggered to result in the best "recipe" for engaging in interpersonal empathy. But our research suggests that each is important and contributes to the full extent of interpersonal empathy. Each component is related to the others. When all five are engaged, we see the full scope of interpersonal empathy. That does not mean we are not interpersonally empathic without all five components at full speed, but to be able to take in the experiences

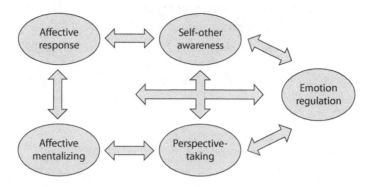

Figure 1.1 Interpersonal empathy

of others most fully, we need them all. Some situations will demand stronger engagement, while other situations will depend on only a few of the components. In figure 1.2 I have added the two components that complement interpersonal empathy and that reflect social empathy, contextual understanding, and macro perspective-taking. These additional components require that we expand our abilities to take in

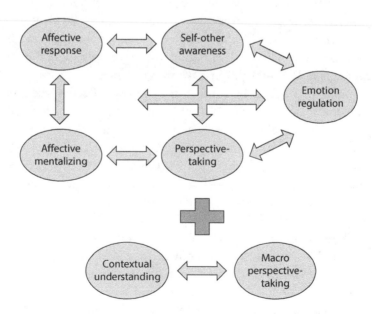

Figure 1.2 Social empathy

information about others that includes their differing life situations, the history of their life experiences, and the history of the groups to which they belong. What is valuable about understanding the full scope of empathy as the expression of these seven components is that we can track and monitor our own experience of connecting to others. We can also teach about empathy in understandable ways, component by component.

Affective Response and Affective Mentalizing

Suddenly an ambulance siren wails and we jump; we see a baby fall and we pick him up; we turn a corner and smell fresh bread baking. All of these signals touch us through our senses, such as our hearing, sight, or smell. We immediately have a reaction, and it is initially unconscious—we are unaware. This reaction is referred to as *affective response*.[20] Sometimes there is no actual physical stimulus like a sound or smell, but we have an affective response anyway. This is because we can imagine the sound or smell. Think back to the earlier description of a hammer hitting a hand—that description might have invoked your own feeling of being hit by a hammer. When we are thinking about an experience or told about another person's experience, we can go into *affective mentalizing*. Affective mentalizing can take place without direct experience. This is what happens when we read a good book. We enter into the character's situation and develop a mental image of the experience. We might even have physiological reactions that mirror the imagined affect. Like affective response, affective mentalizing is neurologically observable.[21] Much of what happens with these two components is unconscious; we are not aware that our brain is firing neurons that imitate the action we are seeing or imagining.

Affective mentalizing is a bridge between affective experiences and cognitive reasoning, the connection between what we might think about while we are experiencing feelings or sensations. Take the example of hearing an ambulance siren. When I lived in a big city, I heard sirens often and got to a point where the sound did not even register in my conscious mind. When I moved to a small town, it was rare that I heard a siren. When one went off, I consciously tuned in to hear if it was getting louder and closer and would visualize a vehicle racing off with lights flashing. What is the difference? Awareness of context. The circumstances surrounding the affective response you are unconsciously processing can cause you to shift into cognitive or conscious thinking. So too are the next three components engaged more consciously.

Self-Other Awareness

We have *self-other awareness* when we identify with another person but still have a clear sense of our self. This may sound simple, but at times it can be difficult. Have you ever gotten caught up in the moment of someone else's emotions and later wondered why you were so emotional when it was not your concern? You might have been swept up in the affective response of the moment. Having self-other awareness means we can separate the experiences, feelings, and meanings that belong to others from the feelings that belong to us.[22] To do this requires a good sense of self, or agency, and at the same time insight into how others are in charge of their own agency. In professional behavioral health settings, this is called having "strong boundaries." Psychotherapists who hear people's life stories in the most intimate and emotional ways need strong self-other awareness. Who wants a therapist who just mirrors all our emotions? It might make us feel heard and understood, but we want that professional person to stay separate and objective.

Why is self-other awareness so important to empathy? It keeps us from becoming overwhelmed or distracted by our own emotions. It helps us to shift our focus away from our own feelings to consider others. In fact there is a term for the lack of self-other awareness: "emotional contagion."[23] Emotional contagion is a feeling that we "catch" from others. Remember in grade school when someone started giggling and then others "caught" it and started giggling too? You may not have known what was going on, but you were swept up with the emotions of others. And it can be awfully hard to stop, even when you know that there is no reason to be giggling. There is a dark side to emotional contagion; when it happens in big groups and includes anger, we refer to it as "mob mentality": an emotional response spreads through a crowd of people, many of whom do not even consciously understand the reason for their behaviors. Being able to distinguish between ourselves and others when there is an external stimulus is the difference between empathy and emotional contagion. But self-other awareness is not enough to move us from having an affective response to having empathy.

Perspective-Taking

Keeping our self-other awareness strong while figuring out what is happening to another person requires an additional skill: *perspective-taking*.[24] We often refer to perspective-taking as "walking a mile in another's shoes." This means we can imagine what it would be like to be in the situation of another person. It is a form of mentally toggling back and forth between being in someone else's situation and being in your own. However, we may think we are taking the perspective of someone else, but without strong self-other awareness, we process the experience as what it means to ourselves and not to the other person. The difference here is very important. We might think we are empathic, but instead we are viewing things from our own point of view.

I find a common example of this when I teach students about people receiving public assistance, often referred to as people on welfare.[25] I often hear points like this: "Why don't they get a job? I know working at a fast food restaurant is not ideal, but I do after school, so why can't they? That's the way out of poverty." This is what I would call weak perspective-taking. We start with walking in another's shoes, but then there is a switch. We think "what would I do if I were *me*" and not "what would I do if I were *you*." This is a difficult distinction to make. It may be the hardest part of empathy. There is no way that we can know everything about another person, especially a stranger. It is very understandable to use our own experiences when imagining being in a different situation, but that is not empathy. If it is true that we can never fully know about the situation and experiences of another person, how can we ever be empathic? We can, but it takes work.

Let's go back to the example of people receiving welfare. Students who have never lived the life of someone on public assistance may be at a loss to understand what choices there are to make and what forces there are that block those choices. This is where social empathy comes in. The two components of social empathy help us overcome the tendency to think about what might fit for us in a given situation rather than what might fit for the other person. But before we get to those components, there is one more interpersonal empathy component that makes all the others work: *emotion regulation*.

Emotion Regulation

In figure 1.1 emotion regulation is out to the side with arrows pointing in all directions. That is because emotion regulation tempers all the other components. It is the calmness or balance that we achieve when entering the world of emotions. Rather than getting swept up with emotions, as with emotional contagion, we still feel emotions, maybe even very strongly, but we don't get swept away by our emotions. We are able to take control and adapt our feelings appropriately to whatever is happening around us. For example, if someone says something to make us angry, we may want to hit that person, but with effort we do not. The reason emotion regulation is so important is that when we stay in control of our feelings, we are more likely to be empathic.[26]

Getting all these components to engage with balance is not easy. Doing so and taking it beyond our individual world is even harder. When we do that, we engage in social empathy. To be empathic on a broader scale, we need to include two more components, gaining contextual knowledge and moving our perspective-taking skills to a broader level.

Understanding Context and Macro Perspective-Taking

Social empathy is broader than interpersonal empathy. We live in a complicated social world. The numerous events and people we come into contact with daily present a lot of information to process, which it turns out can impact our experience of empathy.[27] Social empathy has us look at context so we can fully understand the lived experiences of groups different from our own. And context includes the historical events that shaped the group and contributed to its members' identities today. It is especially important to recognize the challenges and obstacles that other groups have faced. When we talk about "walking in another's shoes" from a social empathy perspective, that means trying to fully comprehend what came before that may have influenced the way groups behave today. For example, in the United States, we need to ask what impact the experience of slavery may have had on the way African Americans are treated or see our society today. This is not easy. It may require looking at historical events we would rather not review because of the discomfort it may bring. We may also feel that the past is long ago, and events that happened to people who lived decades or centuries ago is not part of today's world. It requires both the desire and the interest to learn about people who are different. The resistance to do this can be great, due in part to our evolutionary tribal fear of others, which we will talk about more in depth in chapter 3.

If we can master contextual understanding, we can use our interpersonal empathy perspective-taking skills (and self-other awareness) to walk in the shoes of another. But social empathy perspective-taking is broader; it is taking in a macro or large-scale view of situations. We consider the impact of external factors. One way to do this is by putting ourselves in the situations of others who are different, whether by race, gender, sexual orientation, ability, age, class background, or other characteristics.

Although this is hard, it has a lot of positive potential. Research shows us that broader perspective-taking increases social connections and decreases group stereotyping.[28] When we apply perspective-taking to larger social groups, we can build positive social engagement. For example, the U.S. Army, in order to better prepare personnel to serve in other countries, introduced "social perspective-taking" by military trainers.[29] This training was designed to help soldiers understand the host nation's perspective without their own personal biases. While we might argue whether this has been effective, it is a huge jump in military preparation from centuries of military conflicts in which personnel took little heed of the cultures in which they were immersed to today acknowledging cultural differences and that we are entering another country's culture.

With the full understanding of all the components of interpersonal and social empathy, we can return to the welfare example. How much do we really know about what it is like to grow up poor and rely on public assistance to meet all our survival needs? In 1996, the U.S. Congress passed sweeping welfare reform legislation, the Personal Responsibility and Work Opportunity Reconciliation Act (PRWORA), which famously claimed to "end welfare as we know it." The changes placed many limits on existing welfare programs. At the time, I had done a lot of research on poverty and had interviewed many people who lived financially on the edge and relied on government assistance to feed and shelter themselves and their families. I was taken aback by the direction of the new legislation. The people I had come to know worked hard to make it through each day and were not living a life of luxury. I remember one woman I worked with who spent a lot of time tracking the price of a pound of rice at all the surrounding grocery stores and then calculating how much the bus fare to each store would cost and whether it was worth it to travel for lower prices with the bus fare figured in. And she did this for every item she bought for her family by finding discarded copies of newspaper ads. This was years before personal computers! I was impressed. Even in my poorest student days, I never worked that hard to make my money stretch. I did not have to—I had a safety net, my family. This mother barely finished high school. She had no safety net. She had two young children. In fact, two-thirds of the recipients of welfare were children, most under the age of seven. The end of welfare as we knew it was the end of a program that was, for the most part, serving young children.

I looked at the lived experiences of the people on welfare as I analyzed the reform legislation. In 2006, ten years later, there was a lot of publicity about the "success" of the reform. The goal of ending welfare as we knew it was "proven" by the decrease in numbers—from 12.3 million recipients in 1996 to 5.1 million in 2005. But deeper analysis I did proved disturbing—before welfare reform, 80 percent of poor families who were eligible received aid; by 2006, only 48 percent did.[30] There were still poor families. We did nothing to change that, we just found a way to get them off welfare. But where did they go? A lot did find employment, but most had low-income jobs. The number of children who were poor did not change, and these children fared the worst. Welfare used to serve two-thirds of poor children, but now we only cover one-fifth, and the rest must fend for themselves. How could we develop a new policy that so completely ignored the needs of young children? Where was the empathic insight that might have informed policy makers?

I went back and looked at the political players in Congress who passed the 1996 welfare reform.[31] While adult welfare recipients at the time were 90 percent female, the members of Congress who passed the legislation were 85 percent male. These women on welfare averaged thirty-one years old, almost all of them only had a high school education, and none of them were millionaires. The members of Congress were on average fifty-five years old, 93 percent of them had more than a high school education, and 30 percent of them were millionaires.

Two-thirds of welfare recipients were people of color, while almost 90 percent of the members of Congress were white. Finally, the majority of recipients overall were younger than eight years old. Who took their perspective? This research was a social empathy "aha" moment for me. The politicians who were making these legislative changes lived lives vastly different from those who were the recipients of these changes. I was struck by how little contextual understanding was involved. Where was the help for young children that these families so desperately needed? Instead, now the adults on the program had to be away from home for more hours a week trying to find jobs. Who would take care of their young children? In fact, while the bill was debated in the House of Representatives prior to the final vote, only eight legislators (out of the 435) even mentioned children.[32] Instead, the adults receiving welfare were seen as freeloaders. Frank Riggs, a member of Congress from California, remarked that the bill "addresses a fundamental issue in American society, and that is the resentment of working individuals toward able-bodied individuals who refuse to get off the dole." John Kasich from Ohio commented that now the system "is going to ask the able-bodied to get out and begin to work themselves" because, as Tom DeLay of Texas stated, "welfare should not be a way of life . . . welfare has not worked." Who were these able-bodied folks on the dole? Two-thirds of all welfare recipients were young children who of course could not work. The other third were their parents, most of whom were single mothers who lacked education. Where were child care, health insurance, and educational opportunities for mothers? The only thing these legislators were interested in was getting people off welfare. Thus, for the first time in the sixty-year history of the program, legislators put a time limit on receiving benefits.[33]

It should not be surprising, then, that almost 80 percent of the men in the House of Representatives voted for it, while only 54 percent of the women did. I had research that showed the value of contextual understanding and macro perspective-taking, or at least the lack of it. This study on welfare reform was the impetus for me to study empathy on a broader, societal level. I could not get the memory of the families I had personally come to know to square with the changes being made in welfare legislation. I was searching for a way to explain how policy makers could be so out of touch with the lives of people for whom they were making policies. I began to delve into studying empathy more broadly. Now, more than ten years later, I think I have a better understanding of one of the factors that contributed to the passage of the legislation: there was a lack of social empathy. This book is the full explanation of what social empathy means, what happens when we lack social empathy, and what good can be done when we use social empathy.

Pulling All the Components Together

Thanks to cognitive neuroscience studies, the brain regions, neural pathways, and reactions that physiologically contribute to the experience of empathy have been identified. Cognitive neuroscientists have mapped brain activity that corresponds with what researchers, after decades of observing animals' and people's behaviors, have called "empathy." Fifteen years is a short time for scientific discovery, so we are likely only beginning to combine neurology and psychology to advance our understanding of empathy. But this beginning helps us to understand the biological imperative to survive and how empathy fits in that struggle.

It is important to remember that empathy is contextual, both on the personal level and in our larger society. Contexts change, and so do our interpretations. Even for the same person, empathic awareness can vary depending on the situation. Consider how hard it is to feel someone else's sadness when you are sad yourself. Or you might be in a great mood and don't care to hear about someone else's trouble. Maybe you are very tired and don't have the energy to engage in all the complexity of being empathic. It may take years and a lot of conscious effort to fully develop empathic abilities. Empathy is not easy to master, but understanding the components gives us a picture of what the full scope of empathy looks like. We can train ourselves and others to become skilled empathically, component by component. And now that we have the ingredients for empathy, we can identify emotions and behaviors that are often confused with empathy.

What Is Not Empathy?

Of course not every emotion we share with people is empathy. There are a number of different terms people use that they think refer to empathy but do not. Pity is feeling bad for other people or having sorrow about their situations. For example, when we see pictures of malnourished children in Africa or earthquake survivors in Haiti, we may feel terrible about their life conditions but have no connection to those images in a putting-ourselves-in-their-place perspective. Besides only conveying sadness (as opposed to feeling a full range of positive and negative emotions belonging to other people), pity involves feeling *about* another person, not with or in their shoes. Pity might move you emotionally to delve deeper and engage in empathy, but not necessarily.

Similarly, "personal distress" is a term that has been used in the empathy literature to describe feeling another's pain or discomfort. In some earlier work on empathy, personal distress was considered a key attribute of empathy. However, personal distress is when we feel someone's pain but then focus on the uncomfortable or distressing feelings that it creates in ourselves.[34] Suppose that a colleague at work comes over to your desk to talk to you about how depressed he is about the death of his mother. You have a deadline to meet, which is stressing you out, and you are uncomfortable about the topic because your own mother is getting older and you don't want to think about her dying. This experience does not make you feel empathic; instead it feels upsetting and disruptive. The result is that you experience personal distress. In fact, when we are in personal distress, we are more likely to try and avoid contact so we don't have to deal with the discomfort or anxiety of feeling pity. Avoiding other people's feelings and being self-focused are not empathy.

The idea of personal distress as a key aspect of empathy was so strong that one of the most well-known instruments to measure empathy, the Interpersonal Reactivity Index (IRI) created in 1980,[35] includes personal distress as part of empathy. However, over the years, many researchers have chosen to drop the part of the instrument that measures personal distress. We now know through cognitive neuroscience research that capacities for self-other awareness and emotion regulation are needed for empathy. These abilities help us to not get overwhelmed with personal distress or feelings of pity.[36]

"Sympathy" is another term that often is used when people mean empathy. When we feel bad for a person, we are sympathetic, but without any of the other components that create empathy. Only feeling bad for someone else because of the situation the person is in lets us stay removed from actually sharing their feelings. Without self-other awareness and perspective-taking, we stay apart from the other person.

We might be moved to help, but the distance can also make us come across as condescending or patronizing rather than achieving and communicating true understanding. For example, I have no doubt that the former First Lady Barbara Bush was a wonderful, loving woman who could be very compassionate. But after Hurricane Katrina, when people were evacuated from New Orleans and temporarily put up in the Astrodome in Houston, she visited as part of an effort to raise money to help the victims. While there, she commented that "so many of the people here were underprivileged anyway, this is working very well for them."[37] I am sure she did not say that with any malice; she simply had no idea that although people were poor, they still had places they called home that were destroyed and they had lost whatever life possessions they had. She was there to raise money, showing that she was willing to help people in need, but she was not at all relating to their situation or lives. Without any real personal connection to those who live in poverty, how can we possibly understand what their lives are like?

A more recent example of this lack of connection to the lived experiences of others was on display in a tweet posted by Speaker of the House of Representatives Paul Ryan in 2018. Speaker Ryan, who has often talked about his concern for those who are financially less fortunate and struggle to make ends meet, retweeted a post to show how great the recent tax reform plan was for Americans.[38] He retweeted a post by a high school secretary in which she had noted her surprise that she would be getting an extra $1.50 a week from the big tax cut plan. Ryan took it as evidence of the tax cut plan's success. But the backlash on public media was swift and severe. He was chastised for being out of touch because an extra $78 a year was so very little, especially compared to the tax breaks and extra money that would come to high-income earners and the wealthy. Ryan must have heard his detractors because he deleted the tweet within a couple of hours and said nothing. His post on Twitter demonstrated a lack of empathic insight, particularly a lack of contextual understanding. This example also reflects the dynamic of power impeding empathy, and that is discussed in more detail in chapter 4.

We can be compassionate but still not be empathic. Compassion evokes charitable feelings about the plight of others, but it too is concerned only with distressing situations. We do not have compassion for people who are happy and doing well. Compassion is focused on people's pain or distress. Some of the components of empathy, such as self-other awareness, perspective-taking, and even emotion regulation, might come into play, but there is not a shared experiencing of another person's emotions or life situation.[39] We tend to have compassion for those less fortunate, often because we are in a better situation. I am not saying empathy is better than compassion or sympathy, just that these are different emotions and should not be confused as meaning the same thing. Two prominent empathy researchers from the Laboratory for Social and Neural Systems Research in Zurich, Switzerland, Tania Singer and Claus Lamm, state it well: "The crucial distinction between the term *empathy* and those like *sympathy*, *empathic concern*, and *compassion* is that empathy denotes that the observer's emotions reflect affective sharing ('feeling with' the other person) while compassion, sympathy, empathic concern denotes the observer's emotions are inherently other oriented ('feeling for' the other person)."[40]

Is Empathy Too Emotional?

The title of Paul Bloom's book *Against Empathy* is certainly provocative, and in it he argues that empathy is too emotional and leads us to make bad decisions.[41] His position is that we should not rely on empathic feelings; instead we need to be rational but compassionate. Bloom bases his arguments on the view that empathy is "the act of coming to experience the world as you think someone else does"[42] and that this emotional sharing is subject to bias, unfairness, and overly emotional reactions. Instead of empathy, he advocates compassionate rationality: "I want to make a case for the value of conscious, deliberative reasoning in everyday life, arguing that we should strive to use our heads rather than our hearts."[43] I don't disagree with Bloom's goal of recognizing our biases and the need for us to control our emotions to make sound and compassionate decisions. I disagree with Bloom in that I think the full scope of empathy does just that. Thanks to the work of neuroscience, we know that empathy is complex and includes multiple skills, which I describe as components. Missing from Bloom's characterization of empathy is self-other awareness, which helps us to not assume we know what another person is feeling; emotion regulation, which helps us to be calm and level headed and not get swept up in the other person's emotions or situation; contextual understanding, which broadens our view of what the other person is experiencing; and macro perspective-taking, which has us imagine what it is like to live the lives of members of other groups different from our own, pushing us to take into account all the historical and social experiences that shaped that group. Bloom wants us to use our head, not our hearts. That is exactly what empathy does—we take physiological inputs that happen to us unconsciously and process the meaning of those sensations using our brain. That is empathy.

Empathy is a tool; it provides us information. What we do with that information is up to us. It can open a door to take action. A great deal of research shows that empathy-induced action is often positive (which is discussed in detail in chapter 2). But taking action is learned as a result of empathy as a next step. Empathy itself is the process, it's what we do with it that is the conscious decision making that we learn over a lifetime. But if we do not recognize the full process of empathy, the physiological triggers, the split-second processing that goes on in our minds, the pitfalls to interpreting our empathic feelings, the need to take in context, then we will fall into the space of irrational emotionalism that Bloom describes.

Together the Components Make Us Fully Empathic

We are empathic when all the components come together. That is not to say it is all or nothing. Each component of interpersonal and social empathy contributes to deeper awareness and understanding of others. Building each part can help us better understand others, even if we cannot command all components fully all the time. But that building process should be directed toward engaging in the full scope of empathy. We know that our bodies react without thinking. This reaction is triggered by our brain mimicking what we see. If we have the neural pathways for empathy, we share the feeling, realize it is not our own but try to step into it as if we are the other person, and do all of this without losing control of our emotions. We are then open to understanding what the other person is feeling and experiencing. We might go further and seek to understand what historical events contributed to who that person is today and what it might be like to live as that other person. Once we do all that, we can decide whether to take action, action that is based on what the other person might need. Such action connects us to others and, repeated over and over by millions of other people, can lead to living in a world of caring and understanding between people of all different backgrounds and experiences. We will see in chapter 2 that empathy can be the driver of good behavior. Because of that connection, understanding empathy and how to share it with others can be the tool to make our world a better place.

CHAPTER TWO

Why Do We Need Empathy?

Beyond Survival

We need others to help us survive, and our ability to "read" people enhances the likelihood that our survival will be successful. The survival of a species like ours requires two important skills related to empathy. First, we must be able to pick up the cue of fear from others. Second, we must recognize that our offspring have needs that we must take care of, and we must follow through with that care. But feeling and responding to fear and reading another person's needs do not necessarily make us empathic. Those are important tools, but they do require further training and abilities to fully develop into empathy. In addition, having our basic survival needs met thanks to the efforts of a caregiver does not necessarily mean we have experienced receiving someone else's empathy. Empathy goes beyond the mirroring of others or the recognition of basic needs, although both are very important as building blocks for empathy.

After years of research, I believe that empathy is a very advanced ability. As human beings, empathy gives us more than our survival; it also supports our growth and prosperity. Empathy takes us beyond adapting for survival to thriving, which can lead us to a fully lived life. Thriving, the opportunity to prosper and flourish, is what pushes human beings to accomplish great things. Being skilled in interpersonal and social empathy means that a person is more likely to successfully navigate social situations, and in the process feel a sense of well-being. This is a tall order. Developing the full array of empathy is not easy. Even with all the components of empathy developed, at times we face situations in which it is difficult to call on those skills. I am not saying that empathy is the perfect answer to a better life, but it certainly helps us to live in a more cooperative, safe, and fulfilling way. And research tells us that the lack of empathy is an obstacle to adapting and thriving. We need empathy to achieve the highest sense of ourselves as individuals. When we enhance empathy across groups, we create communities that are cohesive, caring, and successful. That may seem too simplistic, but in this chapter I will walk us through the ways that empathy enhances our personal lives, our communities, and ultimately our global connections.

Belonging

Feeling like you are part of something larger than yourself, part of a family, tribe, team, religious group, or community, is a reflection of our deeply engrained sense of how best to survive. It starts with the earliest sense of making a connection with another person. The theory most referred to when we talk about people connecting with each other, typically learned at an early age, is *attachment theory*.[1] Attachment theory posits that being able to connect emotionally from a young age leads to healthy development. It helps an infant, and later a child, feel secure in his or her surroundings. Building a bond with someone who cares for us helps us to make sense of the world around us. We can go out and explore knowing that if it gets too scary, we have a secure base to return to, literally and emotionally. What makes attachment so important to empathy? When we are secure in our sense of connection to others, it is easier to consider the feelings of others, while when we are insecure, we have little emotional room to think about and take in the feelings of others.[2] In fact, this connection between attachment and empathy starts early in life, as early as birth.[3] Built on mirroring and response to needs, empathy is reflected in the way care-takers interact with babies. When infants cry and then are held or fed, babies begin to experience a connection with those around them. This connection shows them that they are heard and that their needs will be met, and a sense of security develops. It is also a modeling of empathic response—you have a feeling and someone consistent in your life reads that feeling correctly. Of course, as any parent can tell you, correctly understanding exactly what a baby wants can be very difficult at times. But the effort to stay with it and assure the infant that a protective response is there builds the sense of attachment.

How do we know that attachment is key to thriving from a very early age? In the kind of social experiment that no one would ever conduct because it is unethical and horrible to consider, we would see if babies who were not responded to emotionally would not thrive and develop empathy. Unfortunately, such a social experiment did occur, although it was not done intentionally. In 1989, the people of Romania revolted and overthrew the government of the dictator Nicolae Ceaușescu. His regime had, among other things, warehoused children who were considered orphans in institutions that took care of the children's physical needs but, due to staffing shortages and a phi-losophy of care that was focused almost entirely on basic physical care, neglected to provide emotional support and the kinds of caretaker/child interactions that foster attachment. For example, the style of care included feeding done on a uniform schedule, not according to the babies' needs, with bottles propped up in place without the touch of a human being. Children were clean, but there were no organized social or emotional interactions. A team of experts in child development chronicled the experiences of the children raised in these orphanages and followed their development for almost twenty years as some were moved into foster care and others remained institutionalized.[4] It is the kind of research that probes the depths of human development in con-ditions that provide for physical care but are devoid of the emotional interactions that build attachment and emotional security. Among the findings was that the neural development of these children, especially the ones who remained in institutionalized care, was significantly less than seen in noninstitutionalized children. Their brain matter was actually smaller, and they experienced delays in cognitive development and socialization. Their ability to attach was also disrupted, likely as a result of emotional neglect and poor brain development.

For the children in the Romanian orphanages, the emotional connections to caretakers and the physiological development of their brains were greatly diminished. Socialization for attachment and the neural development of the brain are critical for the development of the components necessary for empathy. Children need to experience mirroring in order to tap into their affective responses, develop understanding of the self, learn to take the perspective of others, and develop emotion regulation. Recent research on children and their relationships to their parents found that those children who were secure in their early attachment demonstrated greater empathy.[5] This research went further and looked at how well they got along with their peers. Children who were both insecure in their attachment and unempathic interacted poorly with their peers. That is not surprising. But here is what was most interesting: for those children who were unempathic but securely attached, their behaviors with peers were more positive. This is fascinating research because it suggests that it is attachment security that helps children interact in positive ways, even if they have not yet developed strong empathy. While much more research needs to be done, it may be that the positive socialization of secure attachment comes first or may not depend on empathic abilities, at least in early childhood. However, we are fairly sure that empathy is aided by secure attachment and may even need that security to fully develop as children age.

This suggests that the relationship between empathy and attachment goes both ways. Having attachment abilities allows us to be empathic, while receiving empathy allows us to learn how to be attached. Secure attachment encourages and supports empathy, and it is the efforts of a caretaker to respond to our needs that models empathy, all of which promotes security. For the most part, the process of building empathy starts with the adult being able to recognize the child's needs. Without some level of caretaker empathy, it is very difficult to develop strong attachment and pass on the learning of empathy.

Empathy Is Key to Why We Do Good

So why does empathy matter? One very important reason is that empathy promotes positive behavior. Doing "good" can mean a lot of different things to different people. It can be helping others, contributing to a larger cause, performing acts of kindness, or simply being nice to other people. Psychology calls positive interactions between people *prosocial behavior*. Having empathy does not guarantee that a person will act in a supportive and helpful way, but it does push us in that direction. A number of behaviors that we consider positive and prosocial are associated with empathy: altruism, cooperation, compassion, morality, and justice. There is even research suggesting that empathy is related to happiness and deepened by adversity. Not all good behaviors involve empathy. We behave in prosocial ways, such as by doing good so people will think well of us or so we will feel good about ourselves, neither of which requires empathy. Although prosocial actions do not require empathy, with empathy we are more likely to act in prosocial ways.

Altruism—"I Did It for You"

Sometimes people do good things for other people when the actions do not directly benefit them. We refer to this as *altruism*.[6] A great deal of research has been conducted on this behavior because it seems counterintuitive that we might put ourselves at risk for the sake of others given our human desire for personal safety and security. One theory about this tendency is *kin selection*, which holds that the best means for your genetic long-term survival is to be sure that your offspring and closest kin survive. The strong desire to pass on the genetic line may be built into us as the result of those with strong kin selection survival drive keeping their descendants alive to go on and reproduce and thus maintain the species over time.[7] Because empathy is the skill that helps us to read the needs of those who we might risk our lives to protect, it plays a role in kin selection. Kin selection helps to explain why parents would put their lives on the line for their children.

In addition to genetic continuation of the species, there are more biological dimensions to empathy. The world-renowned primatologist Frans de Waal regards empathy as the emotional connection that makes altruism possible,[8] and it is rooted in our biological evolution.[9] We know that from a biological perspective we have evolved as a species that wants to connect with others. Empathy provides a way to create deep and lasting bonds, fulfilling our underlying need to belong and creating connections. That empathic connection is what motivates us to engage in the costly individual sacrifices of altruistic behavior.

In other words, if over time we get closer and closer to another person (typically in early life that would be with our adult caregivers) and form an attachment that is enhanced by reading each other's needs and feelings, we are more deeply concerned with their survival as well as our own. This deep concern will prompt us to do things to protect and care for those who we are close to, as they will do for us.

Although empathy and altruism are connected, a word of caution: that relationship is stronger for those we know rather than those who are strangers, likely as a result or in some way related to kin selection and the tribal background of human beings. This distance we feel from strangers is often referred to as "otherness" or the degree to which we do not see ourselves reflected in the other person.[10] There are numerous reasons we don't see ourselves in others, and we will fully explore those reasons in chapter 3. But for now, think about the distance between different races, ethnic groups, and religions. Those are examples of otherness in our world today. When we do not see a similarity or shared humanity with others, we are less likely to be connected through empathy. Lacking this connection, we are also less likely to behave in prosocial ways. So altruism is definitely related to empathy, and barriers to empathy contribute to barriers to altruism.

Learning to Be Empathic

Kin selection suggests something happening at a deep unconscious level. It may have originally been learned in the sense that only those who practiced it passed on their genetic material, building the inclination into each successive generation. But we also learn how to read others, which enhances our chances for survival. When knowledge of how to behave is taught, we regard this as social learning. Social science has long debated how much of who we are is a result of our inherited genetic makeup and how much is a product of what we have learned while growing up. As with other human behaviors, this is a difficult distinction to make in terms of empathy. Are we born with the ability to be empathic or do we learn it? The likely answer is yes to both. We are born with the mechanisms to mirror others and we physically develop brain matter and neural pathways needed for cognitive processing. Learning to use our cognitive processing, the thinking parts of our brain, gives us the mental capacity to think outside ourselves, which is needed for empathy.

Over thousands of years, human beings inherited the genetics best suited to survival and learned from each other what to eat, how to be safe, and how to work together. Thus, we have a dual inheritance, some of it biological and some of it learned behavior.[11] Empathy reflects that duality. The challenge is for us to pay attention to the physiological triggers to empathy and then to process in our minds what those triggers mean. For example, imagine hearing a loud sound in another room, being startled and fearful at first, and then quickly remembering having placed a heavy box on a shelf, which likely fell. This example is a simple view of this process.

We have a stronger ability to put these skills together when it comes to kin, those we know and especially those who we know well. Today kin may extend beyond physiological relationships, including blended families, gay unions, and adoptions—families created by choice. The strength of these kin bonds can be very powerful and nurture deep empathy. Empathy is less likely to happen with people we view as strangers. It is more difficult to connect the physiological reactions we have to others with a well thought out understanding of what our reactions mean and what the actions of others mean when those others are distant or foreign to us, as is discussed in more detail in chapter 3. Making the connection of kin selection to the entire human species has been and continues to be a struggle. Those connections rely more on social learning, so we have to be much more deliberate about being empathic with those who we do not know well or do not know at all compared to those who we do know. Thus, biology is the foundation, but social learning is what brings empathy to a wider swath of people.

Cooperation—Play Well with Others

From our earliest years in preschool, we are not only encouraged to get along with others but also measured on that ability. I remember my early report cards from school. My teachers graded me on my "ability to play well with others." The emphasis on this skill as we grow up is to reinforce cooperation through social learning. Cooperation means that we work together; we interact in ways that are beneficial to all who are involved. Empathy can help that process. We can understand the situations of others so we can connect better and minimize misunderstandings; this can help us to cooperate.

When I read through the research on empathy and cooperation I found that with empathy we are more likely to overlook negative unintended behaviors of others; that is, we cut people slack when we have empathy toward them.[12] This reminded me of an experience I had in college that made a lasting impression on me. When I was studying social work, we were often put in groups with the goal of simulating situations we would face in the workplace that would require collaboration. I liked my classmates a lot, so I enjoyed working in groups. But one thing I disliked was the prospect of getting everyone to contribute. In one class, our final project was a very involved group presentation that required a lot of work. Our group got along well, but we had one member who was older, had children, and worked outside of school. He did not attend all our planning and work sessions, and as this was before the internet and video conferencing, he was simply absent. I could feel myself getting upset that we were doing all this work and he was going to benefit without doing as much. This was a huge project, worth an entire semester's grade. But I was reluctant to say anything. Who wants to be the tattletale or seem bossy? And making an issue of our workload would create a distraction from the task we were focused on. I am glad I didn't say anything. We found out later that he had a very sick child and also was the sole support of his family and needed to work. The information helped me to understand his situation, which was very different from the rest of us who were young, single, and did not need to work full time. We figured out ways to get his work that did not require his presence at our meetings. It gave me a chance to walk in his shoes in a way that made it possible to overlook his difficulty in working with us according to our schedule. We did our presentation and got a good grade, and he did what he could and was grateful to have had classmates who were supportive. I learned from this group project to be sure to hear other people's stories before interpreting their actions or, as in this case, lack of actions. This does not mean that everyone in groups with me gets a free pass, this just stands as a reminder that people have different abilities and circumstances and we can work better together if we have greater empathic insight into others.

Morality—Knowing Right from Wrong

When we ask if something we do is moral, we are asking if it is right or wrong.[13] There are numerous ways we can learn about morality: from our parents, from religious leaders, or even from the law. If something is outlawed by society, we are likely to see it as wrong. Of course, not everyone subscribes to the same interpretation of what is right and what is wrong. In our modern society, we have major behaviors that we agree are wrong, such as killing another person. But even killing is not clearly wrong, as in cases of self-defense or when a nation goes to war with another nation, justifying the killing of others as enemies. Morality is subjective; it depends on situations and circumstances. The enemies of today may be the allies of tomorrow, so the rules of conduct can change over time. Psychologist Martin L. Hoffman has written a great deal on empathy and its impact on our moral development.[14] He considers morality in large part to be consideration for others. Human beings would not have survived as a species if people only cared about themselves. Our survival is secured through our interactions with others, and morality is the code we create to monitor these social interactions. Our moral code is informed by empathy.

In his book, Hoffman makes an incredibly insightful point when he writes about how we can teach morality to children through empathy. If we ask children how their actions will affect other people now and in the future, we teach them to engage empathically and imagine whether what we do feels right or wrong. That is probably something we are all familiar with, both as adults teaching children about right and wrong and as children who were taught. He goes on to suggest that we go further and teach children to do "multiple empathizing" for the other person, which I find really valuable. Multiple empathizing has us make a switch in our minds and place someone we care about deeply in the other person's situation, then imagine how that person we are close to might feel. For example, imagine you are walking down the street and see a homeless person who is pushing a cart full of her belongings. What if that person were your mother, sister, or best friend? The feelings we have can be very different and powerful when we engage in multiple empathizing. If you start doing this with issues you hear in the news, it can start a process of thinking differently. When I have discussions about immigration, I think of my grandfathers, one who came to this country as a young man, the other as a boy with his parents in what family lore suggests was not a legal entry. Would I want my grandfathers, who came to this country as immigrants, to have been deported, leaving behind their wives and children, my grandmothers, mother, and father? It connects me in a personal way to the stories of today's immigrants. The process of multiple empathizing helps to remove our tendency to not engage as deeply with people who are strangers or distant from us.

As I was writing this section on morality and empathy, I was confronted by a glaring case of a breakdown in morality and empathy that was being covered in the news.[15] In February 2017, a group of fraternity members at Penn State University were charged with involuntary manslaughter and aggravated assault for ignoring or actively deciding not to call for medical assistance when one of their pledges was pressured into drinking copious amounts of alcohol, then falling down stairs and hitting his head. For the next twelve hours he went back and forth between unconsciousness and consciousness without anyone calling for medical assistance. The leaders of the fraternity were cited as discouraging anyone from taking action to get the young man any help, likely to protect their fraternity—the young pledge was nineteen years old, under the age of legal drinking. By the time 911 was called, he had been lying on the floor for hours and was cold and unresponsive. Worst of all, there were security video cameras recording much of the behaviors, providing glaring evidence of how many members of the fraternity did not call for help. How could twenty young men, all enrolled at a major university in the United States, collectively fail to engage in empathic reasoning to take care of their young pledge? There were likely many competing emotions that blocked the multiple empathizing that Hoffman describes. On an individual basis, I am sure most or even all of these young men have emotional attachments to others, people they care deeply about. What if that young pledge had been someone's real brother in that fraternity house? Or what if one of those twenty young men who were involved had taken a moment and imagined that the young man could be his brother, best friend, or father? What if someone had engaged in multiple empathizing? Would that have moved him to call for help? In chapter 3, we will explore in detail the many reasons that empathy fails, including the sense that the other person is not one of us. Maybe the distance between being a full-fledged member of the fraternity and a pledge who is trying to be accepted is a big enough gap to limit empathic connections. We will likely never know what each young man was thinking or going through during those twelve hours, but we can see that both morality and empathy were not called on until it was too late. This example is not just tragic but also shows how precarious engaging in empathy can be. And when we don't engage in empathy, we are more likely to ignore morality or doing what is right.

On the other hand, Google "stories of helping others because it is the right thing to do" and you will find countless examples of empathy leading people to do good by others, stories that don't necessarily make the nightly news.[16] Many of these stories are about young people who simply feel for others and want to help. Consider the young boy who saw a news story about homeless people living on the streets and asked his parents if they could start collecting blankets for those people, or another young boy who heard about a mother and daughter who died in a fire because they did not have a smoke alarm and used his savings to buy smoke alarms to be installed by the fire department in neighborhood homes that needed them, or the young girl who chose not to get presents for her birthday and instead asked that her birthday money be used to buy supplies for an animal rescue shelter. All these cases show how empathy can be an important part of how we teach morality to children.

Doing Good Without Empathy

While empathy is key to promoting prosocial behaviors, there are times when people do behave in socially positive ways with low levels of empathy or even in the absence of empathy, although it is less likely to happen. There are many reasons we might help other people without being prompted by empathy. We might feel obligated to help others because of some rule our parents or religious leaders taught us. Or we might see our good deeds as transactional—if I do you a favor, you will feel more inclined to return the favor later. Another reason we might be moved to do good is to pay someone back for help he or she gave us before in order to even up the sense of obligation. We might also do good things for others because it builds our reputation and gives us status. The thought of public recognition, of people seeing how generous and thoughtful we are, can be a motivator for doing good. There may even be a mixture of reasons for doing good that involves empathy in part but is triggered for other reasons. For example, one study found that empathy moved people to help others in distress in multiple ways, but when the help required personal interaction, there was a preference to aid those who seemed more socially desirable. The study created two scenarios with hospital patients who had the same illness. One patient was described as very sad and distressed and the other was described as joking and upbeat about the situation. What happened was that participants were more likely to help the sad patient with indirect help, like donating money, but preferred directly helping the happy patient.[17] This research suggests that empathy may be key to picking up someone's need for care or concern and making us feel good about helping, but that if we are asked to provide personal assistance, we are drawn to help those who we find to be desirable social partners. This is not surprising. If you have a friend who is sick and needs to be driven to the doctor, it is easier to be in the car with someone who is upbeat and feels like the illness is beatable versus driving someone who is depressed and miserable about the situation. That is not to say that empathy can't be present in both situations, but the way we do good in response to our empathy can differ, which adds to the complexity of understanding when and how we respond empathically.

Knowing exactly why someone behaves the way he or she does is incredibly complex and probably involves a combination of reasons. Some of those reasons may be triggered by empathy, and some not. Even those helping behaviors that are preceded by empathy may look different depending on the situation or the personality of the recipient. Thus, while not all good behaviors are motivated by empathy, the chances of good behavior happening are greatly improved because of empathy.

Side Benefits of Empathy and Doing Good—Bringing Us Happiness

We know that empathy can move us to do good things to help other people. We call it prosocial behavior because the recipient of the good deed ends up better off as a result of that effort. (A word of caution here: remember the difference between empathy and sympathy or pity—being the object of someone's sympathy may result in receiving help, but the relationship may be so patronizing that the recipient does not feel at all valued in a meaningful way.) The good news is that more and more research suggests that in addition to the recipient, the empathic person also benefits.

While it may not be surprising that doing good things for other people makes us feel happy, what is surprising is that it may be a deeply imbedded connection that starts early in life. Toddlers involved in experiments in which they had choices about sharing treats were happiest when giving to others, even happier than when they received the treats for themselves.[18] The researchers argue that although we cannot completely rule out social learning as the reason for a preference for sharing at such a young age, it is likely that being prosocial feels good from a deeper place than something we learn as we grow older. The very young age of the children in the experiments suggests that they were sharing because it felt good, better than getting the treat themselves. It seems that by the time we are young adults, the connection between happiness and empathy and altruism may be well established.[19] But this raises some questions. We do not know for sure the direction of that relationship. Does empathy lead to doing good things, which makes us happy? Or are happy people by nature more empathic and likely to act on their feelings to follow through with doing good things? We need to do more research to know exactly which comes first. Based on what I have studied, I would argue that doing good things promotes happiness more than the opposite. A person can be very self-absorbed and be happy to ignore the needs of others. However, an empathic person who feels the needs of others has to make a conscious decision whether or not to respond. Over time we learn from previous experience what it feels like to help others. Those who link doing good with feeling happy will be more likely to do so the next time empathy kicks in. Sometimes an empathic response is difficult and may not feel as rewarding, but we do it anyway. Thus, I would argue that helping others can make us feel good, although it is not a guarantee. I also take it a step further and feel strongly that social empathy, using our empathic abilities on a broader societal level, can make us all feel better.

Over the past several years, a group of highly respected independent researchers has compiled an annual happiness report covering thousands of respondents from 150 countries. Comparisons among the countries are made based on measurements of the respondents' assessments of their current lives, including health, economic well-being, and social support.[20] We would think that the high level of economic well-being in the United States, compared to many other countries, would place us rather high on the happiness scale. However, that is actually not the case. In spite of overall growth in income and national wealth as measured by gross domestic product, happiness in the United States has fallen over the past ten years. The items that contributed to this fall were decreases in social support, a lower feeling of personal freedom, and stronger perceptions of government and business corruption. These are social ills. One of the authors of this study, Jeffrey D. Sachs, draws the conclusion that to improve the level of happiness in the United States, we need to focus on strengthening social capital. This means improving social relations and social support. Sachs specifically calls for building better relations between those who are native born and those who are immigrants, shrinking the income and economic gap between those at the top and those at the bottom, restoring faith in government and elected officials through campaign finance reform, and improving the social safety net through greater access to and quality of health care and education. Dr. Sachs makes the connection between social change and individual well-being; that is, addressing larger social problems will improve our personal levels of happiness.

While these recommendations may not be surprising, we can create a greater commitment to these efforts through social empathy. Social empathy requires greater attention to our surroundings and how groups have fared over the course of history, urging us to apply our empathic insights to better understand differences among groups. It encourages us to develop multiple empathizing skills. Our insights can help trigger empathic impulses to engage in prosocial behaviors on larger social problems. Viewing public concerns through a lens of social empathy means examining which groups are most affected by a lack of social support, putting ourselves in their places, and using that insight to make changes.

Does a Lack of Social Empathy Diminish Happiness?

When we lack social empathy, we have less insight and understanding of those who are culturally and ethnically different from us. This distance means that we are prone to provide lower levels of social support and prosocial behaviors. A fascinating study on "unplanned helping behavior" was conducted in 2001 and again in 2011 in both the United States and Canada.[21] The study observed people being helpful to strangers without any recognition or reciprocity. The research followed the dissemination of "lost letters" that were strategically placed in select neighborhoods to compare the likelihood of someone picking up the letters and making the effort to mail them. All the letters were the same and were stamped and placed in obvious public places. The goal of the research was to see whether the rate of return had changed from 2001 and 2011 and if any changes differed between the United States and Canada. The findings were very interesting. Only in the United States was there a decline in the rate of returning the letters. When all the differing variables were more closely examined, the most significant change in unplanned helping behavior since 2001 that differed between the two countries was in neighborhoods in which the proportion of noncitizens had increased over the ten-year period. There seemed to be a different perspective on immigrants in Canada compared to the United States. The level of unplanned helping declined between 2001 and 2011 more significantly in the United States than in Canada within communities with more noncitizens. So although both countries had neighborhoods that saw an increase in immigrants living there, only in the United States did those neighborhoods also see a decline in unplanned helping. One possible explanation offered by the researcher was that the impact of the September 11 attacks may have had a deeper effect on people in the United States than it did in Canada. That impact may have been to increase wariness and distrust toward immigrant groups. The study author concluded that both negative political rhetoric and harsh policies toward immigrants in the United States may have contributed to lower levels of trust within diverse neighborhoods that in turn led to a pulling back from community involvement and participating in unplanned helping efforts. Such anti-immigrant rhetoric and policies did not occur to that degree in Canada.

The differences in social support between Canada and the United States might be explained in part through examining what we know about ethnic diversity and its impact on social connections in neighborhoods. An analysis of over ninety studies on this topic revealed some interesting differences between the United States and Canada, as well as with other Western countries.[22] This will likely not surprise anyone who has been following the news over the past couple of years, but public perception of diversity in the United States has been much more negative than in Canada. One theory the researchers who reviewed these ninety studies offers to explain this difference is that the history of the United States is unique compared to Canada and other Western countries.[23] Although we are a country of immigrants, as is true for Canada, possibly our legacy of slavery and legislated segregation for hundreds of years contributes to the difference. The codified public policy of slavery and efforts to separate races may make racial diversity much more difficult to bridge in the United States.

When we examine the historical context of diversity in this country, we see problems with building the social relations and social support that are needed to combat the drop in happiness in the United States. The forced relocation to this country of Africans to serve as slaves, the national divide on slavery that contributed to the Civil War, and generations of descendants of slaves who were barred from access to education and opportunities have all contributed to racialized experiences growing up in the United States. Add to that history the forced upheaval and relocation of thousands of indigenous people, also through public policies, and we have a racial divide that is very deep.

In fact, although many immigrant groups have not received warm welcomes by those who were already settled here, the distance among races is far deeper than among the descendants of early European colonists and the waves of immigrants who came to the United States from countries such as Ireland, Italy, and Poland. The historical context of the racial divide in this country cannot be ignored when looking at multiculturalism and diversity today. What a review of the ninety studies on diversity suggests is that we have a lot of diversity in the United States, but that diversity is still very segregated, and as a result, groups do not interact in significant ways. This gives us a veneer of diversity but not the deeper connections that can build empathy between groups.

Returning to what we know from the annual happiness report, the factors that most influence how people rated their happiness center on building a trusting, supportive, honest, and generous social foundation more than on increasing income or improving life expectancy. Building empathy can be a powerful tool to build social connections that include trust, support, and generosity. Now more than ever we need to address the deep day-to-day separation between groups and create a stronger sense of social support, which will contribute to higher levels of happiness. Empathy can help do that. Interpersonal empathy can tap into our individual sense of feeling good, and social empathy can help build social connections, all of which in turn increase levels of happiness.

Can Empathy Make Us More Civilized?

Since the presidential campaign of 2016 and analysis of the postelection divide between voters, there has been more talk of a need for empathy. I won't disagree with that point in general; there are numerous social reasons why an improvement in empathy would be beneficial. Are we on track as a society to improve empathy? I have good news and bad news. First the good news: over the course of human history, empathy has been on a steady rise with less violence and human destruction. Now the bad news: our national history is not very far removed from acts of violence demonstrating a lack of empathy, and today we can find examples of behaviors that reflect utter disregard for the humanity of others.

Jeremy Rifkin in his book *The Empathic Civilization* provides a comprehensive historical tracking of the spread of people joining together to live in organized governed communities and how empathy played a key role.[24] He wrote the book to document that we have shared characteristics across nations, and if we can tap into our empathy we can build connections and raise empathic consciousness throughout the world. He points to changes over time that have contributed to greater empathic consciousness. The book is very comprehensive and detailed, so it is difficult to reduce the central idea of how empathy has grown throughout the world to one key principle. But several of Rifkin's ideas help to explain the evolution of our empathic civilization.

Rifkin points to the shift in how people lived. Tribal life with little contact between tribes shifted over the centuries to more diverse cosmopolitan living and the establishment of nations and cities. Cosmopolitan living means more exposure to diverse people and cultures and increased economic connections between communities. These connections create familiarity and common bonds. With increased familiarity comes a greater likelihood of empathy. The process of developing urban life began two thousand years ago, and it opened the door to broaden empathy. As Rifkin explains,

> The dense living arrangements invited cross-cultural exchange and the beginning of a cosmopolitan attitude. The new exposures often created conflict, but they also opened the door to experiencing people who had heretofore been considered alien and other. The empathic impulse, which for all of previous history had been confined to small bands of close relatives and clans living largely in isolation, was suddenly presented with new opportunities and challenges. Finding the similar in alien others strengthened and deepened empathic expression, universalizing it beyond blood relationships for the first time.[25]

Of course, this process has not been without setbacks and deviations. The past two thousand years may have witnessed the cross-cultural exchanges that deepen empathy described by Rifkin, but there have also been countless violent and destructive exchanges that demonstrate a lack of empathy.

Psychologist and linguist Steven Pinker has done a comprehensive analysis of violence over thousands of years of human history in his book *The Better Angels of Our Nature*.[26] He echoes Rifkin's view of growing empathy hand in hand with civilization. Although this social progress has not occurred at the same levels in all places across the world, in general and certainly in many regions, empathy has developed far beyond what early civilizations experienced, and with it came greater peaceful coexistence. Pinker also reviews how our evolution has gone from living among tribes and clans to forming city-states, communities of numerous tribes and clans that are organized and governed. In city-states, there are different groups living together who interact for economic gain. These interactions have led to a decline in violence. Tribes are limited in what and how much they can produce. If one tribe attacks another, they may have more resources in the short term by defeating and taking from the other tribe, but the other tribe, left with nothing, will plan their retribution and attack. This creates a cycle of violence with nothing gained over time. If instead the tribes trade and cooperate, both will gain. Pinker thoroughly documents violent exchanges that have occurred over long parts of history throughout the world and how that violence slowly dissipated, leading to cooperation and coexistence.

At the risk of oversimplifying thousands of years of human history, I offer a simple example. Imagine two small communities, one of farmers and another of sheep herders. If everyone in the farming community has enough grain to last until the next harvest, any surplus of grain grown by the farmers will sit and potentially rot. For the sheep herders, they may end up with lots of sheep, requiring more land or shepherds than they have, both needed to maintain the growing flock. If they cannot take care of all the sheep, some will wander off or be lost. For the farmers, taking their extra grain and trading it with the shepherds for their surplus sheep gives both groups more than what they had without trading. They benefit by changing their extras into new resources they can use. This system of exchange is what brought people together to live in city-states and lessened violent interactions between groups.

Once human beings started trading and interacting with different groups, they started to need to understand their trading partners and exchange cultures. Getting the best price or exchange for your products is helped by knowing what is important to your trading partner. This is the work of empathy. And for economic interactions to work well, there need to be systems and rules. Consider what is in our wallets. Most of us have plastic cards that allow us to walk into a store and leave with tangible products. How does this work? How does a small embossed piece of plastic allow me to fill a cart with groceries or choose what I want from hundreds of items of clothing? What we take for granted as part of our daily lives is a complicated system that is based on agreements among producers, merchants, banks, and governments that cross national and international boundaries. This system is a hallmark of civilization and intertwines our lives in ways that are beneficial. Such commerce and other aspects of civilization cannot exist with violence. As systems get larger, personal agreements are enlarged through the creation of governments. Laws are passed to reflect the decisions regarding what is and is not just.

Systems of economic commerce further developed through literacy. Developing ways to communicate among people and record the rules of the emerging economic system were furthered by the ability to read and write. With the development of the printing press, communication could expand beyond commerce and include literature, which Pinker regards as a way for people to engage in perspective-taking, which is entering the life of someone else. How much do we learn today from reading about different cultures or seeing a movie portraying life in another part of the world? Reading opens people to all sorts of experiences, allowing us to take the perspective of others, which adds to our empathic training. By engaging in personal perspective-taking, we build interpersonal empathy, and by using perspective-taking to understand different groups and their historical evolution, we build social empathy.

You might be wondering, if we have all this great progress toward civilization, how do we explain times in history when there were horrific events like the Holocaust or, in more recent years, suicide bombings that include flying planes into the World Trade Center to kill thousands of people? This hardly seems to fit the idea of collaboration through civilization. Pinker provides deeper analysis that helps to explain these occurrences. First, civilization has not developed at the same pace everywhere, and second, other intervening events can derail social empathy and civilization. Pinker's book was published before the rise of the Islamic State known as ISIS or ISIL, yet his analysis describes the events that contribute to a breakdown of civilization and give rise to groups that rule through violence and display a lack of empathy. He warns us that collective misfortune and chaos (such as the impact of war) can open the way for leaders to emerge who promise a perfect world if people follow their ideology and rules. Their ideology is the only way to achieve this perfect world, which means that anyone who does not follow that ideology is in the way, blocking this perfect world, and those people therefore must be stopped or eliminated. When people have little opportunity for jobs or raising families, especially young men, joining such a group becomes an appealing option. Religious fundamentalism, which is the belief that only your religion is right, makes deeply connecting with others who have different beliefs a challenge. The struggle between competing religious beliefs and empathy is discussed in chapter 6.

Empathy as a part of civilization has evolved in uneven ways. We are shocked and distraught by the beheadings that are videotaped and distributed to news media by terrorist groups as part of their campaign to take control of regions and people. The statement they are making to Westerners is violent, clear, and meant to terrorize us. Their methods are brutal, but unfortunately not new. About fifteen years ago,

I was visiting a friend who lived in Pittsburgh. There was a traveling exhibit at one of the museums that she was interested in, and she asked if I would be willing to accompany her. It was a pictorial history of lynching in America. To be honest, I did not know much about the exhibit. I expected it to be disturbing and I understood the horror of lynching from a historical perspective, but I was unprepared for what I saw. To understand what I experienced that day, you can visit the website www.withoutsanctuary.org and see the eighty photographs that were in the exhibit. From 1877 to 1950, over four thousand lynchings across the United States were documented.[27]

Lynchings were violent acts of torture, many of which were done publicly with hundreds of people, including children, in attendance. The vast majority of lynchings were done by whites in power in order to frighten and consequently control blacks. One of the things that shocked me that day at the exhibit was the discovery that the photos that chronicle these acts of torture (including mutilations, hangings, and burnings of African American men, women, and even children) were taken by professional photographers to be sold as souvenirs. The photos were sold by the thousands over the years. In some of the photos, you can see white adults and children smiling, posing in front of the corpses as if they are at a celebration. I wanted to view this as an anomaly, something that was out of place in our history, but that would be naïve and, frankly, untrue.

The power of a noose to represent the terror is still strong today and used to frighten people, especially African Americans. On the morning of the first day that American University Student Government President Taylor Dumpson took office, May 1, 2017, bananas with racist messages were strung up with nooses across the campus. Ms. Dumpson was the first African American to be elected president of American University's student government. The message meant by those nooses was clear. It harkened back to the days of lynching. The person or people who did this had to have known what those nooses would mean; a lot of work went into creating and placing them on campus. The imagery was powerful and purposeful. But there has been progress, as Ms. Dumpson had the courage and position to respond and wrote a very strong and inspiring letter to her university community.[28]

We have additional histories of violence toward groups of people because they were different and not considered human. From the arrival of the earliest European settlers, views of Native Americans were at best tolerant, at worst as savages to be destroyed. The white settlers' sense of entitlement to the land can be seen in the words of President Andrew Jackson when in 1814 he asked, "What good man would prefer a country covered with forests and ranged by a few thousand savages to our extensive Republic, studded with cities, towns and prosperous farms . . . filled with all the blessings of liberty, civilization and religion?"[29] The use of the term "savages" to refer to Native Americans was so common that President Jackson used it in his official speeches and writings. Jackson went on to use the power of his position to put forward legislation that included the Indian Removal Act of 1830, which relocated thousands of American Indians, taking their lands in the east and forcibly resettling them in areas developed as reservations. Under this law, the entire Cherokee tribe was forced to walk west during the fall and winter of 1838 and 1839, resulting in four thousand Cherokees, almost one-fourth of the tribe, dying due to hunger, disease, and winter conditions.[30] This forced march is known as the "Trail of Tears" for the sheer devastation it brought.

What makes horrific violent acts such as these doable is by *not* seeing your own humanity in others. Sometimes we codify the inequality. Ever wonder where we got the "rule" for counting slaves as only three-fifths of a person? That came from the Constitution of the United States, Article I, Section 2. The same section does not even count Indians as people unless they paid taxes, which the vast majority did not do because they lived on their own lands or later on reservations. This section was repealed after the Civil War, but for more than one hundred years it was the law of the land. Codifying blacks as less than a whole person and marginalizing Native Americans through the highest law of the land, the Constitution sends a very powerful message. Lynchings and forced marches leading to death are not easily done if you see yourself in those being killed. If we see those others as outside our tribe or not part of humanity, then killing them is helpful in ridding the world of impure nonhuman savages who threaten our purity. Even when laws change, changing people's learned perceptions of others can be more difficult than what it took to change those policies.

Understanding this history is a painful realization. You may be angry at my bringing it up or at my oversimplification of complex historical events. Or you may be asking, why go over events that happened hundreds of years ago and were done by people who are no longer alive? There are important reasons for revisiting our history. First, it helps to explain the context of race in America, and second, that knowledge informs perspective-taking across races. Both of these reasons are foundations for engaging the components of social empathy. I hope you will stay with me through this examination. In chapter 3, we will look closely at the power of "otherness" and how it blocks empathy. This is difficult for us because we are a nation with "otherness" in our own history. But there are ways to recognize these behaviors and learn from them, hence my reason for spelling it out here. I promise that, by the end of the book, I will share ways to build social empathy to mend relationships, bridge historical differences, and create civilizations that are healthy and productive for all.

Can Adversity Make Us More Empathic?

Life can deal us some heavy blows, such as illness, injury, loss of a loved one, or violence. When we are dealing with such traumas, it may be difficult to focus on feeling empathic toward others. But the good news is that it seems as though with life adversity comes greater empathy.[31] However, timing is important. While we are in the midst of our own struggles, we are less likely to engage empathically, but once we have gotten through them, we are likely to have stronger perspective-taking skills and feelings of empathic concern. There are likely different reasons depending on the person, but we do have a good understanding of why going through tough times and coming out okay can improve a person's empathic abilities. Being in a difficult situation would call on unconscious survival mechanisms, which include hyper awareness of surroundings and what is going on with others in case they can give you cues on what to do or in case they are threatening and you need to defend yourself. Tuning in becomes life sustaining. Once we get through difficult situations successfully, we will have been rewarded for that extra vigilance and ability to read others. We will have learned how to overcome a tragedy or painful experience using self-other awareness and perspective-taking tools in addition to our heightened attention to affective triggers. These are key components of empathy.

I have a colleague and co-researcher, Cynthia Lietz, whose own work has centered on resilience, the extent to which we can bounce back after facing adversity. Over the years she has joined me in some phases of my research on empathy in part because she sees a strong connection between empathy and resilience. In fact, in research on children, those who understand the feelings of others and take their perspectives show more resilience.[32] Cynthia's research focused on families engaged in prosocial activities who have gone through trauma.[33] She was interested in finding out what drove them to help others after going through such difficult times themselves. Among her findings was that resilient families reported having a high degree of understanding of what others are going through based on their own experiences. To them, this was an important ability that developed from their adversity. Note that Cynthia's research was on families who reported having healthy family functioning and had made it through the difficult times. We don't know about those families who were still struggling and did not feel resilient. But for those families who showed resilience, they felt their empathic understanding had improved because of their experiences.

Let me make one last point about adversity and empathy. In chapter 3, we will look at what it means to be an outsider and how that affects empathy. The short version of the relationship between being outside the dominant or majority culture and empathy is that when we are different from the mainstream, we are more conscious of our difference. Although not all minority or outsider statuses involve adversity, they often do. Being in the minority means tuning in to how those in the majority act so we can blend in or at least not stick out. Reading others can become an important skill for outsiders. Thus, forms of adversity in the way of being an outsider or minority can also enhance empathic abilities.

Is There Such a Thing as Too Much Empathy?

Yes, although it is complicated according to new research. In a study of couples who reported instances of not feeling understood by their partners, people with high levels of empathy felt more stress and disappointment at not being understood. This could be a consequence of being able to feel emotions deeply, or it could suggest an emotional oversensitivity due to being highly empathic. The good news is that in a follow-up one year later, the stressful disappointments did not negatively affect their relationships.[34] Another recent study considered whether empathy between parents and their adolescent children is beneficial or might come at a cost within families.[35] Being the parent of a teenager can be stressful as the child goes through adolescent development. We would like to think that being empathic parents would be soothing for children and create a strong family connection. The researchers found that indeed parental empathy was helpful for adolescents. The young people with more empathic parents showed better ability at handling their emotions and lower levels of physiological stress. It may be that having parents who are empathic and can respond appropriately to adolescents' needs creates a less stressful environment at home and may help young people navigate the emotional ride of adolescence. For the parents, higher levels of empathy related to feeling good psychologically but were accompanied by higher levels of physiological stress. Being empathic with children likely does give parents a sense of well-being because they are better connected and can feel the positive emotions that come from being supportive and understanding. However, this empathic connection might be physically demanding for parents. Empathy for their adolescent children can be exhausting. Stepping into the lived reality of others, especially when it is your own child's life, requires a good deal of your own emotion regulation to master what your empathic insights are discovering.

Both studies suggest that there is an intensity to empathy with those who you are very close to, with romantic partners in the first study and adolescent children in the second. Does this mean there can be too much empathy? I would say that it is not a matter of quantity but rather a matter of the strength we have in the part of empathy that relies on our emotion regulation, our ability to handle the feelings we pick up from others and our reactions to processing those feelings. In fact, understanding the components of empathy can prepare us to know that we are likely to mirror strong affective and emotional feelings with our closest family members. These shared feelings can help us to gain perspective and understanding. But to do so well, we need to be sure we attend to our own emotions and develop the skills to handle the intensity of those emotions.

People Who Lack Empathy Make Empathy
Even More Important

There is one last reason that makes empathy so vital to our personal lives and our civilization. As important as knowing that empathy helps us to do good is knowing what a lack of empathy means. Research has linked a lack of empathy to a number of negative behaviors, such as spousal battering,[36] bullying,[37] sexual offending,[38] and overall psychopathology.[39] On a societal level, the absence of empathy has been linked with genocide and ethnic cleansing.[40] I don't need to tell you that these are behaviors that are not high on our wish list as a society.

Psychopathy is defined as antisocial behavior. It is a condition that includes a number of behaviors that come together: a sense of dominance and fearlessness, callousness that is exhibited by self-interest with little to no regard for others, and an impulsiveness that lacks control of emotions.[41] Even if we did not have research showing that those with psychopathic tendencies have little to no empathy, the characteristics that describe psychopathy are opposite to what one needs for empathy. Being fearless means that one disregards fear, which, as I already pointed out, is a key element of attachment and needing others; self-interest with no regard for others blocks the key empathy components of self-other awareness and perspective-taking; and impulsiveness suggests that there is no emotion regulation. While it is difficult to know whether psychopathy is a condition that prevents having empathy or whether not developing empathy contributes to being psychopathic, we do know that where there is psychopathy there is very little if any empathy. Thus, understanding how people do not become empathic is also important to society. In chapter 3 we explore in more depth the reasons why we may see a lack of empathy.

We know that empathy leads to prosocial behaviors, including altruism, generosity, attachment, cooperation, and emotional well-being. Society benefits from having empathic people as its citizens. At the same time, social ills often reflect a lack of empathy. These are compelling reasons to promote the teaching and learning of empathy.

CHAPTER THREE

If It's So Important,
Why Is Empathy So Hard?

THE MINUTE YOU feel fear, your first reactions will be unconscious and will take you into a primitive survival mode. Your body will react to help you to respond without thinking, releasing hormones such as adrenaline to give you immediate energy and deepening breathing and increasing your heart rate to bring more oxygen to your bloodstream, which also gives you more energy. All this is in response to one unconscious question: What do I need to do to protect myself? For some of us, that might be to fight, for others the reaction might be to flee (which is also to not fight back), and some of us might band together with others and protect ourselves as a group. When this happens, you are unlikely to feel empathy. However, if the fear can be reasoned with, thought through a bit, then the instinct will give way to cognitive processing, that is, thinking through the situation you are in. This pause for thinking gives us time to draw on what we might have previously learned about others and ourselves, and we can feel empathy.

In our modern world, feelings for survival can be triggered in different ways from our ancestors. Think of a time you might have had an emotional and illogical argument with someone. Maybe a friend made a snide comment about what you were wearing, a parent criticized you, or a co-worker made fun of you in front of others. If you can look back and analyze the situation from a third-person perspective, not from an emotionally involved place, you are likely to see that you felt attacked and were reacting instead of being thoughtful and deliberative. Your impulses to protect yourself went into gear. Unfortunately, our bodies don't recognize the difference between an attack of words and an attack of physical danger—a threat is a threat. Once you feel threatened, the body reacts to protect itself. It takes a lot of work, including a lot of emotion regulation, to not immediately react and instead process what is going on. Maybe the friend who made the snide comment about your outfit is really insecure about how she looks and tried to make herself feel better by putting you down, maybe your father or mother wants so badly for you to be special that the criticism came from a place of wanting you to do more, and maybe the co-worker who put you down in front of others is jealous of your abilities and wants to lower you to feel higher himself. These are all common human behaviors, and there may be times when we are the one doing the "attacking" because of our own insecure or anxious feelings. Overcoming our primitive fears, which can be triggered in many different ways, is what makes being empathic so difficult. This chapter explores the many ways that fear can block empathy.

How Does the Drive to Survive Block Empathy?

We know that human beings, like other species, are wired with a strong sense of survival. Survival can be secured by our ability to read people. That ability helps us with attachment to others, to recognize danger, and to collaborate with others. These are all important survival skills. We also know that our survival at a young age depends on the care and support of other human beings. Through mirroring and affective responses, we communicate our needs and learn from others, and they in turn mirror and affectively respond and return the connection. Not only does that help us survive, but it also draws people together, which is the foundation of empathy. However, researchers have discovered that there are boundaries to this connection to others. Anything or anyone that gets in the way of our survival is a problem. When our survival is threatened by another species, such as a dangerous wild animal, we humans band together and form protection. Individual human beings could not survive for very long alone, but in groups, survival was greatly enhanced. Thus, living in groups became part of human existence over thousands of years. This is a simplistic way of describing our tribal evolution. But what happens when we perceive our survival is at risk from other human beings? Do we see those others as different from us because they threaten our survival, or do we see them as threatening our survival and therefore different from us? And within our tribe, are we sufficiently alike that we are motivated to protect and support each other, or, because we are in the same tribe, do we see ourselves as the same and it is necessary to support those like us for our own survival? The answers to these questions are key to understanding how difficult it can be to feel empathy for others who are perceived as different.

Human beings vary in different ways. We vary by sex, age, race, ethnicity, class, gender identity, religion, physical abilities, or any number of other categories into which people organize themselves. One common thread throughout the research on empathy is that if we see other people as different, it is more likely that we have a weaker empathic connection.[1] And if we see others as a danger to our survival, we are even more unlikely to feel an empathic connection.[2] On a tribal level, if there is a threat to the tribe, resources and defenses are organized and the tribe fights back to restore a state of safety and survival for the tribe's members. However, outsiders of a tribe are a social construct, a perception or belief that is created by human beings to explain or categorize other human beings. These constructs may have evolved geographically (think Southerners versus Northerners), socially (native born versus immigrants), economically (rich versus poor), or politically (Democrats versus Republicans). Some group identities are entertaining, like fans of a sports team, or are temporary, like being a student. Being a member of various groups is part of being human, so how and why do we perceive or create otherness, and how does that block empathy?

What Is "Otherness" and How Does It Block Empathy?

In research on empathy, the terms "ingroup" and "outgroup" are often used. These terms are used to describe how people divide themselves between those like us (our "ingroup" members) and those who are different from us ("outgroup" members). Decades ago, researchers documented this tendency to divide ourselves between those who we see as like us and those who we see as different.[3] Even when people are divided into rather arbitrary groups, by color, for example (think the blue team versus the green team back in elementary school or summer camp), members form biases against the other team and develop favoritism for their own members.[4] When group members have similarities that are longstanding, such as growing up together, being part of a religious community from birth, or living in the same neighborhood over a lifetime, bonds of similarity are strong. The stronger those bonds of similarity are, the stronger the ability for ingroup members to empathize with each other. But what happens to our empathy when we interact with people who are different?

When neuroscience began using brain imaging to look at our neural activity, scientists discovered that our empathic responses differ when we respond to people like us compared to when we respond to people who are different from us. Numerous different experiments have shown that our brain reacts similarly to the experiences of those who are like us more than it does for those who are different.[5] In some cases, people do demonstrate empathy toward outgroup members but use different parts of their brains than when processing feelings for ingroup members. It seems that we mentally process members from our own group as unique individuals, while we mentally process members of outgroups as part of a whole.[6] What might this tell us? It may be that we process the experiences of others, like pain, in a firsthand way for those who are like us and in a secondhand way for those who are different.[7] These studies suggest that empathy can be there for outgroup members, but it may be a learned behavior using secondhand brain mechanisms for feeling what the other person is feeling compared to unconscious mirroring or firsthand experience when viewing the experiences of an ingroup member. This makes a lot of sense. We can see ourselves in others who are like us, so the unconscious and conscious parts of empathy connect smoothly and allow us to feel empathic. But when we are observing someone different, an outgroup member, we don't experience mirroring in the same way we do for those like us. In addition, group identity can be so strong that the boundary between one's personal self and social self (being a group member) is weak. There is a fusion of identity.[8] On the one hand, this can create tremendous commitment to the group, but on the other hand it can bury individuality and self-reflection. Without self-reflection there cannot be self-other awareness, which in turn limits perspective-taking, which altogether makes feeling empathy very difficult.

Race Is a Strong "Other" in America

Race is possibly the biggest "other" we face in our nation today. Race is a difference that jumps out—we can see it right away. It has been used as a way to differentiate between "us and them" for much of American history. Today racial otherness is deeply engrained in our modern U.S. history. Slavery based on race was outlawed in this country 150 years ago, but racial segregation remained legal for another 100 years. The lived experience of legal slavery and legal segregation in the United States spanned hundreds of years, leaving a strong mental picture of otherness between races. The impact of this otherness can be seen in recent years in the reactions of whites and blacks to the police shootings of young black men and the rise of the Black Lives Matter movement. The standoff between the American Indian tribal members of the Standing Rock Sioux, who were trying to protect their lands, and the builders of the Dakota Access Pipeline reflected hundreds of years of policies imposed by those in power on nondominant racial groups, thereby ignoring human rights and concerns and treating them as others.

Perception of the impact of race differs widely. According to the Pew Research Center, two-thirds of blacks say it is a lot more difficult to be black in the United States than white, while only about one-quarter of whites say the same. And 84 percent of blacks say they are treated less fairly than whites by the police, while about half of whites agree with that view.[9]

Even if you are rich, highly talented, and famous, accomplishments greatly valued in America, racism still follows you. LeBron James is one of the best professional basketball players to have played in the NBA, yet that level of success does not protect him from being viewed and diminished as an "other" due to his race. In May 2017, while he was in the midst of playing for a championship in the NBA Finals, the front gate of his home in Los Angeles was vandalized with spray-painted racial slurs. LeBron James spoke openly about what it meant to him and what it meant about otherness in America:

> No matter how much money you have, no matter how famous you are, no matter how many people admire you, being black in America is tough. We've got a long way to go, for us as a society and for us as African Americans, until we feel equal in America.[10]

In case we are tempted to view this as an example of extreme fan behavior in attacking the best player on the opposing team, we must ask why the spray painting included derogatory racial terms. Would such an attack happen to a white player, and if so, would his race have been spelled out in spray paint in derogatory terms? The act of putting ourselves in the shoes of another from a social empathy perspective demands that we consider not only what it feels like to be in the other person's situation but also what part history has played in that situation.

Michelle Alexander, in her book *The New Jim Crow*, a brilliant analysis of civil rights and the criminal justice system, views racial and ethnic inequality as a part of American life for a long time to come.[11] Although she sees the damage of othering people by race, she also worries that if we strive for colorblindness, we will ignore all the history of differences between races that has been built into the structures of society. She argues that seeing each other's race is not the problem; the problem is being

> blind to injustice and the suffering of others. . . . Refusing to care for the people we see is the problem. The fact that the meaning of race may evolve over time or lose much of its significance is hardly reason to be struck blind. We should hope not for a colorblind society but instead for a world in which we can see each other fully, learn from each other, and do what we can to respond to each other with love. That was King's dream—a society that is capable of seeing each of us, as we are, with love. That is a goal worth fighting for.[12]

Alexander is making the case that we cannot ignore or sweep away racial differences because we need to consider the historical experience of race in America. Understanding the perspective of others in historical context is social empathy. To become socially empathic across races in order to follow her advice and see each other fully, we need to understand what the research tells us about empathy and race.

Empathy and Race

From neural research, we know that brain activity differs when seeing the pain of those who are like us compared to those who are different, especially when race is involved.[13] In one study comparing brain activity, white and black participants viewed three sets of hands being pricked with a needle.[14] The pictures included a set each of white hands, black hands, and purple hands. The researchers wanted to use the purple hands as a way to control for racial biases. They wanted to see if we affectively share pain with those like us, those different from us, and even those different in no prelearned ways, hence the purple hands. The results showed that participants did share the affective pain with all the sets of hands, but it was strongest with those who are similar (ingroup hands), weaker with those who are neutral (the purple hands), and weakest with those who are different (outgroup members). In addition, the mental sharing of pain took longer for the hands of outgroup members than it did when viewing the pictures of ingroup hands. This suggests that not only do we empathize less with people of another race, but we also process it differently in our brains.

In another study, when participants watched videos of people expressing sadness, their brain activity showed stronger sharing of the sadness with people racially like them (ingroup members) than people who differed.[15] The researchers added an interesting piece to their work. They wondered if a person who was already racially biased would have even less empathic sharing with other races. As part of a psychology course, all the participants had completed a racism scale previous to the experiment. When those scores were compared to the levels of sharing in the sadness of others, the higher the score on the racism scale, the lower the shared sadness with the outgroup member. The researchers concluded that while people are less likely to feel the emotions of those who they consider outgroup members, the sharing becomes even more unlikely if that person is prejudiced.

Additional research supports the finding that there is a racial bias in empathy, but it seems to be something we are taught and is transmitted through culture.[16] The fluid nature of our group identity has been seen in other experiments in which group identity is manipulated in ways that are not related to prior identities. This process involves researching human behavior when people are put in "novel groups," such as dividing people in groups by colors or other arbitrary divisions. Novel groups have no prior socialized meaning. Yet, being placed in a novel group can even override long-standing group identities. Identifying with a group is so powerful that a new, rather innocuous identity, such as being part of the blue team in a competitive game, can connect members who may belong to other racial or social groups that, in a different setting, create "us versus them" feelings.[17]

Thus, although race is typically thought of as a key marker of difference among groups and has been proven to differentiate in levels of empathy for others, it seems to be rather malleable. Three group characteristics seem to be encoded in human beings as necessary to our survival: age, gender, and propensity for coalitional alliance, which is the determination of friend or foe. This makes sense based on thousands of years of human survival. What was most necessary for procreation and tribal peace was to determine who might be a suitable mate (hence the need to identify age and gender) and who could be counted on to ensure the survival of the tribe, and conversely who might be a threat to the survival of the tribe. Race as a marker of group differences is relatively new in human history. Hunter-gatherer tribes could only travel small distances and thus likely only came in contact with others who were affiliated with different tribes but looked the same. Thus, the most important factor to consider in those moments of meeting between tribes was whether they were a friend or enemy. Research has shown that assessing the likelihood of an alliance is key. Race as a categorization for group otherness is socially constructed and can be changed.[18]

What seems to happen is that we often encounter race as a group identity that actually covers for the friend or foe perception. We learn to associate the race of other groups as a proxy for whether they are a group that will support and work with us or that is a threat to us. It is a cognitively learned process that research has found can easily be manipulated (think of today's political rhetoric), which is not the case for grouping by sex or age. This is good news because it means that racial bias can be unlearned, and, in turn, empathic sharing across races can be improved.

Social Stigma

Unfortunately, race is not the only ingroup/outgroup barrier to empathy. Just the mere perception of someone as an outgroup member, such as that person being homeless or a drug addict, can lead to lower empathic sharing. Even the circumstances surrounding a person's outside status can impact other people's levels of empathy. In a brain imaging study, participants were measured on their sharing of pain with people with AIDS. There were two different groups presented: some who got AIDS from blood transfusions and others who got AIDS from sharing needles while using illegal intravenous drugs.[19] Sensitivity to pain was greater for those who contracted AIDS through infected blood transfusions than for those who contracted AIDS through intravenous drug use. Using additional measures, the researchers found that the more participants perceived a person was to blame for the situation, the less empathy they experienced for that person. Thus, otherness on a number of levels can impede empathy—race is an obvious difference, but the way a person lives can also set us apart. If we think that his or her lifestyle is immoral or endangers others, then we are less likely to connect on an empathic level.

In fact, this difference in how we view people with AIDS actually played out in public policy. Although AIDS as a public health concern gained attention during the mid-1980s, the federal government response was slow. In fact, the Reagan administration had quietly made it their policy to not mention AIDS to avoid dealing with it because the largest groups affected were gay men and intravenous drug users, groups for whom there was not a lot of empathy.[20] Then came the story of a young boy with hemophilia living in Indiana who had contracted AIDS through a blood transfusion. Ryan White was being banned from attending school for fear of passing AIDS to other children. This brought a great deal of attention to the disease and shifted public perception in a way that made advancing policy easier—caring about a boy who, through no fault of his own, had contracted AIDS aroused much more concern than for those who had previously been identified, primarily people who were viewed with stigma: gay men and intravenous drug users. In 1990, the federal government passed the Ryan White Comprehensive AIDS

Resources Emergency (CARE) Act, the first, and to this day only, federal public policy to address those who have AIDS and related health needs.

Connections Between Ingroup and Outgroup Members

Distance between groups is rather easily cultivated. Recent research has found that just the presence of an outgroup member in a group setting has the effect of dampening neural activity, making the observed person less interested and motivated in the group.[21] This presents a challenge when organizing across community groups. If just the mere presence of someone seen as an outgroup member can limit neural activity, then the likelihood that empathy is blocked increases. If feeling different from others is not addressed, there will be little hope of sharing experiences and creating empathy between groups.

The research is telling us that getting to know people and finding ways to understand each other are important first steps to building empathic exchanges. Although the perceived differences between ingroup and outgroup members are powerful enough to limit empathy, it seems that when confronted with an outgroup member, if we can see individual characteristics that seem similar to us, we are more inclined to act empathically.[22] What does this mean? It means that if we connect on some shared aspect when confronted by someone who seems very different or foreign to us, we can evoke empathy between us. I was indirectly taught this human ability by a story my father told while I was growing up. Although I had heard the story numerous times over my lifetime, the connection to empathy only came to me while writing this chapter.

My father was a soldier in the U.S. Army during World War II. He shared many of his experiences through his stories, spanning joining the army, training throughout the United States, transferring to Iceland and then England, landing on the beaches of Normandy, fighting through France and Belgium, being captured by the German army, spending time as a prisoner of war in Germany, and finally being liberated. As you can imagine, as much as all those experiences influenced my father, hearing stories of that journey from him influenced my growing up. One story he told strikes me as a strong example of the power of bridging the ingroup/outgroup gap through humanizing oneself to the other person, powerful enough to have saved his life.

As the end of the war was drawing near, my father and his fellow prisoners were forced to march away from the front lines, sleeping in fields at night. Food for prisoners had become even scarcer than it had already been, and starvation was a constant threat to my father's survival. Occasionally, prisoners were assigned to local farmers to do menial tasks. One day my father was told to go help a farmer with some work on his farm. As he did so, he could smell cooking from the farmer's kitchen and saw that a woman (likely the farmer's wife) was making potato pancakes. She had the kitchen door open, and as my father walked by, in his broken German, he mentioned to her that his grandmother had been in Hamburg (a major city in Germany) and had also made potato pancakes. The woman looked at him and, likely from a place of connection, thinking my father had family from Germany and was missing his grandmother, gave him one of the potato pancakes she was making. When the farmer came back and found out, he was furious because helping a prisoner could have put his family in danger. For my father, he would say that potato pancake gave him nourishment that lasted for weeks, keeping him alive.

What my father's story taught me is that his survival instinct, linked with his self-other awareness and perspective-taking, guided him to find a personal way to connect with the German woman and get her to feel his hunger. What is even more incredible about the story is that my father's broken German was a result of having grown up Jewish and learning Yiddish, a Germanic-influenced language. Here was this Jewish prisoner of war making a personal connection with a German civilian in the midst of World War II. The story was full of other lessons. My father's German was elementary, but he made clear to us that he said his grandmother had *been in* Hamburg, not that she had actually *lived* there. She had been in Hamburg as one of many stops along her travels as an immigrant from Eastern Europe in the late 1800s while making her way to the United States. And she did make potato pancakes. My father was very proud that in no way did he lie about any of the information he shared. I heard my father tell that story dozens of times. Only now do I realize that he was describing a way to connect with people on a personal level even when the differences were so vastly and dangerously different. It is a credit to him that he did so with full honesty, although the impression he was trying to make was clearly stronger than what may have been. What a lesson! Now, after studying empathy, I see that what my father's intuition did to survive was in fact a well-developed social skill designed to increase empathic connection between ingroup and outgroup members. That was a skill I watched growing up. My father was a master of talking to all different types of people; for him it was a genuine interest. We used to joke that my father knew one sentence in every language because over the years, as he would meet people from different cultures, he would ask them to teach him something. As a young girl, I often felt embarrassed, like when he would ask the busy waitress who was trying to take our order how to say "how are you?" in Polish, Swedish, or Italian. But now I understand that I was watching firsthand a way to bridge otherness and connect with people from different groups, as well as how valuable that skill can be.

When Empathy Goes into Hiding: Genocide, Apartheid, and Slavery

What about when the distance between people is so great that not only is empathy absent, but people also do horrible things to other people? Here is the most frustrating aspect of empathy: We have the biological building blocks to become empathic, but we also have the biological drive to divert us from empathy. We have the mental abilities to learn to be empathic, but we also have learned mental obstacles like prejudice that block empathy. It is a major struggle, and one that we as human beings experience more deeply than other species. Worst of all is that human beings throughout history have taken their fear of others to extreme levels and developed sophisticated plans to eliminate those who are different. We have historical examples of genocide and cultural wars so numerous that Steven Pinker filled almost eight hundred pages of his book *The Better Angels of Our Nature* with accounts of such behavior throughout human history.[23]

It seems that if we can dehumanize another and completely divorce that individual from the human race, then we can sever any connection.[24] That helps to explain how slavery and atrocities such as genocide can occur without empathy between the perpetrators and the victims. If the slave or the enemy is less than human, then empathic connection is blocked, and any pain or humiliation inflicted on the other is not felt. Social psychologist Peter Glick has done extensive research on the social breakdown that leads to genocide.[25] He finds that when there are social, political, or economic conditions that are problematic and difficult to understand, people seek answers that make sense to them. The desire for comprehendible explanations contributes to being swayed to blame others for the problems, what he calls "ideological scapegoating." Such stereotyping and blame can find an easy home when there are longstanding mistrust and negative beliefs about the other group. The Holocaust is a glaring example of this phenomenon. Coming out of World War I, Germany struggled economically and had trouble regaining status as a leading nation, while at the same time sharing the longstanding European undercurrent of seeing Jews as outsiders with no allegiance to their nation or values. These conditions contributed to what psychologist Ervin Staub sees as a psychological need for security, safety, and an understanding of the world.[26] He argues that when these needs go unmet, stronger attachment to one's own group feels comforting and promises solutions. The stronger the group identity, the stronger the feelings of being part of an ingroup and the stronger the difference with outgroups. Not all societies resolve complex social or economic problems with stereotyping and dehumanizing others, but we can see variations of it when certain groups are blamed for problems, such as immigrants taking jobs and thus causing economic problems or unreligious people not respecting the values of marriage in their support of same-sex unions. We'll look at some of these growing group differences and what it might mean for our future at the end of this chapter.

Overcoming Our Group Bias

Not all social problems are viewed through ideological stereotyping. Empathy for the needs of others can be found among many groups in our nation. Empathy in spite of our needs for security, safety, and understanding can happen. Neuroscience research and analysis of history suggest that we may rely more on our hardwired biological parts to empathize with someone who is like us, a member of our ingroup, but we have to call on learned behaviors (cognitive processes) or interact with others in different ways in order to have empathy for those who are different from us.[27] If this is the case, it tells us a lot about how to cultivate empathy within groups and between groups because different neural mechanisms are needed in each case. For example, when we are faced with observing those who we like and those who we do not like, there seems to be different neural activities that are called upon to process empathic feelings. In a study with Jewish male participants who were introduced via video stories to people who were designed to be likeable and people who were designed to be offensive as anti-Semitic hateful people, there were significant neural differences in how they viewed these subjects' experience of pain (being shown each subject getting an injection in the palm of the hand).[28] While the participants mirrored pain for both groups, the intensity was greater for the hateful group, and there was also greater brain activity for emotion regulation, as well as evidence of activity in the brain area that senses rewards. The participants felt the pain of both groups but may have felt a sense of satisfaction that the hateful group was getting what it deserved. That mix of emotions gave rise to the need to regulate those emotions. Hence the brain activity was different for observing the pain of likeable people versus the pain of hateful people.

Thinking in terms of the components of empathy, this means that empathy for those who are like us draws more on our affective mirroring responses so we can more easily feel and see ourselves in the other person. But empathy for people who are different may rely on the learned thinking part of our brain, on self-other awareness, micro and macro perspective-taking, emotion regulation, and contextual understanding.

Learning to Not Have Empathy

As I was doing research on how and why people commit atrocities, particularly on the Holocaust, I came across some interesting studies discussed in Roy F. Baumeister's fascinating but dark book about evil and human violence.[29] One of the atrocities committed during the Nazi rule of Germany was rounding up Jewish civilians, having them dig large pits, ordering them to undress and stand at the edge of the pit, and shooting them. If the body did not fall into the pit, the soldiers had to physically move it into the pit. As described by Baumeister in his analysis of human violence and cruelty, this would seem to be "easy" for soldiers, as it did not involve combat or threat to their own lives. However, reports of anxiety, depression, and sleep disorders were common. Those ordered to do these killings would often find ways to get out of the task, which is not surprising. But many did it and found ways to manage doing it. What seemed to be more universal, and is found in research on other perpetrators of violence such as serial killers, is that the perpetrators experienced significant physical reactions initially, including literally being sick to their stomachs. Baumeister summarizes from the research that inflicting severe harm on another person is upsetting and physically disturbing, although with repetition it becomes easier. "The distress associated with hurting or killing seems to be different from the moral or spiritual objection that might be expected. It is not that people feel that their principles have been violated, although some may indeed have such objections. Rather, it seems to be more of a gut reaction."[30]

It seems that physically, emotionally, and psychologically we have a natural tendency to be opposed to killing other human beings. Lt. Col. Dave Grossman has spent years studying the act of killing in combat in order to understand how we train soldiers to overcome their resistance to killing.[31] He documents a long history of soldiers in combat who found ways to avoid actually killing another human being. This aversion seems to be deeply seated in our human psyche. We recognize ourselves in the other in ways that make killing abhorrent. But people figure out ways to overcome this resistance; we have legions of examples. Foremost is physical distance: the more remote the contact, such as through long-range artillery or bombing from the air, the easier it is to kill. It is a target and not a human being. Obedience to authority can also push people to kill: "I was just following orders." This allows for a psychological distance, not being personally responsible. Other research suggests that killing as a loyalty to your own group can be justified. If we don't kill them, they will kill us. Perhaps most effective for close-range killing is to create emotional distance, or to portray others as less than human. Grossman summarizes this process:

> It is so much easier to kill someone if they look distinctly different from you. If your propaganda machine can convince your soldiers that their opponents are not really human but are "inferior forms of

life," then their natural resistance to killing their own species will be reduced. Often the enemy's humanity is denied by referring to him as a "gook," "Kraut," "Nip," or "raghead." In Vietnam this process was assisted by the "body count" mentality, in which we referred to and thought of the enemy as numbers. One Vietnam Vet told me that this permitted him to think that killing the NVA and VC was like "stepping on ants."[32]

When I read Baumeister's story of German soldiers and Grossman's analysis of the learned ability to kill, I was struck by what may happen to empathy when we are taught to kill. We know that dehumanizing others makes it easier to kill, as well as treating others as slaves and using torture and other forms of violence against them. Constructing others as not like us and less than human is a cognitive process; it can be taught. Seeing otherness can be strengthened with fear and threats to survival: "We can't let *them* destroy us." What cannot be shifted easily are our unconscious physical reactions, our mirroring or affective responses. What I see in the history of human atrocities is the social construction of dehumanizing enemies as a way of getting people to fight and kill these others. But the involuntary physical reaction of being sickened happens. Mirroring means that inflicting pain on another person will likely trigger some physical sharing of the pain. With repetition, that physical reaction gets easier to handle. Strong mental otherness imaging of others, such as calling them inhuman terms and presenting "evidence" that shows their intent to harm us, dehumanizes others so that committing violence against them becomes easier. Combine the mental image of nonhuman others with all sorts of ways that these others threaten the ingroup's survival and we have all the ingredients needed to help perpetrators learn to tamp down the unconscious physical affective response.

There is a high cost to desensitizing people to the humanity of others. Grossman goes on to warn us that once this kind of racial, ethnic, and cultural hatred is unleashed during wartime, it can be difficult to retract for decades and even centuries afterward. He cites all the posttraumatic stress that affected soldiers on both sides of the Vietnam War as a recent example of the high personal and social cost. In chapter 5 we will explore how such stress can dampen and even cost us our empathy, creating an unfortunate, long-lasting impact of all that unleashed otherness.

However, we might be able to reverse the sense of dehumanization. In a study of real-life enemies (Jewish Israelis and Palestinians), when people were told about help that their group had given to the other group, their recognition of the outgroup's humanity increased.[33] Telling stories of help from ingroup members to outgroup members may have tapped into empathic feelings between the groups. Based on what we know about all the components of empathy, maybe a key way to address violence and enhance empathy is to stop the efforts used to dehumanize others. This includes between individuals, which might include bullying and stereotyping, and on larger social levels, in which public policies contribute to demonizing certain groups and pitting people against each other (for example, immigrants versus native born, heterosexual versus homosexual, or Muslims versus Christians). Recreating humaneness shifts the balance from "us versus them" to "we are similar and in this together." This means that we can have empathy for all people. But it takes more work to develop empathy for those who we perceive as different from ourselves. Or, if we can shift the way we see ourselves away from ingroup and outgroup identities and instead create more global "us" identities, like being part of world humanity instead of discrete citizens of a particular country or ethnic group, then we have less of a barrier to feeling empathy for others. For me, the realization that empathic feelings are malleable reinforces the need for social empathy, taking perspective-taking deeper and broader to encompass social, economic, and cultural differences across all communities, nationally, and globally.

Empathy Is the Antidote to Otherness

While we have tremendous biological, historical, and humanly constructed ways of perceiving the danger others may pose to our safety, when we develop strong enough empathic abilities, we can change the way we see other people and other groups and then change the way we interact. Simply put, empathy is the antidote to otherness. Empathy is the solution to how we overcome prejudice, discrimination, and oppression. If empathy is the way we can overcome the otherness of prejudice, discrimination, and oppression, then it would be helpful to better understand what happens when we face those who are different from ourselves and what it means on the larger scale of communities and cultures that differ yet share our global space.

We are currently going through major social changes in the United States that increase the need for safety, security, and attachment. The potential to tap the fear from those changes is great. We hear about group differences on the news, talk radio highlights an "us versus them" mentality to create loyal listeners, and our political processes create extreme divisiveness between political parties. What we need to do is to understand those changes and then find ways to give security to those who are alarmed by them so we don't have further growth in the distance between different groups.

Demographic Change and Why It Scares People, Triggers Survival Mode, and Blocks Empathy

The 2016 presidential election brought up many issues that were polarizing. The "us versus them" feelings were tapped in the portrayal of immigrants versus native born, race differences accentuated by police shootings of young black men giving rise to the Black Lives Matter movement, and the class difference between those at the top and those struggling to make ends meet. While watching some of Donald Trump's campaign rallies on TV, these are some of the handmade signs I saw audience members holding up:

"Build a wall"
"Take back our country"
"Make THEM leave"

My first reaction was that this was an example of a complicated issue, immigration, reduced to ingroup versus outgroup. Using my best perspective-taking skills, I tried to understand the opposing sides on immigration in the 2016 presidential election. But promising to build a wall between the United States and Mexico was a powerful example of separating the ingroup from the outgroup. We already have portions of the wall built. I have visited the wall, and it is not a sight that makes a warm or empathic impression. It may project an image of security, but only as a physical barrier. It presents a physical divider that reinforces otherness. The wall invokes a strong message

Figure 3.1 "The Wall"—The border between the United States and Mexico

that people who are different from us should stay away. Here are some photos of the wall between San Diego, California, and Tijuana, Mexico (taken in 2013, before building it became a campaign promise). It looks like a wall around a prison. By the way, we don't have walls like this on the border we share with Canada.

Even though the sign in figure 3.2 is on the United States side, there no need for English, only Spanish—we know who it is meant for.

We know that invoking otherness is a tactic that can bring your own group together. Typically such otherness involves demonizing the outside group. It creates an "us versus them" mentality and suggests that survival depends on sticking together and fighting off the outgroup. Calling outsiders names, like criminals or rapists, helps to separate them from the ingroup, making *them* less than human and consequently entirely different from *us*.

Donald Trump was not the first politician or leader to tap into the deeply imbedded fear of others. Part of our biological survival depended on being wary and careful about those who are different until we knew for sure whether they were safe or would harm us. We know that a sense of "otherness" exists in all of us. Wait a minute—so people screaming at each other "go back to where you came from" is biologically driven? To a certain extent, yes it is. However, the behavior to act aggressively or violently based on otherness, although possibly triggered by fear of others, is more likely a learned reaction, particularly in our modern world. Chances are that most of the people

Figure 3.2 "WARNING—High Security Zone—Barb Wired—Passage Is Prohibited"

who worry about harm that will come to them from people who look different from them actually have no real personal experience with those who are different and whom they fear. It is a learned response that comes from a place of fear, fear that your comfortable survival zone is at risk. What triggers this fear? Change that feels like a disruption to your equilibrium, what you know to be right, and your safety. Although the United States has been shifting demographically for hundreds of years, the fears of otherness today are based on changes that have been rather significant over the past fifty years. Some of the demographic and social changes that have upended the status quo have come quickly, over the past ten to twenty years.

The United States Is Changing Very Fast

The proportions of different groups in the United States were relatively constant for two hundred years. In fact, the U.S. Census Bureau did not even track categories such as mixed race or Hispanic until 1970. That is not to say that different races, ethnicities, and cultures were absent. Rather, they were considered insignificant in terms of the total society. Segregation by race and class meant people could go a lifetime without having a meaningful exchange with someone of a different race. Prior to television and media, where people lived was the total sum of their experiences. Until the civil rights movement and the passage of the Civil Rights Act in 1964, separation between groups was the norm and was in full effect. Thus, the demographic and social changes that catapulted the political ascendency of Donald Trump were in part based on the rapid social changes of the past fifty years of U.S. history, changing a social landscape that dated back to the 1600s. Robert P. Jones of the nonpartisan Public Religion Research Institute chronicles these changes in his book *The End of White Christian America*.[34] He discusses two major trends in our country that have contributed significantly to the shift: demographic changes in our population and the growth of those who identify as religiously unaffiliated.

Until the 1980s, the proportion of the population that was identified as white was a large majority, almost 90 percent. From 1980 to 2010, according to the official census (which many argue undercounts members of nondominant groups because they can be harder to locate due to more frequent moves and are less likely to respond due to mistrust of authorities), the proportion of the white population in the Unites States declined by almost 13 percent, while those identified as black, mixed race, or other grew by more than 60 percent (see table 3.1 and figure 3.3). The Latino population, which can be white or black, also grew by more than 150 percent. Looking at 2010, we can see that the population of the United States was more than one-quarter people of color. Based on the changes of the past fifty years, the Census Bureau estimates that by 2060 one-third of the population will be people of color and almost 30 percent will be Hispanic.

If we add to these actual changes in numbers a shift in the visibility of different races and ethnicities due to the growth in media and racial

TABLE 3.1
Population Distribution from 1940 to 2010 According to the
U.S. Census Bureau

	White (%)	Black (%)	Other/Mixed races (%)	Hispanic or Latino (%)
1940	89.8	9.8		
1950	89.5	10.0		
1960	88.6	10.5		
1970	87.5	11.1	1.4	4.5
1980	83.0	11.7	5.3	6.4
1990	80.3	12.1	7.6	9.0
2000	75.1	12.3	12.6	12.5
2010	72.4	12.6	15.0	16.3

composition of popular pastimes such as sports teams, the impact likely feels even greater. Other demographic changes have added to the shift. The number of foreign-born people in the United States has more than doubled from 1980 to 2010 (see table 3.2 and figures 3.4 and 3.5).[35] The overall addition of immigrants has steadily climbed since the 1970s.

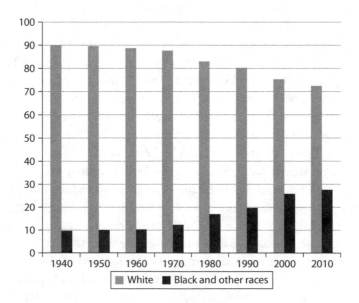

Figure 3.3 Changes in U.S. population, 1940–2010

TABLE 3.2
Net Immigration

1931–1940	121,000
1941–1950	754,000
1951–1960	2,090,000
1961–1970	2,422,000
1971–1980	3,223,000
1981–1990	5,655,000
1991–2000	6,743,000
2001–2010	7,396,000

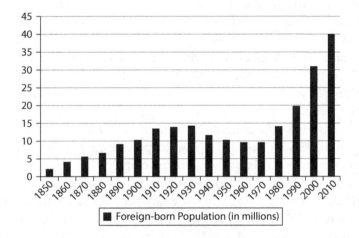

Figure 3.4 Foreign-born population (in millions)

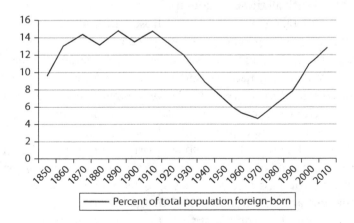

Figure 3.5 Percent of total population foreign born

We have also seen shifts in our values, as more than 60 percent of all Americans support same-sex marriage.[36] These demographic and social value changes, while overall representing significant proportions of the population, are not evenly distributed geographically. Much of the demographic changes have taken place in urban areas, and the acceptance of value shifts, such as support of same-sex marriage, is also geographically split and divided by political party.[37] Consider the political divide among the states most supportive of same-sex marriage (Washington, Oregon, Colorado, Vermont, New Hampshire, New York, Connecticut, Massachusetts, Rhode Island, New Jersey, and Delaware) and the states least supportive (Mississippi, Alabama, Tennessee, Arkansas, South Dakota, Louisiana, Utah, and North Dakota). All the high-support states voted for the Democratic candidate, Barack Obama, in the 2012 presidential election, and all the least supportive states voted for the Republican candidate, Mitt Romney.[38]

Another area of demographic change that has likely contributed to unease with how the country has shifted in recent years is the place of women. In 1950, one-third of women participated in the civilian labor force compared to almost 90 percent of men. By 2010, the rate for women had almost doubled to 60 percent of women actively engaged in the civilian labor force, while the rate for men had actually dropped to just over 70 percent. Overall, from 1950 to 2010, the rate for men dropped almost 18 percent over the sixty years and increased for women by almost 73 percent.[39] A shift in religious identification has been coupled with all these demographic and value changes. According to Gallup polls taken over the years, those who identify as Christian has declined from 91 percent in 1950 to 72 percent in 2015.[40]

Perhaps the most telling statistic about these changes comes from another Pew Research national survey.[41] In response to the question "Compared with fifty years ago, life for people like you in America today is better, worse, or the same?" 81 percent of Trump supporters said it was worse compared to only 19 percent of Clinton supporters, and only 11 percent of Trump supporters said it was better compared to 59 percent of Clinton supporters. The way our country has changed over the past fifty years has split us between those who feel those changes are for the better and those who feel they are for the worse. These numbers show that fear of how our country has changed became linked to a political candidate.

The Cost of Being an Outgroup Member

What do all these changes mean? For those who are not accustomed to living, working, and socializing with other racial, ethnic, religious, or sexual identity groups, it means the safety of their ingroup dominance is being challenged. Members of dominant groups are not used to being challenged in this way. Being on the outside as a minority typically means one has to be able to cross social and economic divides. Belonging to a nondominant group tends to make one more empathic compared to those who are part of the dominant culture because one has to understand both one's own culture and that of the majority.[42] The ability to emotionally and cognitively understand both one's own culture and those that are different from your own is often referred to as "intercultural" or "ethnocultural empathy." For example, if you grow up poor in a community of color and want to go to college, you will likely have to learn how to navigate the world of the dominant culture. I learned this lesson from one of my first students. It was my very first time teaching. I was a graduate student teaching an introductory course. Like most first-time teachers, I was very nervous and wanted to do well. I had some diverse students; in fact, what I loved about the university was that I found it very diverse, especially compared to the small liberal arts college I had attended as an undergraduate. It was a public university on an urban campus with thousands of students, with people from different racial and ethnic backgrounds. After I handed back an assignment, I noticed a young African American women who sat in the back. She did not speak in class, and I was worried about her body language. At times she looked bored and at times she looked annoyed. I was not sure how to reach her, and I was especially nervous about it because of my very limited experience teaching. I was thinking about asking my advisor for some direction.

That week I was on my regular subway commute to school, and at the transfer stop, who do I see but my student. I said hello and asked her how things were going. She shrugged and said something about not understanding my class. I jumped on the chance and suggested she come to my office, where we could talk about what was not clear. Thankfully she took me up on the offer. We started reviewing the course material, and she told me about her journey to the university. She had been a straight-A student at an all-black local community college. She was the only person in her family to go to college. She had just transferred to the university, and this was her first quarter. Over the course of numerous meetings, I learned a lot from her. For her, our university was the whitest institution she had ever been a part of, and she was uncomfortable. All her professors were white, unlike at the community college. She was uncomfortable approaching them, and they did not approach her. It was eye opening for me because I thought we had such a diverse university. She had never seen such a large library and did not know how to use it. All her instructors at the community college let their students hand-write their papers; here she was supposed to type her work. She did not have a typewriter. (This was years before personal computers.)

I was struck by how different life for her was at this urban, public university from what I imagined it to be. It was a humbling experience. We went to the library together, where she learned how to do research for my class; she did very well. She was a very smart young woman. I wish there had been a happy ending. She stopped by periodically after our class ended and gave me updates. She had not connected with any other professors (unfortunately I was only a graduate student, not a professor) and found their courses to be difficult. Biology was the worst; she had never been in a laboratory before. She came by less and less, and when weeks had gone by with no word, I asked our registrar about her. I was told she was on leave. She never came back. She had started to learn the process of operating within a culture that was new and foreign to her, but it was too much. The university had no system of support for students like her. I learned a lot from her experience, and it helped me to understand the huge divide between the dominant and nondominant culture and the cost of being an outsider in my university world. I could not do much on an individual basis, so I was drawn to figure out what should be done on a societal basis. This was one more experience that led me to social empathy.

Can We Bridge the Otherness Divide?

As I was writing this chapter, I was struck by how different urban and rural life in the United States is when it comes to interactions among people who are different in the ways that ask us to demonstrate intercultural empathy, such as with people of other races, ethnicities, and classes. In most urban areas, even when people do live divided by race, ethnicity, and class, there are more interrelations and thus people are more likely to mix in what I call "micro novel groups." Remember that novel groups are those groupings that are arbitrary and not based on shared meaningful differences. In spite of the superficiality of a novel group, membership can override biases based on previous ingroup and outgroup identities. Thus, being divided into the purple team versus the yellow team to play a game or work on a project can create a unified identity that overrides that of each person's individual race, ethnicity, or class identity. Could it be that living in a community in which you move in and out of micro novel groups with mixed identities creates more tolerance and understanding of people who are different? I am thinking of the years when I commuted to work on public transportation in very multicultural cities. Sometimes something quirky would happen, such as a sudden stop or the driver making an announcement that no one could understand. People would have brief moments of unification, asking each other what was going on or sharing surprise at the suddenness of the stop. This moment creates a micro novel group: the riders on that subway train. Living in diverse urban areas means it is more likely that one will work in places with diverse colleagues and interact with people from different backgrounds for day-to-day living tasks such as grocery shopping, moving through multiple micro novel groups.

On a daily basis, living in a diverse community means repeated moments that include people from a variety of backgrounds as part of micro novel groups. Other experiences such as travel or attending a large university open the way to participate in micro novel groups with diverse people. This means that on numerous occasions each day, a person might have moments when his or her main group identity takes a back seat to a new novel group identity. These experiences can add up over time to reorient our neural pathways to accommodate more affective and cognitive reading of people who are different. On the other hand, living in a homogenous community in which the micro novel groups do not include diversity would make the ability to develop intercultural empathy more difficult and unlikely. Could these experiences help explain why urban areas tend to have different political leanings than do rural areas? Looking at the 2012 electoral map from a more detailed perspective of voting districts reveals a much more concentrated difference between political voting. Although an entire state may be considered "red" (Republican) or "blue" (Democratic), what is evident in the map in figure 3.6 is that urban areas are much more likely to be blue, while rural areas are much more likely to be red.[43]

The urban-rural divide was evident again in 2016. Of the twenty-five most populous cities in the United States, twenty-two went to the Democratic candidate in the 2016 presidential election. Of those twenty-two cities, more than half (twelve) were in Republican major-ity states. That includes cities like Houston, Indianapolis, Memphis, Charlotte, Dallas, and Nashville, all in solidly red states.

What does this tell us? First, that urban areas vote differently than nonurban areas. Second, that diversity is more prevalent in urban areas, while homogeneity is more prevalent in rural areas. These geographic areas reflect different experiences, values, and beliefs. These differences make empathic understanding between groups challenging. If we want to promote empathy across different groups, we need to find ways to override ingroup bias. Research tells us that can be done through cog-nitive training: the rethinking of our patterns of ingroup dominance. Having experiences with members of different groups is one way to help us develop the neural pathways that shift views of otherness and group differences. The challenge is finding ways to connect different groups in meaningful ways across geographic and cultural distances.

There are two difficulties in connecting ingroup and outgroups member. One is the obvious problem of connecting people who are geographically distant, and the other is that there is discomfort and anxiety in bringing together members of different groups, particularly for those who are from nondominant groups that already feel the pres-sure of being on the outside of a majority culture.[44] One encouraging approach to counter these two issues is called "extended contact."[45] This approach relies on indirect experience with other groups, pri-marily through the contact one's friends have with other groups. In a study of school-aged children, for both majority and minority chil-dren, greater extended contact with outgroups was accompanied by higher intergroup empathy, more positive attitudes toward outgroup members, and less stereotyping.[46] That is, being friends with people who have diverse friends expands the empathy and understanding of outside groups through that friendship. While the researchers do not consider extended contact to be a replacement for direct intergroup experiences, they consider extended contact a useful way to reduce prejudice and prepare people for future intergroup relations.

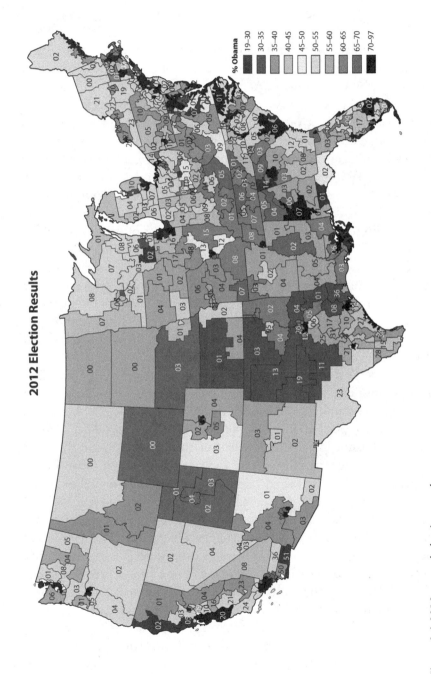

Figure 3.6 2012 general election results

The Need to Bridge Otherness

I had finished the first full draft of this book a few days before white supremacists marched in Charlottesville, Virginia, on the campus of the University of Virginia in August 2017.[47] I watched the television on Friday night as the news showed live images of hundreds of all-white marchers, most of them young men, carrying flaming torches and yelling Nazi slogans. All I could think about were two sets of images I had seen in black-and-white grainy film: of Kristallnacht,[48] the night in 1938 when Nazis across Germany and Austria looted and destroyed Jewish shops and synagogues using torches to ignite fires, and of hooded KKK members over many decades riding on horses at night holding burning torches, circling the homes of African American families while dragging a family member out to be lynched. I knew those images were exactly what those marchers wanted me to see—at least those who planned it. There were hundreds of torches; this was a well-orchestrated message. It's very possible that many of the marchers did not know the historical facts of Kristallnacht or the depth of the legacy of lynching, but they knew that carrying those torches would scare those who were the targets of their hatred.

The visceral fear that I and so many other people felt that night and the next day was intentional; it was a blatant example of using otherness to intimidate and control those who are different. It showed reading other people, but it lacked walking in their shoes. Those marchers did not imagine themselves or their loved ones in the place of those being terrorized, and they did not show that they considered the targets of their hatred to be human beings like themselves. Am I being too harsh or overgeneralizing? There probably were some who marched without fully understanding the implications of what they were doing, but their ability to take the actions they did shows that they saw people different from them as others, people to whom they could not relate or feel similar. And how do we know that? By the slogans they chanted, the symbols they carried, the goals they espoused, and, ultimately, by purposefully taking the life of someone who came out that day to stand against their show of hatred.

Unfortunately it can be easy to be caught up with belonging to a tribe that gains its identity by focusing on hatred of others. It feels powerful to be part of a group that claims selectiveness as a criterion to belong—you need to be like us and not like all those others who are less than we are. It is seductive because it makes us feel wanted and connected. But being wanted and connected at the expense of other people's humanity is tribalism in its worst form. That is why we need to work at understanding what it really means and feels like to be someone else, as if we were living their life, and what the historical experiences of all groups mean.

CHAPTER FOUR

Are Power and Politics Barriers to Empathy?

POWER CAN BE found in a lot of places and in many relationships. It is always found in politics. I learned that firsthand when I spent a year working as a fellow in Washington, DC. My doctoral research was on public policy, specifically the Social Security Act. I always had an interest in actually contributing my research to the making of public policy. I had entertained the idea of doing a city government internship as a way to bring my studies into real-world policy making, but my advisor wisely warned me against doing that while working on my degree. She was worried that I would get side-tracked and never finish my studies. So I finished my degree and, in line with my training, I started teaching at the university level. While I was very happy teaching, the itch to actually "do" policy rather than study it got stronger. After two years of teaching, I was lucky enough to be chosen to serve as a Congressional Science Fellow.

My year in Washington was split between working in the office of a U.S. senator and serving as a legislative analyst in an office sponsored by Statehouse members back home in Illinois. It was fascinating to see and be part of the numerous power rankings. The most obvious power was in the making of public laws. Congress and the president, supported by a massive staff across federal agencies and political offices, were the crafters of the rules and regulations that governed all of our lives. What an incredible seat I had to watch the making of U.S. law! But that was only the official power. What struck me was all the other power that rested in people's hands at so many different levels.

Power in Politics

When I worked in the Senate office, just mentioning my place of employment (even though I was a temporary fellow) meant my phone calls were answered, people were happy to meet with me, and I would receive any reports or data I needed. I was in research heaven. However, in that Senate office, I was constantly reminded of my outside status. I was told that things were different in Washington and not like the life of a university professor. The first memo I was asked to write was an internal memo, only to be read in the senator's office. It was returned to me by the legislative director (to whom I reported) with corrections seven times (and the memo was only five sentences long). He frequently made fun of me for being an "ivory-towered" academic, an outsider. To be sure that I was aware of my position, he moved my desk on three different occasions over six months, all without telling me beforehand. I might have taken it personally (okay, I did a little), but it was simply the way things were done. I watched as staff more senior than I was complained about being treated like lackeys one day (having to carry the senator's coat and briefcase without being conspicuous or saying a word) to providing a briefing on legislative issues of importance the next day. It was a wild ride of being important at one moment and being the lowest outsider in another.

When I worked in the state office, my phone calls stopped getting answered and I never got the reports that were supposed to be sent. I was now in a lower-ranked office in the pecking order of Washington. Senate offices were not only physically higher, sitting on Capitol Hill, but also higher in power and rank. Now I was in a state office, not far away, but off of the prime real estate a stone's throw away from the Capitol. When a member of our Illinois state house came to visit, we were all on call to serve any need the elected official might have. On several occasions I overheard those folks complaining that they were not being treated with respect by the Washington elected officials. My boss in that office was very open with us that our job was to make each state elected official feel important because in the pecking order of Washington, he or she was not as important as was the case back home.

It's not that such power rankings did not exist in every place I had been employed. University politics is not free of power maneuvering; it's definitely there. But what struck me about Washington was that power is at every level, front and center. It really was not personal as much as it was practical. Who you are in terms of what you can get done or who you can influence defines you. And that is very much the basis of power.

Power is having influence and control over outcomes in other people's lives.[1] Power is a process in which the few have the means to enforce their choices or will over the many.[2] The nature of power in most systems is in the shape of a pyramid; there are more people at the bottom and fewer people with power as you go up within the system. Most businesses have managers who report to supervisors who in turn ultimately report to company owners or chief executive officers. Schools have teachers who report to principals who report to superintendents. Some systems, like schools, have outside boards to hold the leaders accountable. But the day-to-day power rests in fewer hands as you go up the chain of command. Many of our larger systems are made up of a collection of pyramids that also narrow as we go up the ladder of influence and control. For example, local governments report to state governments that report to the federal government. Because power affects life outcomes, it matters to our daily lives. That is especially true in the very public arena of politics, in which those in power are watched and analyzed by millions.

At the National Achievers Conference in 2012, Donald J. Trump stated: "One of the things you should do in terms of success: If somebody hits you, you've got to hit 'em back five times harder than they ever thought possible. You've got to get even. Get even."[3] Those are powerful words, spoken by a powerful man. At the time he was simply a multimillionaire. He had the power of riches, fame, and position, and four years later he added to that by being elected to the highest political position in this country, president of the United States. With that kind of power, a person can influence every arena of public life. Getting even means you can exert more power over the other.

There does not seem to be much need or room for empathy. You set a goal, you go after it, and all seems to be within your personal control. Is power over others contrary to the empathy we have been talking about? Can we be powerful and still consider the positions and needs of others?

Many in government do not think empathy belongs with power. The president of the State of Arizona Senate in 2014, State Senator Andy Biggs, gave his answer to that question while he was speaking on the floor of the state Senate explaining why the state budget had cut funds for education and social services: "Government is raw power. Government has no compassion or empathy."[4] Two years after saying that, Mr. Biggs was elected to the U.S. Congress and is now serving as a member of the House of Representatives. Clearly he has succeeded in using his power because the voters gave him a promotion. Equally as clear is that he views government as no place for empathy. He is not alone. When President Obama invoked the value of empathy in choosing Supreme Court judges, saying, "I view that quality of empathy, of understanding and identifying with people's hopes and struggles, as an essential ingredient for arriving at just decisions and outcomes," he was met with stiff resistance.[5] In a 2013 article in the *National Review*, James Christophersen, the executive director of the Judicial Action Group, wrote that "the value of 'empathy' as the primary criterion for selecting judges must be eradicated, as should the practical application of that value, which usually means emphasizing race, sexual preference, gender, and political affiliation over basic qualifications and standards" over concern that Obama would again use empathy as a criterion for choosing a Supreme Court justice.[6] He went on to call it a "subversive trend." To Christophersen, empathy means giving things to people who do not deserve them simply because they are a member of a specific group.

Resistance to empathy by those in power tends to break between conservative and liberal lines. Why? Is empathy a soft, liberal-hearted way of thinking that ignores qualifications and standards? Given Biggs's and Christophersen's assessments, it would seem so. In fact, a survey conducted by the Pew Research Center asked about people's political ideology and their beliefs about what is important to teach children.[7] Over three thousand adults were given a list of twelve traits and asked to choose the three that they thought were the most important qualities to teach children. They were also asked to describe where they fell in their political ideology. Table 4.1 shows the distribution of the responses.

On the one hand, there was a good deal of agreement. All the groups agreed that among the top three qualities to teach children, "being responsible" was important. All five categories cited "hard work" as among their top choices, although to varying degrees. However, only one group identified "empathy" as among the most important qualities to teach children—the group who identified themselves as consistently liberal. The trait of "helping others" only showed up as a top quality for the consistently and mostly liberal. "Religious faith" was very important to the mostly conservative and consistently conservative groups, less important for mixed and mostly liberal, and not in the top for consistently liberal (chapter 6 covers religion and empathy, so we will return to this item). "Obedience" was only cited as important by those who identified as consistently conservative. Much of what is in this chart is not surprising given what we know about the political spectrum ranging from liberal to conservative. But what does it say about our ideological divide that teaching children empathy is considered important only by those with the most liberal ideology? Is empathy a liberal perspective? It might be.

Neurological brain activity actually differs between those who identify as liberal and those who identify as conservative. Those who identify as liberal have a greater tendency to take in social cues and context, while those who identify as conservative are more focused on the individual.[8] Other neurological research found that people who identified as liberal dedicated more neurological activity to processing complex and conflicting information, while the neurological activity in people who identified as conservative was connected to maintaining habitual patterns.[9] Genetics may even play a role. Using behavioral genetics analyses of data from twins, researchers found that more than life experience or environment, genetics influenced political attitudes.[10] This genetic influence may explain how we develop our political orientation from a young age. A study that was able to track preschool children over twenty years found that there was a set of characteristics shared by preschoolers who twenty years later identified as politically conservative and a different set of characteristics shared by those preschoolers who later identified as politically liberal.[11] Among the traits in preschoolers who later identified as conservative were uncomfortableness with uncertainty, rigidity under duress, and compliance with

TABLE 4.1
Three Top Qualities Most Important to Teach Children

Consistently Liberal	Mostly Liberal	Mixed	Mostly Conservative	Consistently Conservative
Being responsible: 47%	Being responsible: 55%	Being responsible: 56%	Being responsible: 57%	Being responsible: 61%
Empathy for others: 34%	Hard work: 42%	Hard work: 46%	Religious faith: 44%	Religious faith: 59%
Helping others: 28%	Helping others: 26%	Religious faith: 29%	Hard work: 43%	Hard work: 44%
Hard work: 26%	Being well mannered: 24%	Being well mannered: 26%	Being well mannered: 21%	Being well mannered: 17%
Curiosity: 23%	Religious faith: 23%	Helping others: 24%	Independence: 16%	Obedience: 15%

following directions, while the traits in those preschoolers who later identified as liberal were autonomy, expressiveness, and inclination toward under control, that is, unconstrained by others. A comprehensive review of over eighty studies done across multiple countries supported these other studies: the psychological underpinnings of political conservatism ideology are based in concerns about handling uncertainty and fear, with conservatives having an overall response of resistance to change.[12]

In a very recent study, the power of fear as a precursor to conservative positions on social issues and resistance to social change was confirmed.[13] When half the participants were first asked to imagine having the superpower to be able to fly, their responses to a social attitude survey were as expected: the Republican-identified participants were more conservative and the Democrat-identified participants were more liberal. But when the other half of participants were told to imagine having the superpower to be able to make themselves completely safe and invulnerable to any harm, the Republican-identified participants' positions on social attitudes were more liberal and similar to the Democrat-identified participants. The researchers had addressed the underlying concerns for safety and survival, moving them to take more liberal social views. This is particularly interesting because we know that fear and concern about safety and survival can block empathy.

These studies suggest that the components of empathy may come more naturally to those who hold liberal ideologies—they are already attuned to context and their brain activity reflects processing of complex and conflicting information, which is similar to the cognitive activity needed to maintain self-other awareness and emotion regulation while walking in the shoes of others. On the other hand, as we know from the previous chapters, concern about uncertainty, fear, and resistance to change can all act as barriers to engaging in empathy. I am not saying that liberals are empathic and conservatives are not, rather that the characteristics that commonly follow those identities can be encouraging or inhibiting to engaging in empathy.

Empathy and Social Hierarchy

Political identity is not the only ideology that might have an impact on empathy. People's beliefs and values in how societies are best structured, that is, how the social hierarchy or status of groups is ordered, can play a role. There are varying terms, but the two most basic competing structures are between one that stresses social dominance, in which people prefer their own group to dominate others, and the other view that stresses collectivity and egalitarianism, in which people prefer practices and policies that flatten the hierarchy and promote equality. These two views often relate to conservative political ideologies and liberal political ideologies. Conservative political thinking tends to see society as hierarchical and view groups as not all equal, and liberal political ideology tends to want society to be more egalitarian with more equality between groups and less hierarchy.

Researchers measuring brain activity found that for those who prefer social dominance hierarchy over egalitarianism, there is less neural activity in the region of the brain that is key to the ability to share emotions and feel concern or another person's.[14] This lower activity in sharing emotions has been found to impact how well people can read others. Furthermore, those who believe that social hierarchies are good and that social inequality is normal demonstrate lower empathic accuracy.[15] These same researchers found that even when people themselves lacked power, holding the *belief* that social inequality is part of our natural order was still related to lower empathic abilities.

This raises a key question. Does believing that social inequality is a normal part of our society make one less empathic and thus strive for power over others, or does having lower empathic abilities facilitate the attainment of power, which includes seeing social hierarchy as a key view? For example, lower empathy might make it easier to make tough decisions about subordinates, such as disciplining or firing someone. Thus, those with lower empathy are able to take on the difficult side of being in charge and feel comfortable with the hierarchical relationship they have with their subordinates. While this likely plays a role in the lower empathy of people with a social dominance orientation, it seems that having that perspective may dampen empathy more than empathy tamping down the social dominance preference.[16] Other research seems to back this up. Students with a communal orientation were compared to students with a self-interest orientation (a form of social dominance in which the individual is more important than others). When given power, those with a communal orientation completed tasks in a socially responsible way by choosing to take more of their time and consider others, while those with a self-interest orientation completed tasks faster with their own interest at the forefront.[17] All the students were given power and choice on how to complete the tasks. The difference in how they did it reflected their social orientation. Those who tended toward beliefs that reflect social responsibility used their power for others, while those who tended toward beliefs that reflect focusing on their own needs and interests used their power for themselves.

Power Does Affect Empathy

The research on power and beliefs suggests that the way we think society should be structured, either in a vertical hierarchical order or in a horizontal egalitarian fashion, affects our levels of empathy. There may be several reasons for this difference. Power and being at the top of a social hierarchy may not require attention to others or awareness of the social context. Unlike the powerless, who live with the decisions of the powerful that impact their lives, those who are powerful do not need to pay much attention to those who are powerless. The powerless have no impact on the life outcomes of the powerful. Also, the powerful have more demands for their attention because of their roles in the hierarchy. They have something to offer subordinates. Because of the demands on their attention, they are more likely to use stereotypes. Stereotyping is a quick way to judge people. It serves as a shortcut to understanding others. Psychologist Susan Fiske states it best: "The power*less* are stereotyped because no one needs to, can, or wants to be detailed and accurate about them. The power*ful* are not so likely to be stereotyped because subordinates need to, can, and want to form detailed impressions of them. The powerless need to try and predict and possibly alter their own fates."[18] There seems to be a one-way direction of interest: those with less power are more interested in those with more power.[19]

In addition to less interest in understanding the uniqueness of others, high-powered individuals have a lower capacity for compassion and empathy.[20] This may not be because they are hard-hearted, but instead may be due to a selective use of their attention. High-powered individuals attend less to the social environment, to context. This keeps them from being distracted and makes them more capable of staying on task. There is more to gain for the powerless in understanding peripheral information, while high-powered individuals can focus on the task at hand. This may be in relation to the way high-power individuals approach processing information—high-powered individuals are able to ignore nonrelevant information and focus more deeply on the task, which improves their pursuit of goals because they pay less attention to context or "peripheral information."[21] The powerless, on the other hand, take in all sorts of information and form more complex pictures of people and situations. They actually have higher executive functioning, that is, the mental cognitive processes that help us plan, organize, and make sense out of our surroundings.[22]

In addition to the lack of attention to social context by those in power, another key skill of empathy often gets missed: perspective-taking. Research shows that power actually impedes perspective-taking.[23] There may be two reasons for the lack of perspective-taking for those with power.[24] The first may be the result of a "disinhibiting" effect of power. People with power feel freer to take actions that satisfy their needs or desires. It can be anywhere from being more likely than those with less power to turn off an annoying fan that is blowing in their face[25] to a greater likelihood of committing adultery.[26] In fact, those of higher social class are more likely to behave unethically, including cheating, stealing, and lying, than those of lower social class.[27] These behaviors typically have social norms that place them as misbehaving. But having a sense of power frees people to act more on their impulses with less worry about what others think.

The second reason those with power are less likely to engage in perspective-taking is their self-focus. When participants in a study looking at power and inspiration were asked to talk about and write about an event they found inspirational, those who scored higher on power ratings were more likely to feature themselves in the inspirational event than those who rated lower in power. The researchers came to the conclusion that "the powerful prefer to entertain their own rather than other people's experiences and ideas, because they are more inspired by their own internal states than by those of others."[28]

The behavioral differences between the powerful and the powerless are more than just feelings or desires. We can actually see differences between individuals with power and those without power in their brain patterns. The areas of brain activation of those who feel powerful differ from those who feel powerless.[29] EEG brain scanning (electroencephalography) used to assess the neural activity of participants writing about a situation in which they had power over another person, when compared to participants writing about a situation in which someone had power over them, revealed different brain activity. Those who were in the power group used the system in the brain that stimulates approach (a form of disinhibition) and goal achievement, while those in the powerless group used the part of the brain that is reactive to external events. The researchers concluded that these reactions make sense: those with power are less constrained by the environment or other people and act on their goals and desires, while those with less power pay attention to the environment, likely monitoring any unexpected changes because of their more precarious situation of lacking power. It may be that the powerless, because they are more dependent on others by nature of having fewer resources or control, tend to have a more communal focus.[30]

Thus, we see that having power minimizes perspective-taking, places the self as most important (ignoring self-other awareness), and distances us from our social context. Given these tendencies, power does not move us toward interpersonal or social empathy. While we may feel distressed at the prospect that people in power are unlikely to have empathy, it is not all bad.

The Plus Side of Power

The focus of those in power can result in positive outcomes. Power decreases procrastination, promotes focus and prioritization, and increases persistence, flexibility, and readiness to respond. Together these abilities/behaviors promote goal-directed behavior.[31] These skills can be invaluable when major projects are taken on and deadlines need to be met. However, although power can improve outcomes, it can come at the cost of processing the feelings of those with less power. As I was studying this aspect of empathy and power, I finally got some clarity on an event that occurred in my professional life fifteen years ago.

Years ago we had a major change in leadership at our university. With new people at the top come new directions, which can be both exciting and terrifying. One such change was that our department was one of several that was to be moved off the main campus, our home since the inception of the program thirty years before. We were going to be located twenty miles west on a to-be-built campus downtown. At the time, there was virtually nothing there, an area needing revitalization, and very few of us, especially the support staff, lived in the area. In fact, most of us had bought homes to be close to our jobs, and now our jobs were being moved. That was a very disruptive and anxiety-provoking experience.

The new president of our university held an open forum to answer questions. Over a hundred people showed up, many of whom were frontline staff like secretaries and clerks, some of whom barely made wages above the poverty line. After the president presented the plan, one of the first questions asked was about parking: Would there be affordable and safe parking close to our new workplace? That question set off the president, and he proceeded to berate us that we were small minded by worrying about such an unimportant detail when the big picture was about progress, serving more students and developing a new kind of campus. While that was true, he completely missed the anxiety of those he had tasked with making this move. Most of our students, staff, and faculty were women who were concerned about working in an underdeveloped urban area (at night it was deserted) without knowing if they would have safe parking that they could afford. We had built our lives around our jobs, and now we were being mandated to uproot. On top of that, we were being reprimanded for focusing on the details of the move and not appreciating the bigger, grander picture of what could be.

I learned a lot about empathy and power that day, although I still did not have the deep research-based knowledge that I have today to help me understand what happened. Here was an example of someone in power who was a visionary, completely committed to his vision, but not tuned in to those less powerful than he who were not looking for change and were very content in the current structure. In fact, many of us had lots of friends and working connections forged over many years that were part of where we worked. Moving would change all that. There was no ownership or sense of belonging to this greater vision because it came from the top and was mandated. There was fear of the change, and there were genuine, important life concerns. Those at the top were not picking up any of those emotions. At the same time, knowing what I know now about empathy and power, had the president attended to our needs, he would not have been able to swiftly and efficiently bring to life this new endeavor.

To bring about rapid and dramatic change, people's feelings have to be minimized. Empathy actually can be a barrier to sweeping change, because if you are in charge of those changes, tuning in to all the concerns of those affected by the changes would be overwhelming. But not tuning into those changes has a cost. The cost is that people feel unheard and alienated, and although they may do what you want, they will not feel connected to the mission, the vision, or to you as leader. So it becomes a choice about how much we want to care about others and what we want to accomplish. I do not think that both are impossible to do at the same time, but I am certain that both cannot be done quickly. Processing people's feelings takes time. Attending to empathic insights takes time. It means figuring out what feelings are behind someone worrying about a parking space. That can slow down the big process. It is a question of your priorities. Do you want to engage with people to build a caring and connected community, or do you want to create buildings, programs, and outcomes that are tangible in an efficient and timely manner? Some of us leave a place behind hoping that people remember that we made them feel important and cared about, and others leave a place behind hoping that people remember what we created and what we built. Sometimes you get to both touch people's lives in a personal way and build tangible outcomes. If being empathic is important to you, then doing both looks different than what we are used to.

When empathy is part of group living and working, outcomes can be significant but are more unexpected and unplanned. What do I mean by that? Let me share another example. In my first year as a university professor, I was asked to teach a class about working in communities. As is true for a lot of new professors, you often get asked to teach courses that are not covered, and therefore you may not actually have the expertise to teach that class. That was the case for me. I did my due diligence and prepared a list of readings and included the assignment from the previous instructor that required a community project. I did not have a specific project in mind; I was new to the community and the truth was that, although I had some community work experience, it had occurred years earlier and was not a major part of my professional training. Rather than try to be the expert I was not, I invited the students to choose a community topic about which the class could do research and plan some action to take related to the topic.

It was a small class, and the group began a discussion of what they might want to study. They began to focus on the issue of homelessness. Well, I had just moved from Chicago, a city with a lot of problems around homelessness, to teach in this small, rural community that was primarily a college town. My first thought, and I remember even saying it out loud, was that homelessness was not something that was a real problem in a college town like it was in Chicago. The students got quiet. Although they were polite and did not argue with me, I sensed that they were deflated because I had made a judgment about their perceptions. Luckily being a new teacher made me more tuned in to my students because I really wanted them to like my class, so I wanted to know what they were feeling. They thought they had a good idea, and I thought it was a dumb idea. I decided to shut my mouth and let them go off and begin their community research to come back in another week and report what they found. I actually was so sure of myself that I thought they would return and we would have to come up with a different topic. I was concerned that we would lose a week and that everything I had planned would have to be rearranged. I was wrong. I was very wrong. Over the course of a semester, those students created the most amazing research project, documenting for the first time the extensive hidden homelessness in a rural, small town. The project got lots of local press coverage, and the students even got asked to meet with the state representative from the community to share their research with her. It was astounding, and I was totally wrong to discourage them from pursuing their interest. Had I not sensed their feelings, a great opportunity would have been lost. How many great ideas get lost because those in charge have an agenda and are not willing or comfortable with letting the emotional flow take place?

Finding the Middle Ground: Making Power and Empathy Work Together

The motivations and actions that accompany power make powerful people less likely to engage the components of interpersonal and social empathy. The skills most at risk of not being used are perspective-taking, self-other awareness, and attention to social context. This seems to portend badly if people with power are the ones developing laws and rules to guide social living. I have already recounted numerous policies and actions that demonstrate that problem (recall the example in chapter 1 about welfare reform and the Twitter story of the Speaker of the House not realizing how little an extra $78 a year is): those in power simply don't get what it's like to live a less powerful life. Are we doomed to have those in power only think of themselves and act without restraint? The good news is that not everyone in power behaves that way, and there are clues as to why having power is not a fait accompli to lacking empathy. Thankfully there are good examples of when people in power do get it, make decisions that take others into account, and are not self-focused.

Earlier I quoted former president Barack Obama and his call for using empathy when choosing judges. Before he became president of the United States, he expressed his belief that empathy was important for making sound decisions when he wrote in his book *The Audacity of Hope* that he considered a sense of empathy to be "at the heart of my moral code." He wrote that empathy was more than sympathy or doing charity; he described it as "a call to stand in somebody else's shoes and see through their eyes."[32] Politicians before him walked that walk and used their understanding of others to create lasting and meaning social policies. In 1852, Harriet Beecher Stowe published the book *Uncle Tom's Cabin*, which empathically conveyed the pain and tragedy of living life as a slave. It sold millions of copies, and as expert on the psychological development of morality psychologist Martin L. Hoffman wrote, "it probably did as much as any book could" to convince people of the moral choice to abolish slavery. In fact, President Abraham Lincoln is famously said to have acknowledged the impact of the book's message of antislavery when he met Stowe with the greeting, "So this is the little lady who started this big war."[33]

The Great Depression of the 1930s impacted millions of people in distressing and painful ways. President Franklin D. Roosevelt tapped numerous people with empathy to help move his New Deal agenda to respond to the catastrophic economic upheaval. He appointed as his Secretary of Labor the first woman to hold a cabinet position, Frances Perkins.[34] Perkins grew up in a privileged New England family, which afforded her the opportunity to attend Mount Holyoke College. Her intention, like many women at that time, was to become a teacher. In her last year, she took an economics course that, unlike her other studies, required her to visit local factories. She saw firsthand the working conditions of women and children in the factories. This experience was her first empathic view of labor. After teaching and then working in a position helping immigrant and African American girls find work, she decided to become a social worker and study political science. Following her advanced studies, while working in New York City, she personally witnessed the Triangle Shirtwaist Factory fire of 1911, the worst factory fire in New York's history. Because the stairwells were locked to prevent breaks and the factory was overcrowded in order to get the most work done in the cheapest way possible, the women and children working there were trapped. Witnesses, like Frances Perkins, watched in horror as women jumped out of windows to escape the flames, only to fall to their deaths. The images left an indelible mark on Frances Perkins. She went on to work in state and federal government for passage of regulations to improve labor conditions. First as a member of Roosevelt's governor's cabinet and then as a member of his presidential cabinet, Frances Perkins shepherded numerous labor reforms. Foremost among her work was chairing the committee that crafted the Social Security Act of 1935 and gained passage of the Fair Labor Standards Act of 1938, which included the prohibition of child labor.

Perkins was not alone at that time in using empathy to guide policy making. The two men who worked with her and sponsored the Social Security legislation in Congress, one in the Senate and the other in the House of Representatives, knew poverty firsthand. The well-regarded historian of the New Deal era Frank Leuchtenburg wrote, "The administration's bill was introduced in both houses of Congress by men who had felt keenly the meaning of social insecurity. Robert Wagner, who steered the social security measure through the Senate, was the son of a janitor; as an immigrant boy he sold papers on the streets of New York. David Lewis, who guided the bill through the House, had gone to work at nine in a coal mine. Illiterate at sixteen, he had taught himself to read not only English but French and German."[35] These men, along with Frances Perkins, used their personal insight into what financial insecurity and lack of employment feels like to advocate for legislation to address the problem. Today, Social Security is the most powerful piece of social welfare policy in the United States, keeping millions of retired seniors out of poverty. The legislation includes programs that cover health care (Medicare and Medicaid), disability, and unemployment insurance.

Although not an elected official, Martin Luther King Jr. is perhaps the most moving example of a person who called on his life experiences to inform his efforts at social change. The moving account of his life describes a man who knew firsthand the limitations caused by prejudice and discrimination as well as the opportunities that can come with gaining power and recognition.[36] He never lost sight of his experiences or those of his friends, family, and the many people he met through his ministries and travels. Those experiences shaped and informed his advocacy. In his famous "I Have a Dream" speech delivered on the mall in Washington in August 1963, his personal connection was vivid in his remarks when he acknowledged people's lived experiences and connected them to his own family:

> I am not unmindful that some of you have come here out of great trials and tribulation. Some of you have come fresh from narrow jail cells. Some of you have come from areas where your quest for freedom left you battered by the storms of persecution and staggered by the winds of police brutality. You have been the veterans of creative suffering. . . . I say to you today, my friends, even though we face the difficulties of today and tomorrow, I still have a dream. . . . I have a dream that my four little children will one day live in a nation where they will not be judged by the color of their skin but by the content of their character.[37]

These powerful words were spoken from personal experience and reflected his ability to understand the perspective of others and the social context in which they lived.

As in the case of Frances Perkins, not all powerful political actors with empathy personally grew up with disadvantage. Even with a young life of privilege, some with power have gone on to gain empathic insights that moved them to advocate for public policies that reflected those insights. Robert Kennedy came from one of the most powerful and privileged families to move within political circles. In 1967, in response to the growing public awareness about hunger and economic deprivation that gave rise to the War on Poverty, Robert Kennedy visited some of the poorest communities in the South. Those with him reported that following one visit to families living in a very poor community in Mississippi, he was moved to tears. This man of great wealth and privilege returned to Washington and pushed Congress to expand the Food Stamp Program to better provide for those in need. Kennedy cited those experiences of seeing poverty in person as the motivation behind his advocacy to create programs to feed the neediest.[38]

These examples are but a few showing that empathy can inform power and move the powerful to take action that is beneficial to the many, not just to themselves. While there are likely more examples, unfortunately they are not typical. In fact, many politicians have great skills in reading people, but that does not necessarily translate to having empathy.

Can You Have Perspective-Taking Without Empathy?

We often marvel at the ability of some people to read others but see them do it in a way that is manipulative and anything but empathic. That is because reading people and being responsive to what you think they want is not the same as being empathic.

In experiments with supervisors and those who reported to them from a variety of companies and organizations, each person was tested on how well he or she could assess the emotions of others. The results were that the supervisors scored higher on accurately recognizing the emotions of others.[39] This is not surprising. In a positon of leadership, it is very helpful to be able to read the emotions of those who work for you, as well as on a broader level, which may include customers, business partners, suppliers, or voters, all the others with whom a leader is likely to interact. So we know that those in power positions can read other people's emotions, but what those readings mean to them and what they do with that knowledge can be anything but empathic. Reading people is not the same as walking in their shoes. It is not taking the time to learn about and understand the context of their lives and imagining what it would truly be like to be in their place.

What does it look like when you have someone with incredible ability to know what others are thinking and feeling, but who does not show interpersonal or social empathy? The obvious examples on a one-to-one basis are con artists (people who appeal to what you want or feel but do so without any concern for your well-being) and, in a worst-case scenario, sociopaths (people who read others well enough to mistreat them in ways that exploit their vulnerabilities). These are the extreme examples. Others in power can use these skills as well, although not for such nefarious purposes. Politicians use these skills all the time. Some might call it "playing to the crowd" or telling people what they want to hear, making them feel like you are connected to them, one of them. This skill can help one get elected to office.

The tactic of telling people what they want to hear in order to get elected has been used by many politicians, none more so recently than Donald Trump. While running for president, he famously promised things like "drain the swamp," suggesting that he would get rid of insiders in government, and that he would stay away from big donors, as he was going to fund his own campaign. He criticized his opponent for being close to Wall Street, particularly the investment firm Goldman Sachs. Well, neither promise was actually delivered, nor were several others.[40] Key roles in the Trump administration were filled by insiders, such as the former head of the Republican National Committee, and Goldman Sachs executives, including the firm's president, who was appointed to lead the White House National Economic Council. Almost one-third of his cabinet positions were given to top donors, people who gave millions to his campaign. He also complained that Hillary Clinton would not do news conferences, blaming it on her dishonesty and her desire to not answer questions about it from the press. Then he stopped holding press conferences in July 2016 and did not give another one for six months. Telling people what they want to hear to get elected is not new at all. And it can be done with the highest of abilities in reading other people. But that is not empathy. It is not walking in another's shoes and seeing the world through their eyes. It is not perspective-taking as used in empathy. In fact, as discussed in chapter 3, it is more tapping into people's fears and telling them what they want to hear to make them feel better and, as a result, want to vote for you.

Power at Its Worst Can Lead to Dehumanization

As if I have not depressed you enough about power lacking empathy, there is more bad news. Power and dehumanization, degrading people by taking away their humanity, are essentially linked. Dehumanization is "the act of denying humans their human nature and treating them like objects."[41] At its worst, dehumanization allows people to suppress their emotions so they do not connect as human beings, allowing behaviors that include abuse, torture, and even genocide, as discussed in chapter 3. But there are other reasons to dehumanize, such as distancing oneself from behaviors of one's ingroup for past injustices to other groups or making tough decisions such as sending soldiers to war. Dehumanization can be a tool for powerful people to make difficult decisions by minimizing the suffering of others to justify their own behaviors or decisions. As previously discussed, power is associated with a) lower perspective-taking skills, b) social distance between those in power and those who are powerless, and c) a tendency to stereotype, group people, or deindividuate others by those in power. All these characteristics support dehumanization. Across three different experiments, participants were placed in powerful positions and asked to make difficult decisions. One decision involved residents of a very poor country with severe unemployment in which most people lived in slums having to be forcefully moved to an uninhabited new area for their own good. The other decision was to choose between two medical treatments for a patient, one that was painless but less effective and the other that was very painful but more effective. Across the several groups participating, those with higher power were able to make tough decisions and in doing so were more likely to dehumanize those for whom the decisions were being made. This research suggests that the powerful use dehumanization to remove any emotionality raised by their choices. They can live with causing short-term suffering for what may be a long-term benefit.[42]

But is dehumanization a tool used to make tough decisions, or is it built into being powerful? Other studies suggest that it is power itself that leads to dehumanization. By virtue of being in power, one tends to see less humanity in the less powerful. This view may in part be due to the nature of powerlessness: those who lack power typically exhibit fewer attributes assigned to being human such as ambition, imagination, passion, and being analytical.[43] There is a superiority attached to power that leads the powerful to see those without power as lacking abilities, which can include their humanity. In some cases, this is problematic, as when those in power make decisions about others with disregard for their feelings or needs. In other situations, it is beneficial, as in making tough medical decisions that focus on the treatment and not the patient's feelings or making employment decisions that adversely affect some while helping others.

Back to Power and Politics

The political skew of this chapter might be disturbing to some of you or make you feel like I am taking sides, being biased. Because of this concern, I and members of my empathy research team engaged in some studies to look at political ideology, political party affiliation, and empathic abilities.[44] We surveyed students anonymously, asking about their political party affiliation, their view of social responsibility (being more liberal) on key policy issues (such as protection of the environment, immigration, health care, and government assistance), and compared their policy views to their levels of interpersonal and social empathy. We suspected, consistent with research cited previously in this chapter, that empathy would be stronger for those who held a more collective view, and wondered if that would also split across political party affiliations: more empathy and a stronger social responsibility view would lean toward Democrat, while less would lean toward Republican. What we found was somewhat different. There was no significant relationship between identifying as Democrat or Republican and being interpersonally or socially empathic. Yes, those who viewed policy issues as more of a social responsibility had significantly higher levels of social empathy, but it was not tied to their party affiliation. From our research we concluded that empathy, particularly the macro view of social empathy, is not bound to a political party but rather bound to a political ideology (and we saw this in the Pew Research Center report that those with liberal viewpoints prioritized empathy as an important trait to teach children). So while empathy may be more common among those who hold liberal social views, it is not necessarily more common among those who identify as Democrats.

Political Correctness

What does political correctness have to do with power and empathy? There is a lot of angst these days from all sides of the political spectrum over the idea of political correctness. The history of the term and its use varies. The term may have originally referred to being on the right political side of an issue or group, but it transformed in the 1970s, primarily on college campuses, to become the term used to refer to the practice of curbing language that might be offensive. The definition that I think captures this concept best is "the idea that people should be careful to not use language or behave in a way that could offend a particular group of people," which comes from one Merriam-Webster's dictionaries.[45]

What may have started out as a way to be sensitive and understanding moved to feel like control of language and censorship—people were no longer free to say what they felt. Political correctness was seen as a form of power and control. This reaction to the original intent of political correctness was front and center in the 2016 election. This quote from candidate Trump during the Republican debate summed up the prevailing sentiment in opposition to political correctness: "I think the big problem this country has is being politically correct. I've been challenged by so many people and I don't, frankly, have time for total political correctness. And to be honest with you, this country doesn't have time, either."[46] His election as president seems to have sealed the deal: many people feel they no longer have to deal with this policing of our language.[47]

I am actually sympathetic to both sides of the argument—we need to be careful to not use words that are offensive, and we also need to be free to speak our minds. The problem is that what is free speech to you may be offensive to me, and vice versa. Language is fluid and what was once acceptable may no longer be. Those changes in language may happen in places in which not everyone lives, like universities.

Early in my social work training, I was taught a very simple technique for how to refer to people: ask them. Of course we cannot always ask people; we may not know anyone to ask who is from a certain group. But the principle strikes me as taking a step toward empathy. Particularly, using social empathy as a guide may be the answer to political correctness. Understanding historical context and macro perspective-taking can help us to assess what may or may not be offensive to a particular group of people. And this goes both ways, for those who support certain language and those who resent it as a control and barrier to their freedom.

Decades ago, I was invited to give a guest lecture in the class of a colleague. He and I were hired at the same time, had finished our degrees at the same time, and were of the same rank. We had become good friends, and I felt very supported by him and supportive of him.

I was happy to speak in his class, and I thought it went very well. Later that day he came into my office and was noticeably upset and concerned. Two of his female students came to him after class and were upset with him. They felt he had not treated me with due respect. Why? Because when I was introduced, my colleague used my first name. The previous guest speaker, a man, had been introduced by his title and referred to as doctor so-and-so. My colleague was so apologetic and hoped I wasn't insulted. He was genuinely concerned and wanted me to know that he had great respect for me. To tell you the truth, I had not noticed. He and I were friends, and the class was an informal graduate seminar. But the students had a point—as a woman among male colleagues, referring to me by my first name made it seem as if I did not have the rank and credentials of the men. It was my first overt moment of political correctness from a faculty position in academia, and I was torn. I knew my colleague respected me and that he did not think I was less than he was, but his way of speaking suggested that to his students. The lesson he learned was that if he was going to use ranks and titles to introduce guest speakers, he should be consistent and use them for all of his guest speakers. In part it came down to fairness, and his students had called him on that. I know his intention was not to be unfair, but it came out that way.

Since that time, I have tried to make it a practice to ask people how they want me to introduce them or how they want to be addressed in one-on-one discussions. At least that way I have their guidance to use words that are not offensive to them. It is my awareness of self-other differences (not everyone wants to be addressed in the way I might want to be addressed) and starts the process of perspective-taking. Of course, this is not expedient. It requires the time and opportunity to ask. That is why empathy is not as efficient as power.

Part of the struggle around political correctness is that those in power do not take the time or effort to find out about how those who are powerless want to be addressed. It takes time and takes attention away from getting to the task at hand, getting things done. This is why political correctness usually feels constraining for those in dominant cultures. They feel that their freedom of expression is curtailed when they have to learn new ways of addressing people in different, non-dominant groups. They are being pushed to spend time in ways that may not seem particularly useful to them in getting their own things done. Those who are powerless feel unheard and offended when those in power are not interested in learning about them enough to use terms that are not offensive. The person who feels put out because there is no way to know what is and is not offensive and thinks he or she has no one to ask (there is always the internet) should try this: test out what you are saying. At a minimum, take the same term or phrase you are thinking of using for another group or member of that group and use it to refer to your best friend, mother, pastor, or boss, and then use it to refer to yourself. Say it out loud. Say it face to face. If it is ugly, abrasive, or offensive, it will likely show, and in the process, you will have taken a new perspective, which is a step toward empathy.

How Do We Promote Empathy While in Power?

Even though there are positive sides to power without empathy, such as the ability to make tough decisions without emotions getting in the way and the focus of being goal directed and getting things done, a lack of empathy seems a very high price to pay for those benefits. Who is to say that being empathic and being in power cannot help someone to make difficult decisions and stay goal directed? We have the examples of Abraham Lincoln, Frances Perkins, Martin Luther King Jr., and Robert Kennedy.

We know that the full scope of interpersonal empathy includes skills in emotion regulation, which is an ability that can help keep one's emotions in check so one can make those tough decisions and stay focused on the task at hand. Thus, that may be one interpersonal empathy skill that comes more easily to people in power. Power seems to amplify those tendencies that are characteristic of the individual. It gives us the resources, control, and position to be who we want to be. That means that whoever we are before going into positions of power will frame how we behave when we have power.

For those who are already motivated to care about social conditions and the situations of other people, power seems to enhance or improve empathy.[48] We know that power is disinhibiting; it moves people to be freer to act as they want. If their underlying personality and beliefs reflect a prosocial orientation, they will maintain those values and behaviors when in power. Because power gives people more resources and control, if they are prosocially oriented, they will use their power to tune in to others. And the opposite is true. Research on power and unethical behavior suggests that those with an orientation that sees people in power as corrupt and unethical, will behave more unethically when they have power themselves,.[49]

There is another dimension to being in power: staying there. To hold power requires maintaining the respect of those whom you lead. Guess what skills come into play while leading? The ability to correctly assess the emotions, thoughts, or intentions of others, which are key attributes of being empathic.[50] This is especially true in leaders who consider power to be a socially positive role.

These research studies tell us several things. Teaching people that those in power should act ethically can actually influence behavior. When they have power, people will use that ethical social standard for their own behavior. Furthermore, if staying in power is desirable, it helps to read people so you can be responsive to those who you lead. The opposite is also true. Teaching people that everyone in power is corrupt and in it for themselves encourages people to behave unethically if they get a chance at being in power.

The Upside of Being Powerless

You probably didn't see this one coming. It can be good to be powerless? Sort of. Those less powerful can infuse empathy into power relationships by controlling their respect for those in power. Social status is typically assessed by others through prestige, respect, and esteem bestowed on one. Knowing one has high status is a form of power, but it is given and taken by others through their perceptions and assessments. This differs from high power that is defined as influence and control over others, which tends to be more concrete (you are the CEO, boss, etc.). While research demonstrates that high power reduces perspective-taking, status relies on the esteem held by others. To maintain that status, it is important to "read" others. "Status, in general, heightens attention to social relations and related emotions."[51] Maybe we need to remind people in power that we hold the reigns of their respect, esteem, and prestige.

Nobody likes to be reduced to a stereotype, but maybe there is a way that being seen as a stereotype works to help the powerless. There might be a hidden power in being a stereotype because those in power do not know or understand their subordinates. These unknown subordinates can try and organize in ways that are surprising. It is a humorous and rather silly example, but think of the movie *9 to 5*, in which the lower-level women in the office outsmarted their sexist boss who could not fathom that women could be smart in business. They secretly took over, controlled him, and improved the business. They tricked him by letting him believe his stereotypes of them, while behind his back they were using their abilities to create their own new power.

Another strength of powerlessness is accountability. Watching and observing as the outsider is a skill of the powerless. They can use those skills to keep track of those in power. Accountability can hold those in power in check, reminding them that we hold their public reputation in our hands.

Using our powerlessness creatively can change the dynamics. Once we tap into the upside of being powerless, we can actually feel empowered. Understanding people and their motivations and context better than the powerful gives those on the outside a different kind of power.

We also need to change the dialogue around power. It should not be acceptable to say that we expect people in power to behave badly. We have a right to expect that those in power should be responsible and ethical and care about the welfare of others. As one of the most privileged and powerful men in modern history John F. Kennedy stated, "For of those to whom much is given, much is required."[52] I would suggest that empathy is part of that requirement, and we have a right to expect those in power to include empathy in the ways they wield their power.

CHAPTER FIVE

What If Stress, Depression, and Other Health Factors Block Empathy?

WHILE I WOULD not say that empathy is a full-contact sport, it is also not a sedentary, in-your-head experience. Empathy starts in our body. We know that we are capable of picking up affective reactions when we see or imagine the behaviors of others. These perceptions trigger similar physical reactions in our own bodies, initially without our awareness. We have a physical sensation, and then our brain goes to work figuring out what that physical sensation might mean. Our mental awareness might kick in strongly enough for us to actually be aware that we are thinking about what other people are going through and how we might feel ourselves if we were in their shoes. Thus, empathy is both physical and mental.

A lot of the physical activity accompanying empathy goes on in our brains and requires a variety of nerve centers to connect and communicate. This means that if the full physical functioning of our brain activity is blocked or impaired, so too is our empathy. Because of this physiological connection to empathy, we need to consider what happens when there are competing demands on the same parts of our brain that are needed for us to engage empathically. To complete this examination, we need to go a bit deeper into the biological process of empathy in the brain. Once we have a good idea of the neural mechanics, we can consider whether common human experiences that involve similar parts of our brain, such as stress, depression, grief, or even intoxication, compete with our engagement in being empathic. In other words, can we experience empathy when we are stressed out, in a deep funk, grieving the death of a loved one, or overdoing it with cocktails at a party? Of course we humans can multitask, but these human experiences involve emotional and psychological demands that can be very powerful, so we need to ask if the intensity of other tasks closes off pathways that are used for empathic processing.

Brain Biology

We have already talked about cognitive neuroscience, the study of our brain activity, and how we can read the brain activities that reflect empathy through advances in technology. This ability and study is relatively new. Back in the 1990s, researchers in Parma, Italy, were examining the brain activity of Macaque monkeys.[1] The neurological monitoring they were doing involved electronic nodes attached to the monkeys that tracked all their brain activity. They were interested in identifying brain patterns that corresponded to physical activities such as grasping items, holding things, preparing food, and actually eating. One day, while they were taking a lunch break in the lab, they were surprised to see that the monkeys watching them had the same brain activity as if the monkeys themselves were eating, except they were only watching the action of eating. These Italian researchers had discovered mirror neurons, the nerve cells that transmit imagery into the feeling of action.[2] Their discovery paved the way for neurological research on empathy.

The proof of mirror neurons in humans is a bit controversial, in part because there is no one place in the brain that conclusively conducts mirroring.[3] Because the mirroring process seems spread across numerous areas of the brain, it is often referred to as the mirror neuron system, suggesting a process conducted by groupings of neurons.[4] Although there is debate as to whether there is an organized system that is responsible for mirroring, the action of mirroring is well accepted in empathy research. Although we still may not know exactly how it plays out neurologically, we do know that our brains trigger for actions we see, even if we are not doing the action ourselves. As discussed in chapter 1, there is no specific empathy center in our brains; instead a number of actions come together that can be traced to various neural regions. Thus, many different parts of our brains are involved in empathy.

There is a wonderful TV series, *The Brain*, on PBS that features the neuroscientist David Eagleman. I highly recommend his work because he makes a very complicated topic, the working of our brains, understandable and captivating. You can also read his book *The Brain*, which provides an even deeper look at our neurological functioning. To appreciate the complexity of our brain and the magnitude of its functions, it is worthwhile to consider the following facts: the human brain has about eighty-six billion neurons; a neuron is a cell that transmits messages between the brain and other parts of our bodies, including other areas of the brain; each neuron makes about ten thousand connections; if we could track each of these connections, it would be an incredible amount of data. "Reconstructing the full picture of all the connections in a human brain is such a daunting task, and one that we have no real hope of accomplishing anytime soon. The amount of data required is gargantuan: to store a high-resolution architecture of a single human brain would require a zettabyte of capacity. That's the same size as all the digital content of the planet right now."[5] I learned that a zettabyte is a billion terabytes, and one terabyte is over a thousand gigabytes, which is to say that we have a lot going on in our brain! To me, this point makes it clear that the human brain is an incredible "computer" of its own, far beyond the ones we have built, and we have just begun to scratch the surface of mapping what happens with all the processes that go on in our brains.

I am not a neuroscientist, so my understanding of the brain is rather elementary. Even at my introductory level, I am struck by the power of our brains. Weighing in at a mere three pounds of neural tissue, the brain controls and guides all our actions—conscious and unconscious. We don't have to think about our breathing, blood flowing, or heart beating. Our body hums along in ways that are unconscious to us, and then may or may not become conscious for us. The brain is our center for taking in information and making sense of it to help us negotiate our surroundings.

In general, the process starts with information taken in through our senses, such as sight, smell, or hearing. That information is processed through our internal systems to figure out what the information means for our bodies at that moment. Then the information gets routed to other parts of the brain for more advanced cognitive processing. For example, I am writing this while sitting at my computer during the summer with the air conditioning on. Because the air conditioning fluctuates, my body has to adjust to the slight temperature changes, cooling itself when the temperature is a bit high and readjusting when the air conditioning kicks on and I get a little blast of cool air. These are internal, unconscious adjustments. Sometimes, especially as the day gets warmer and the sun starts to hit the window in my study, I will all of a sudden become aware that I am hot and uncomfortable. I tune in mentally and realize that it is now afternoon; the sun is strong and facing my windows. I understand this process because I have learned over my lifetime about the power of the sun. I have also sat at my desk for many summers and learned specifically that my study gets hot in the afternoon. I also understand the working of the thermostat and that I can control the air conditioning. With all this processing of physical sensations, the science of the sun, and the knowledge of how air conditioning happens in my house, I get up and adjust the thermostat. Although empathy is complex and involves understanding the more abstract emotions and behaviors of other human beings, in a very simplistic way this example outlines the process we use to empathically experience sensations in our bodies and then process in our brains what those sensations mean.

Embedded in the center of our brains is a group of brain parts that we refer to together as our limbic system, which is the main processing center of the information from our senses. It includes the amygdala, hypothalamus, and hippocampus. Each part plays a crucial role in helping us to operate within our environment. The amygdala is the part that detects what we sense and then directs that information on for further processing. It is most concerned with detecting fear and anxiety, which are key to our most basic survival. The amygdala sends the information to the hippocampus, which draws on what we already know from our memory or stores new information in our memory and then sends the relevant information to the hypothalamus, which directs the body to do what it needs to do in response to all the information. All this is done unconsciously and is our basic survival mechanism. Once all this initial information is processed, it can be sent on to other regions of the brain for more advanced cognitive processing, basically what we might experience as the thinking part. For our purposes in understanding empathy and brain functioning, know that the brain takes two actions for empathy to occur. The unconscious reading of outside stimuli, typically processed through the limbic system, is first. Then the information is sent to the cognitive areas of our brain for us to figure out what it all means. When either action is blocked, the physical sensing or cognitive processing, we have difficulty in tapping in empathically.

I have tried to understand the various parts of the brain in order to teach about the neuroscience of empathy. To help myself place empathy within the workings of the brain, I developed table 5.1, which lists the activities related to empathy and the corresponding parts of the brain based on a review of dozens of neuroscience research studies.[6] Because the field of cognitive neuroscience is expanding and tools for reading brain activity are advancing all the time, consider this listing dynamic and evolving. But hopefully it gives you a broad overview and demonstrates how neurologically varied and complex engaging in empathy can be.

I was in the process of developing this chart as preparation for a class I was teaching on empathy when it hit me: What if one or more of these brain parts did not work well? I started thinking about what happens to our ability to empathize if there is damage to the brain or underdevelopment of one or more of the many parts of the brain. There are a number of studies on brain damage and empathy. An overall review of almost thirty studies that looked at specific damage from a brain lesion and the ability to recognize, share, and understand the emotions of others does provide clinical research on the impact that brain damage can have on empathy.[7] Indeed, the ability to read others and make meaning out of that information can be compromised with damage to parts of the brain. For example, in research on patients who had a stroke, particularly those with damage on the right side of the brain, there was impairment in their cognitive abilities, and they scored lower on empathy than did a comparison group of people who had not had a stroke.[8] This deficit was also found in patients who had undergone surgery to remove slow-growing brain tumors. However, there was evidence that the brain can compensate under these circumstances and develop other ways to engage in cognitive processing, which we know is necessary for empathy.[9]

TABLE 5.1
Empathy Actions and Where They Happen in the Brain

Empathy Component	Corresponding Parts of the Brain
Affective response	Amygdala Hypothalamus Hippocampus Mirror neurons, which seem to be located in the part of the brain that handles our motor abilities
Affective mentalizing	At least four different parts of our brain, two in the front, the ventromedial prefrontal cortex and dorso medial prefrontal cortex, and two in the back, the temporo-parietal junction and the bilateral superior temporal sulcus
Self-other awareness	Some of the same regions as for mentalizing, including the ventromedial prefrontal cortex and the temporo-parietal junction, another part of the front of the brain, the medial prefrontal cortex, and the right supramarginal gyrus, which is found at the junction of three lobes in the center of the brain
Perspective-taking	Uses the regions found under affective mentalizing as well as the perigenual anterior cingulate cortex, which spans sections in the middle of the brain
Emotion regulation	Shares the anterior cingulate cortex used by the mirror neuron system, the medial prefrontal cortex used in self-other awareness, and the ventromedial prefrontal cortex used in mentalizing
Contextual understanding	All of the regions above, with greater emphasis on the actions of the prefrontal cortex to process the multiple sources of input
Macro perspective-taking	Uses the regions found under affective mentalizing as well as the perigenual anterior cingulate cortex, which spans sections in the middle of the brain with attention to the parts of the brain activated with self-other awareness

Because of the complexity of the brain and the fact that lesions and other forms of brain damage can vary greatly from patient to patient, we have a long way to go to be able to identify the exact relationship between damage to a specific part of the brain and its impact on empathy. Because empathy involves multiple tasks and numerous parts of the brain, injury in one part may have an impact but not necessarily a total blockage to empathy. For example, the parts of the brain that help with recognizing emotions in others might be damaged, but not the brain parts that help a person to take another's perspective once the other person's emotions are identified. In practice this might mean that if a person has a brain injury that impairs reading the emotions of others, telling that person how you are feeling can fill in for that deficit. The ability to read other people may be impaired but not the perspective-taking to understand what those feelings mean. I may not be able to feel that you are sad, but if you tell me that you are sad, I may then be able to think about what being sad means and comfort you. The complexity of empathy means that there can be disruptions in the brain to parts of but not the entire process. Although it may be challenging to zero in on which parts work and which don't, in addition to compensating for what we can identify as problematic, the brain can recover or reroute processes. Learning and practicing alternative ways to take in and process information makes the return of empathy very possible, albeit possibly in a different way than before the injury.

It is not surprising that damage to the brain impacts empathy. But what about fluctuations in our mental state? Are there conditions that can throw us off our empathy? For example, I wondered what happens if we are temporarily impaired in one or more of the empathy-related brain parts. If we drink too much alcohol, our ability to walk a straight line or follow a conversation is diminished. (Ever tried having a serious conversation while you are sober with someone who is drunk? It is not an easy task.) Once the alcohol wears off, we can walk that line and share a conversation. Might this temporary decline be true with empathy as well? What about stress? When we are under deep and prolonged stress, our body chemistry changes, and that impacts our brain functioning. Could this also affect our ability to be empathic?

The possibility of permanent or temporary brain changes or dysfunctions having an adverse effect on empathy intrigued and concerned me. What if no matter what we teach about empathy, the person we are working with has brain parts that are not working well? Asking someone to feel something for another person when the brain pathway to do that is impaired means empathy would be impossible. We would have to figure out a way to help people get rid of the conditions that impaired their brains or compensate and work around such brain issues. The question of whether there are barriers to empathy due to brain functioning led me to look at the extent that other neurological demands might affect the empathy brain parts. The first area that caught my attention was stress because I already suspected from my own life experience that when stress levels are high we are consumed by our worries and don't think much about other people.

Stress

Robert Sapolsky, a biologist and neurologist, wrote a must-read book for anyone who wants to understand stress and the impact it has on our bodies.[10] The book title *Why Zebras Don't Get Ulcers* is the lead in to how stress differs for us as human beings than in animals. We are similar to animals in that our bodies are capable of recognizing threats to our survival and process that information in ways that help us to deal with the resulting stress. Sapolsky argues that our bodies have evolved to handle periods of stress, which is how we survived as a species. If you see a saber-toothed tiger prowling in the distance, your eyes feed that information through your limbic system, and in an instant your body processes that input to determine the level of threat. Your body is likely to immediately go into a different physical state—messages are sent to release stored energy and power up your body to react. We can feel that process in the quickening of our pulse and breathing. We often talk about a "rush of adrenalin." The hormone that is secreted, epinephrine (the scientific name for what we call adrenalin), is the switch to turn up these functions. This process is unconscious, stimulating reactions that provide us with the resources to respond, giving us more oxygen, protein, and glucose, which altogether power us to run off or to fight.

Another hormone is released if the stress is not resolved quickly: cortisol. Cortisol is the hormone that continues the production of resources for energy but also shuts down body processes that are not needed in the immediacy of dealing with the stress. While running away from or staying to fight that saber-toothed tiger, we don't need our body to work on growth, reproduction, regenerating our immune system, or high-level thinking. The hippocampus is activated, calling on our prior knowledge of saber-toothed tigers, either from previous personal experience or what we have learned from others. Cortisol plays a part in activating the hippocampus for retrieving those memories. Once the stress passes, presumably we have survived the saber-toothed tiger and are now catching our breath, returning to our calmer life. The body stops secreting hormones in response to stress, and we absorb those so the messages created to move the body into stress response mode stop. Epinephrine seems to be absorbed more quickly than cortisol. That is why after a particularly upsetting experience it takes some time for us to calm down, get our breathing and pulse back to normal, feel less on edge, and fall into a resting state.

If you had never seen a saber-toothed tiger before and never learned about one, you might not react as strongly or not at all. Of course, over the course of human history, those who did not react, lacked the ability to react, or never learned to react most likely did not survive and did not pass on their shortcomings in those areas. Those who were most successful at surviving were also those most likely to pass on their abilities to future generations.

Readying the body to face an emergency or survival threat by minimizing other functions that take energy but are not vital to the immediate stressful event is a very healthy response. Focus all energy on the task at hand, and then once it passes, return to the more involved long-term body work and higher-level thinking. Understanding this process has been helpful for me. It explains why I get a rush of energy because I have a deadline approaching. This energy boost is helpful; it gets me motivated and focused. But thinking about that deadline for days and days just interrupts my sleep, makes me cranky, and, when it drags on too long, I find myself getting a cold and not able to think clearly.

So our bodies are well equipped to handle periodic stressful events. The problem lies in that we are not well adapted to handle prolonged, chronic stress. Our ability as human beings to retain strong memories about the past and think about the future means that we can hold onto stress for long periods of time, including beyond its usefulness. For some people, their lives are in constant states of stress, such as not living in a safe place, not having enough to eat, working for a bullying boss, or being raised in a dangerous and unpredictable environment. Physiologically, the changes our bodies make for short-term stress are not good for us if maintained over long periods of time. *Why Zebras Don't Get Ulcers* provides an extensive explanation of the biology of stress, which I do recommend reading if you want to understand the details. Perhaps one example can help to illuminate the downside of long-term stress. A lack of sleep can turn on our stress response, which in the short term may not be problematic, and it also makes sense—imagine being on alert for danger at night. Or in my case, that sleepless burst of energy is what helps me to meet a pressing deadline. But when there is a cycle of pressing deadlines, financial worries, or family problems that keep you awake night after night, your stress response stays activated, and you continue to toss and turn or sleep poorly. Lack of adequate and good sleep does not allow the body to recalibrate to its healthy, balanced state, leaving us open to illness, disease, and ultimately less sharpness in our mental functioning. Sapolsky sums it up well:

> If you constantly mobilize energy at the cost of energy storage, you will never store any surplus energy. You will fatigue more rapidly, and your risk of developing a form of diabetes will increase. The consequences of chronically activating your cardiovascular system are similarly damaging: if your blood pressure rises to 180/100 when you are sprinting away from a lion, you are being adaptive, but if it is 180/100 every time you see the mess in your teenager's bedroom, you could be heading for a cardiovascular disaster. If you constantly turn off long-term building projects, nothing is ever repaired. . . . If you are constantly under stress, a variety of reproductive disorders may ensue. . . . The same systems of the brain that function more cleverly during stress can also be damaged by one class of hormones [cortisol] secreted during stress.[11]

When too much cortisol remains in our body or continues to be produced, the neural messages for emergency operations stay on. Over time this is detrimental to our functioning. It is particularly problematic for children who need to develop and grow. According to the National Scientific Council on the Developing Child, when children experience frequent and prolonged stress, such as severe, chronic abuse, their cortisol levels stay elevated.[12] This state of elevation in cortisol can change the functioning of the entire neural system, suppress immunity, and disrupt the actual structure of the brain. Such disruptions can have adverse effects on learning and developing memory. These are particularly harsh outcomes for children who will have a very difficult time later in life if their brain development is compromised by severe or prolonged stress at a young age.

If the process of long-term stress interrupts our ability to think clearly and operate at full health, does that bode poorly for our chances to be empathic while under stress? Many of the areas of the brain that we rely on for empathy are disrupted by long-term stress. We need the limbic system to experience affective response. For all the cognitive parts of empathy (mentalizing, self-other awareness, micro and macro perspective-taking, emotion regulation, and contextual understanding), we rely on various parts of the prefrontal cortex. This is the part of our brain where we perform sophisticated thinking. Unfortunately, it is also the part of the brain that is most sensitive to the negative effects of stress.[13] For example, in one experiment, people who grew up in harsh families had different brain activities when viewing threatening faces than did those who grew up in nurturing families.[14] The differences showed lower amygdala activity in those from harsh families. The researchers considered this response to reflect their ability to tune out or avoid the threatening stimulus. However, when both groups were asked to write about the picture, the opposite happened: those from harsh families had greater amygdala activity; they were overstimulated. On top of that, they also were not able to effectively activate their prefrontal cortex for emotion regulation. It is possible that once those with harsh family backgrounds engaged with the pictures, it triggered previous experiences that were stressful, hence their neural overreaction. This study gives us some important findings to think about in terms of prolonged early life stress and what that means for the brain parts crucial to empathy.

What about short-term stress, the kind that we all go through and that can even give us energy and motivation? Studies are mixed on that. There is some evidence that being exposed to a stressful event and then shown pictures depicting painful procedures (such as a needle being inserted into a hand) diminishes empathy, particularly because the prefrontal cortex shows impaired function.[15] There may be a gender difference, with women responding to stress with stronger ability to engage in perspective-taking than men.[16] Another possibility is that short-term stress improves our ability to affectively respond to stimuli, but not necessarily on the other parts of empathy.[17]

What the research suggests is that an acute or short-term incident of stress may heighten our attention to the actions of others but not have much of a positive effect on the cognitive parts of empathy. We can grab people's attention through stress, but if it goes on for prolonged periods of time, that initial spike in awareness will become problematic and the hormonal releases activated will shut down the brain process necessary to tune in empathically. Does this mean a poor start to life sentences a person to living without empathy? Not necessarily, but it does require reworking one's abilities with self-other awareness, perspective-taking, and emotion regulation. In fact, there is some research that suggests the key to overcoming the impairments from chronic stress turns out to be emotion regulation.[18] Developing emotion regulation in children who have grown up in poverty with chronic stress can improve their prefrontal cortex functioning. And the prefrontal cortex is where so many of the components of empathy are processed, including emotion regulation. As we will discuss in chapter 8, the reworking of brain patterns can be done throughout life, giving us all a chance to overcome any early deficits and become fully engaged empathic people.

Posttraumatic Stress Disorder

One form of stress that has gained a lot of attention in recent years is posttraumatic stress disorder (PTSD). According to the National Institute of Mental Health, PTSD is an anxiety disorder that can develop after a person sees or lives through a threatening or harmful event.[19] It is characterized by symptoms that last longer than a month and disrupt the person's functioning in relationships and in life tasks such as holding a job. The symptoms can include reliving the trauma, avoiding feelings associated with the trauma, feeling tense and unable to sleep or relax, being easy to startle, having memory problems, engaging in negative thinking, and experiencing a loss of interest in enjoyable activities. While these are symptoms we would expect any person to have after a traumatic event, it is the ongoing duration and interference with day-to-day life that make such symptoms a disorder.

There is not a lot of research on empathy and PTSD. The research that we do have identifies an interesting difference in the neural processing of empathy for people with PTSD compared to people without PTSD. The researchers in two different studies found that for people with PTSD, the affective part of empathy, which includes mirroring, registers in their brains as less intense, but the cognitive parts that include perspective-taking are not different.[20] This is similar to the research on stress in general. One possibility for the difference in affective response is that a lower reaction to emotional stimuli might be a good coping mechanism for people who have PTSD. Their state of being is likely on high alert because they may still be reliving the trauma or are on guard to protect themselves from another traumatic event. While they may be low on affective response, they are fully capable of engaging in the more deliberate thinking aspects of empathy, like perspective-taking and self-other awareness. This strikes me as a logical response to trauma. The body is still on high alert and the impact of the trauma still lingers, but that is exhausting. Tamping down the reaction to external stimuli can give the body a chance to rest and heal. However, outwardly that tamping down comes across as being distant, removed, and unconnected to others, which are some of the behaviors associated with PTSD.[21]

Knowing that people who suffer from PTSD are fully capable of cognitively processing the feelings of others but that getting there through affective response is more difficult means that engaging in empathy might take a different route than what is typical. One possibility is to help people increase their emotion regulation skills so the physical stimuli are not overwhelming. By taking in external stimuli in a calmer state with the help of greater emotion regulation, the cues can then be used to engage the cognitive components of empathy. Another possibility is relying more on the cognitive processing so that we engage empathy through discussions. For example, explaining what I am feeling, how I would like you to understand that feeling, and doing that by talking it through with you can bypass the shared physical affective response. This approach relies more on mental processing and less on physical sharing. Remember, empathy is a process, so how we get there and for how long can vary for each of us. Recognizing barriers to empathy, such as those that PTSD and other forms of stress may present, provides insight as to which component may need more attention and alternative ways to do that.

Where We Live Matters

Some forms of stress are brought on by our surroundings. Poverty is one form of environmental stress that affects millions of people, a huge portion of whom are children. The United States may be the richest nation in the world, but more than forty-three million people are officially categorized as living in poverty.[22] That's about one in every seven people.

What impact might poverty make on empathy for those who grow up poor? We know that poverty is not good for physical health. Sapolsky's work on stress includes a warning about the poor health outcomes from stress induced by poverty:

> If you want to increase the odds of living a long and healthy life, don't be poor. Poverty is associated with increased risks of cardio-vascular disease, respiratory disease, ulcers, rheumatoid disorders, psychiatric diseases, and a number of types of cancer, just to name a few.[23]

This is a public concern about the future of people's health and well-being. To what extent does the physiological damage from poverty also impact people's ability to tune into others? The research on brain development and poverty is limited, but what is out there is not optimistic. Comparisons of brain development between higher- and lower-income students found that the actual thickness of brain matter was greater for students from higher-income backgrounds, and greater brain matter was correlated with higher academic achievement.[24] More detailed research found that the picture may be more complicated. While some parts of the brain are less developed for lower-income children, other factors may be at play. In other studies, when a parent's level of education was factored in, that was more important in explaining the difference.[25] It seems that parent education in situations with better income levels still was a strong predictor of a child's brain development. The researchers suggest that a higher level of parent education may be a strong contributor to enhancing brain development for children. Thus, living with an educated parent, or one who can provide an intellectually stimulating environment, could override growing up in poverty.

If the key to brain development is creating intellectually stimulating environments for children, which in turn develops the neural abilities needed for empathy, we have an intervention to improve empathy: provide intellectual stimulation for all children so they develop healthy brains! While there may be a moral imperative to provide stimulating learning for poor children or those with parents of low education as does exist for children of higher economic and social classes, there is also the benefit of better brain development. And better brain development can improve health and cognitive functioning, which also allows for the development of empathy.

We can conclude that the link between poverty and brain development certainly plays a physiological role. If there is tremendous stress, not enough nutritious food, and unhealthy living conditions, brain development is compromised. But if we can provide interventions that include nutritional support and opportunities for intellectual stimulation both within and outside the home, then the impact of poverty on the brain can be ameliorated. In terms of empathy, this suggests that some of the physiological aspects of the brain involved in empathy may be compromised by a child's environment and lack of mentally stimulating opportunities, but that does not mean children cannot grow up to be empathic.

What About Class?

Somewhat different from income, although related, is the concept of class. Usually income and class are synonymous: if you have little money you are likely categorized as a member of the lower class in our society, and if you have a great deal of money you are categorized as a member of the higher class. The research on class and empathy is very interesting. Although poverty may impact brain development, which might inhibit empathy, being a member of a lower class may actually increase one's empathy. Numerous studies have found that there is evidence that lower-class individuals are more attentive to their social context, more interested in interpersonal engagement, and demonstrate higher empathic accuracy than higher-class individuals.[26] The research shows that people from higher classes are simply not as interested in others or their surroundings to the extent that people from lower classes are.[27] We don't know if their lack of interest is the reason for lower empathy or if their ability to empathize is underdeveloped. The first condition is addressed by creating a stronger interest in others, while the second requires more effort in training and development of empathic abilities. It is likely that even if people from higher social classes have the abilities needed to be empathic, if they are not interested in observing others and paying attention to the context within which we all interact, they are not going to be using their empathic abilities very much.

As noted earlier, when looking at class background and empathy, research finds that those from lower-income backgrounds show higher levels of correctly judging the emotions of others compared to people from higher-income backgrounds.[28] So ironically, poverty may not be a barrier to empathy if the physiology of the brain is not compromised because those who grow up as part of lower social and economic classes have greater interest in context and social interactions. Being from a lower socioeconomic group means it is more likely to be outside the circle of power, which, as discussed previously, means it is more important to understand context and watch the behaviors of others. That interest may provide more opportunities to develop the skills of contextual understanding and perspective-taking, making empathy, particularly social empathy, actually more developed among those from lower-class backgrounds than among those from higher classes. Of course, the foundation for this is a healthy brain. If we can support the physiological development of healthy brains for all children, then empathic development can follow.

The Maltreatment of Children

In 2016, more than four million allegations of child maltreatment were investigated by professionals with child protective services agencies across the United States.[29] This was more than a 10 percent increase over the previous four years. And of these millions of cases, almost seven hundred thousand children were confirmed to have been victimized, three-fourths of whom were neglected and one-fourth physically or sexually abused. Each year more children are added to the list of those we know have experienced stressful and threatening events at the hands of adults who either did not protect them or were abusive. Based on what we know about child development and empathy, it should worry us that every year millions of children are at risk of maltreatment that compromises their emotional attachment and brain development. Abuse threatens to create a negative starting point for empathy.

We know that stress in childhood has adverse effects on engaging the parts of the brain needed for empathy. For some children, constant stress is part of a traumatic childhood. It may be impossible to separate stress that emanates from a childhood of neglect and abuse from the impact of other harsh childhood experiences. But given the extent of the abuse and neglect of children in this country, it is important for us to consider how that start to life may impact the ability of people to fully engage empathically. Numerous studies have found that childhood maltreatment is associated with structural brain changes. Those changes include abnormalities in the prefrontal cortex, as well as the amygdala and hippocampus.[30] We know that these regions of the brain are critical to empathy. It also seems that these are the same parts negatively impacted by stress. It is likely that the experience of maltreatment evokes the same bodily responses as chronic stress. This is not surprising. Maltreatment is extremely stressful and can stretch over long periods of time. Although the majority of cases of child maltreatment involve neglect, which may sound less severe, the impact is significant and can set the stage for problems later in life. Children raised in families with chronic neglect are at greater risk for severe cognitive impairments that contribute to emotional, behavioral, and interpersonal relationship difficulties later in life.[31]

In terms of empathy, emotional damage from maltreatment early in life compromises a child's ability to develop empathy, with the biggest deficit in emotion regulation.[32] Maltreated children live through situations that are unpredictable and frightening without emotional support. Living in such an environment requires that a child constantly be vigilant and watchful for warnings of mistreatment. Their lives are lived on edge. That level of stress produces all the negatives we discussed earlier, especially compromising the neurobiological ability to regulate emotional responses to stressful stimuli.[33]

Even if we did not have evidence of neurological differences in children who have experienced maltreatment compared to children who have not had such trauma, we know enough about empathy to worry that their empathic abilities would be compromised. The state of overarousal and constant vigilance with unpredictable emotional support would make developing self-other awareness, perspective-taking, and emotional regulation difficult. That is not to say that children who have experienced neglect and abuse are not empathic or capable of developing empathy. What child maltreatment does is make that pathway more challenging. Developing empathy after a harsh childhood requires the unlearning of behaviors that were protective while being maltreated but are not helpful in becoming empathic. In fact, there may be evidence that even a stressful early life, such as being institutionalized, can be overcome with predictability and support that come with adoption and a stable home.[34] One of the most encouraging things to know about our biology is that our brains are malleable; we can unlearn things that are not helpful to our well-being. It's not easy, but it is possible, and we will talk more about that in chapter 8.

Grief

The literature on empathy and grief is concerned with having empathic feelings for those going through the difficulties of grief and bereavement. Needless to say, that is important. But when I was thinking about physical states that might block our ability to be empathic, I was wondering whether grief has physical demands that might interfere with our ability to be empathic. To my knowledge, this is an unanswered question. I did find some research that compared cognitive performance and brain matter volume across three groups: people with no grief, people with normal grief such as bereavement for a loved one, and people with persistent and prolonged grief that is categorized as complicated grief.[35] Although the differences were not great, those with prolonged and complicated grief performed poorly on cognitive tests and had a smaller amount of brain matter than those in the other groups. This suggests that there could be neural effects of grief that might diminish our cognitive processing, which we need for the full array of empathy to occur. I am reminded of my colleague Cynthia Lietz's work on resilience that I mentioned in chapter 2. People who have come through very difficult events, which includes grieving a loss, have found ways to make meaning through their understanding of what others have gone through. They show resilience over time by engaging in empathy. So it is possible that the immediacy of grief might create a kind of brain drain that initially affects empathic abilities, but that empathy may be a part of working through our grief. Mind you, this is a theory, but it would make sense that one tool to deal with grief is to connect with others who have gone through a similar circumstance and to share emotions and insights. Such actions would involve the components of empathy.

What About Alcohol and Drugs and How We Process Empathy?

There is a lot of research that looks at the impact of alcohol and drugs on our brains and neural systems. Of course, a review of such research is far beyond the scope of this discussion and my expertise. One helpful way to get a sense of this much research is to consult work by experts in the field who review many studies, often referred to as a meta analysis, which is a comparison of multiple studies. In a review of 140 studies that used brain imaging to track the effect of alcohol on the brain, the overall finding was that heavy alcohol use does adversely affect our brains, both in the physical structure and in the abilities to carry out mental functions.[36] It is possible that the brain changes found in heavy alcohol users are in part a consequence of time, that is, using alcohol for years and years. To address the question of whether it is a matter of long-term use, another review of multiple studies focused on younger people.[37] These researchers wondered if heavy alcohol use in younger people whose brains were still developing and were not exposed to alcohol use for many years showed abnormal brain changes. These studies also showed diminished brain structure, particularly in the prefrontal cortex. Overall, there was evidence that brain development for adolescents may be affected adversely by heavy alcohol use.

A very small study did examine the parts of the brain related to cognitive and affective processing in people with alcohol use disorder compared to people without the disorder.[38] Indeed, they did find a reduction in brain matter (cortical thickness) in the areas of the brain that are used for processing empathy in those with alcohol use disorder compared to healthy participants. They even divided the healthy participants into two groups, those with a family predisposition to alcohol use disorder and those without, to be sure that it was not a genetic or inherited difference. The only participants to have the reduced brain matter were in the group with alcohol use disorder.

Although we do not have large-scale research that tracks alcohol use and empathy, we should worry that the damage to the brain that can come from heavy alcohol use affects a key region for cognitive processing: the prefrontal cortex. This means that we should at least be aware that changing the structure and ability to function of the brain due to alcohol could negatively impact one's ability to use those brain regions to engage empathically.

Like with alcohol, there is scant research on drug use and empathy. However, we can assume that if drugs impact our brain, neural actions related to empathy will be affected too. Of course, we would likely think that such interference in empathy would be as a result of using serious drugs, ones that really alter our brain chemistry. That relationship has yet to be studied closely. But there is one recent study that did look at empathy and the use of a common, over the counter drug, the painkiller acetaminophen (which can be found in brands such as Tylenol, Excedrin, Nyquil, Sudafed, and Dristan).[39] Given that acetaminophen is a legal and easily bought medication, the fact that it might alter our empathic abilities is rather surprising. Acetaminophen is a relatively common, low-level painkiller and is often included in mixtures for other drugs such as cold medicines. We would not expect a dramatic impact on our brain activities. However, the researchers confirmed that acetaminophen works to suppress physical pain, but that in that process, it also reduced the extent to which people felt others' pain. These findings might reinforce the physical actions of mirroring. What if painkillers can lessen both the actual physical sensation of our own pain and the body's sensation of pain triggered by viewing or imagining someone else's pain? We might have proof that the mirroring of pain is a real physical sensation. In other words, feeling someone else's pain is not just in our heads, we really do feel it. While these findings may confirm the power of mirroring, might they also raise the risk of lowering our empathy for others because we use medications to lower our own physical reactions? Or is it that only our mirroring for pain is impeded and we can still fully engage in perspective-taking, self-other awareness, emotion regulation, and assessment of context? That is, we may not be unconsciously triggered by the sharing of pain, but if we have learned how to think about what happens to others and what that means, we will move into cognitive empathic processing. One limitation of this study was that it used healthy, pain-free participants. What about people who really are in pain and use acetaminophen to alleviate it? Maybe in those cases, if their pain is eased, they can focus on others and go from a state of less empathy to more.[40] This recent research raises these questions and opens a very large area of study that needs to be considered in the future.

New emerging research on the neurochemical aspects of empathy has begun to look at the natural hormone oxytocin. Our bodies produce oxytocin, and it seems to be present when we are engaged in prosocial actions. There is evidence that oxytocin is linked to prosocial human behaviors, including empathy, social cooperation, group participation, and trust.[41] Although we know our bodies produce oxytocin and it is linked to prosocial behaviors, we do not know biologically how it works.[42] It may act as a messenger of empathy that already exists or enhance the building of empathy. At this point, all we really know is that when it is active in the body, so too are prosocial actions like empathy, cooperation, and sociality. Can we administer medically manufactured forms of oxytocin to help stimulate empathy and prosocial behaviors? So far there is minimal research on this. There is one study that administered oxytocin (through nasal sprays) to both patients with PTSD and healthy controls and found no significant changes in their empathic abilities.[43] More research is needed, but it does raise an interesting possibility for intervention. Can we alter neurochemical hormones to encourage empathy? I confess to being skeptical that we can take a pill and, voila, have empathy. But if there are neurochemical transmitters that help the brain to better engage in learned empathic processing, it certainly would be worth pursuing.

Psychopathy

I left the discussion of psychopathy and empathy for last. It is likely that when we hear "he's a psychopath," we think of someone without empathy. However, "psychopath" is a loaded term and is often used to describe many different things without reflecting a clinical assessment. Although the definition and identification of the mental health condition of psychopathy has evolved in different ways over the years, there is general consensus that three traits come together to form the condition of psychopathy: a sense of boldness and fearlessness tied to dominance, a degree of self-interest that exhibits a meanness or callousness with a disregard for others, and a lack of self-control or inhibition that reflects a lack of emotion regulation.[44] These characteristics are not in tune with empathy. Self-interest and dominance are not compatible with thinking about the feelings of others and walking in another's shoes, and a lack of emotion regulation means it is unlikely that a person can process emotions that might arise from affective responses or mentalizing. In fact, several neuroimaging studies have found that the way the brain works for empathy does not seem to happen for people who exhibit psychopathic traits.[45]

Several brain differences have been found in people with psychopathy, particularly the processing of the amygdala and part of the prefrontal cortex (specifically the ventromedial region).[46] The differences are characterized by a reduced response by the amygdala to stimuli followed by less discrimination of what those stimuli might mean. It is unclear if both areas are dysfunctional or if the amygdala takes in less input, leaving the prefrontal cortex with insufficient information to process. The result of these deficiencies plays out in poor learning of what behaviors are good and what behaviors are harmful.[47] Perhaps most important is research that finds that people with psychopathic personalities can *identify* others' emotions but do not *feel* others' emotions.[48] This is not empathy. This is a skill at reading other people, which can be dangerous without empathy. Reading other people can make it possible to identify their motives, desires, and fears but not take their perspective, and instead take advantage of them or treat them with disregard. This is why people with psychopathic personalities often act in ways that are callous, dominating, and lacking in empathy.

While we may have evidence that the brain functioning of people with psychopathic characteristics differs from people who do not demonstrate psychopathy, we do not know whether this is a biologically inherited condition or is created from the environment in which a person grows up. It is interesting to note that we have already discussed that chronic, deep stress can suppress the amygdala, dulling the intake of stimuli. While this can be a good coping mechanism for someone who has experienced a traumatic event, what if the amygdala is suppressed from infancy? Might that compromise the ability over time to judge what stimuli mean and lead to a lack of understanding what those stimuli mean to others? Might these early deficits leave emotion regulation underdeveloped? One of the behaviors often seen by people assessed with psychopathy is poor impulse control that contributes to inappropriate responses to stressful stimuli. They lack good emotion regulation. We have a lot to learn about the conditions that might lead to psychopathy, but there is one thing that holds general agreement: those who fit the category of psychopath lack empathy. Without empathy, it is more likely a person will behave in ways that disregard the welfare of other people.

Can We Overcome Physiological Barriers to Empathy?

The question that prompted me to write this chapter was: What happens to our ability to be empathic if parts of our brain are blocked, disrupted, or damaged? I don't feel like I have a definitive answer yet, but I do have a strong belief that we need to pay attention to our brain functions and be aware that alterations in our neural structure and abilities can have an impact on whether we can be empathic or not. But what if brain development is compromised? I do not think it is a done deal, that if there is brain damage, poof, we will never be empathic. The brain is changeable; we can learn to think and behave differently. But like so many entrenched behaviors (how many diets or workout plans do we promise to follow with each set of New Year's resolutions?), changing the tracks of our brains can be very difficult. We can't defend against every stress to our brains, but in the cases of maltreatment, trauma, and alcohol abuse, we can work toward prevention so that the ability to engage empathically is not compromised.

Prevention is ideal because then problems never develop. But for all of us, the full development of empathy needs to be learned. Even with healthy childhoods, learning to be empathic spans our lives. There will be times that we are disengaged from our feelings, we are highly self-focused, we are stressed out, or we are frightened, all conditions that throw us off our empathy. Learning to become empathic can be achieved in multiple ways; some of us can get it from a young age, and others of us will need to catch up. I believe we can all develop high levels of empathy. The challenge is figuring out what abilities we are strong in and what abilities could use more work. If there are biological and neurological barriers that impede sharing and processing the actions of others, we need to understand those too. That is why I included this chapter in the book. We can offer all sorts of support, training, and modeling to enhance empathy, but if there are physical reasons that our brains do not gain input in ways that we can process empathy, then training and intervention may need to be specially tailored to compensate for those biological differences.

CHAPTER SIX

Where Is Religion in Empathy?

WHEN I SAT down to work on this chapter it was the first time I had written about empathy and religion. To me, religion was more personal than professional. Research on religion in relation to empathy did not seem to fit the academic work I was doing. But over the years I have done a lot of thinking about religion and empathy. After all, to fully engage in social empathy I have needed to take in other groups' perspectives and contexts, and that includes understanding a very deep part of many communities: their religious beliefs and practices. As I touched on in chapter 1, every major religion has embraced in their liturgy and teachings aspects of empathy; however, there have also been atrocities committed in the name of many religions that demonstrated a complete lack of empathy. How could this be? The mismatch of religion and organized atrocities is what brought me to believe I needed to write a chapter on empathy and religion. I wanted to make sense of the mixed messages about empathy that seemed to come from many religions over the course of human history—love others as you would yourself, but if we deem they are an enemy to our faith, we can wage war and destruction on them. Or the difference in our faiths threatens our way of life, so we need to protect ourselves, which includes fighting those who do not share our beliefs. What do these messages mean? Love them only if they believe like we do? Demand that everyone believe what we believe because we have the one and only truth? For me, the history of religion is confusing in terms of empathy and at times seems to reflect a distortion of empathy. Thus, to better understand the relationship between religion and empathy, I included this topic on my list of ideas for chapters.

Religion Throughout History: The Good, The Bad, and the Worse

It's likely that most of us have been raised with the idea that religion is a positive force in society. Religion serves as a moral guide helping us to be good people. Religious teachings include admonitions to care about people, such as loving others as we would love ourselves. On the surface, this suggests that empathy can be an important part of religious life. To love another as I would love myself suggests that I need self-other awareness, that perspective-taking would be helpful, and on occasions when others do things that I don't like, it would help to have strong skills in emotion regulation. Unfortunately, that is only part of the story of empathy and religion. Over the course of history, including into modern times, religion has not always served as a moral compass or as an example of empathy. Rather, there are surprisingly far too many examples of religion serving as the rationale for actions that are far from what we would consider righteous and empathic. So there is both good and bad in how religion is practiced and the extent to which empathy plays a role.

First, the good part. As discussed in chapter 1, every major religion of the world has some version of rules and guidance to take the perspective of others and treat them as we would want to be treated ourselves. The most popular one that we were likely to grow up hearing is the Golden Rule that in variations calls for treating others as you would want them to treat you. There is reference to this concept across all major religions of the world, including Christianity, Judaism, Islam, Hinduism, and Confucianism. Recall that the Judeo-Christian biblical foundation for this dates back thousands of years to passages in both the Old and New Testaments. Perhaps the most famous line is "love thy neighbor as thyself" found in the books of Leviticus (19:18), Mark (12:31), and Luke (10:27). This suggests that we use parts of empathy, self-other awareness, and perhaps perspective-taking to understand how we might treat others. However, we do not necessarily have to step into another's shoes to show compassion and cooperation. I know how I want to feel, and treating you that way might be kind and compassionate because it would be for me, but it does not necessarily take into account your perspective at all. Thus, loving our neighbors as we love ourselves can be very one sided. While that is not empathy, at least it produces behaviors that should be positive—we usually want to be treated well, so if we use that as a measure of how we act toward others, we have a fairly positive, compassionate, and cooperative system. The Silver Rule that admonishes us to *not* treat others as we would not like to be treated (also discussed in chapter 1) at a minimum also involves projection of ourselves onto others. But it too may not require us to imagine what the perspective of others might be. However, like the Golden Rule, it can also lead to positive human interactions. Thus, although religion teaches us to treat others well, it does not necessarily infuse empathy into that process. From a societal perspective, if we don't treat others badly, even if we don't understand them, that can promote morality and cooperation. So the basic teachings of major religions do help us to create societies that are collaborative and compassionate, even if they are not necessarily fully empathic. That is the good side of religion.

What about the bad side? The basic premise of most religions is that we accept certain beliefs that unite us as a religious group and make us different from others. This is a form of tribalism. We know that being a part of a tribe can be helpful to our survival, and there can be cooperation between tribes to create collaborative larger societies. That is good. However, as we know from chapter 3, when tribalism goes bad, it pits us versus them, promoting otherness. This is bad tribalism. Bad tribalism is not necessarily a required part of religion, but throughout history it has taken on major significance. For the religions descended from the Old Testament, perhaps the strong language of Deuteronomy 13:7–11 reinforces the belief that keeping the tribe together is imperative:

> If your blood brother, your son, your daughter, your wife, or your closest friend secretly tries to act as a missionary among you and says "Let us go worship a new god, have a spiritual experience previously

unknown by you or your fathers" . . . do not agree with him, and do not listen to him . . . you must be the one to put him to death. Your hand must be the first against him to kill him, followed by the hands of the other people. Pelt him to death with stones, since he has tried to make you abandon your Lord who brought you out of slavery in Egypt.

That is strong language and can certainly contribute to bad tribalism if taken literally.

Sometimes being tribal is less overt and takes the form of exclusion, such as membership in social organizations that are restricted by religion. (I remember when I was young that there were certain country clubs that would not allow anyone who was not a member of their religion to join.) Consider the quotas placed on students who were to be admitted to universities, limiting the enrollment of students who might not be from the majority religion. These practices were typically difficult to document, but were actually legal in the United States from the earliest years of our history up to the civil rights movements and court cases during the 1950s and 1960s. Private clubs are still free to do as they please in terms of membership as long as they do not receive public benefits (such as nonprofit tax exemption).

Even the earliest history of the United States, although taught to us as based on groups coming here to practice religious freedom, demonstrated bad tribalism. Digging more deeply into early American history, we find examples of religion used as the justification for taking land, keeping slaves, and even putting nonbelievers to death. The Puritans, the early settlers of New England who came in the 1600s for the right to freely practice their religion, used biblical passages to justify the use of force to take land from the Native Americans who were already settled here. Specifically, they cited Romans 13:2, "Whosoever therefore resistith the power, resitith the ordinance of God; and they that resist shall receive to themselves damnation."[1] There are documented cases of fighting among religious leaders in Colonial America that resulted in violence such as hanging and the burning of nonbelievers. Some whose behaviors were inexplicable (some of which were likely due to medical conditions that caused seizures) were often referred to as witches. The phrase "thou shalt not suffer a witch to live" (Exodus 22:18) was used as justification for the famous witch hunts of early New England, particularly in Salem, Massachusetts.[2]

Religious values were cited as the rationale for both slavery and abolition. Proponents of slavery claimed that all the patriarchs in the Bible had slaves and that there was no mention of God's disapproval, as well as there being numerous mentions of slavery, even in the Ten Commandments (Exodus 20:10 and 20:14). All these cases of slavery were interpreted as God's acceptance of it.[3] On the other hand, for abolitionists slavery was anti-Christian because in the Bible all people are made in God's image, which means they are all of the same family and should be treated equally. Abolitionists also cited the exodus of the Jews from slavery in Egypt as proof that God was opposed to slavery. They even cited the Golden Rule as an important guide for how to treat each other and, as such, how slavery would not be an acceptable way of loving one's neighbor.[4]

Proselytizing, the effort to convince someone to convert to your religion, is a form of holding one religion as the ultimate way of life and believing it so strongly that you want others to be a part of that religion. That can be an affirmation of the proselytizer's beliefs, but it becomes oppressive when that belief assumes that no other form of religion or way of life is correct. The history of missionaries converting Native Americans to Christianity across the United States was done to "civilize the Indians" and was codified into law in 1865 when the U.S. government deputized Protestant groups to administer government boarding schools that forced Indian children to leave their homes and unlearn their native ways.[5]

The use of religion to justify the actions of the early settlers of the United States can be traced back to their countries of origin. Religion being used to oppress others has a long and ugly history throughout the world. Pinker's review of violence throughout history identifies numerous historical atrocities that were committed in the name of religion.[6] In just three pages of his extensive text, he identifies millions killed in the name of religion: the Christian Crusade to take Jerusalem from the Muslim Turks, which was initiated by the Latin Church in Europe with the promise that the Crusaders would erase their sins and have a ticket to heaven for carrying out this holy fight, killed one million "nonbelievers" between 1095 and 1208; the Inquisition designed to clear Europe of Muslims and Jews that was centered in Spain under the Catholic rule of the king and queen of Spain from the late 1400s through the 1600s was responsible for a death toll of around 350,000; and the European Wars of Religion between 1520 and 1648 that included several long periods of fighting between different religious groups is estimated to have claimed the lives of almost six million people throughout Europe. These are just the death tolls of Western European efforts at proselytizing during the Middle Ages.

Wars fought in the name of religion have occurred in modern history as well. Civil wars have frequently involved fighting over religious beliefs, including the fighting in Northern Ireland during the 1970s between Protestants and Catholics and in Lebanon during the 1980s between Sunni and Shiite Muslims. The Dalai Lama is in exile as the spiritual leader of Tibetan Buddhism due to strife with a Chinese government that controls all religion, thereby essentially outlawing practice of their religion. The brutal civil war that broke out after the breakup of the Yugoslavian state in 1992 among Serbians, Croatians, and Bosnians followed a long history of religious differences. While there were political aspects, the civil war included Orthodox Christians and Muslim groups fighting over land that they deemed to be rightly theirs in order to protect their religious heritage. Over a three-year period, one hundred thousand people were killed, mostly Muslims. Despite the war ending, the religious differences are still deep, even today.[7]

We can even find evidence of religions that we do not expect to use violence doing just that to oppress nonbelievers. We usually think of Buddhism as an ideal example of a peaceful and meditative religion. Yet in the Buddhist majority country of Myanmar (formerly Burma) located in Southeast Asia, there is growing evidence of extremist Buddhist monks organized to isolate and expel Muslims. These monks are backed by public policies and the state military. Their organization's goal is to rid Myanmar of Muslims. Unrest has led to riots, ethnic violence, and the displacement of 140,000 Muslims into government camps from which they cannot leave.[8] This is not an isolated case. Extremist Buddhist nationals are also targeting Muslim residents in Sri Lanka.[9] The situations in Myanmar and Sri Lanka further demonstrate that extremism in any religion, even one that seems to be very accepting such as Buddhism, can lead to violence and oppression.

The current most striking example of how religion has been organized to use brutal means to spread its message is the attempt by ISIS (which is an acronym for the Islamic State in Iraq and Syria, also sometimes referred to as ISIL or the Islamic State in Iraq and the Levant) to create an international Islamic State, uniting all Muslims under one religious calling and leadership. The means that ISIS uses include videotaped beheadings of Western prisoners, mass killings of nonbelievers when towns are taken over by their armies, and suicide bombings designed to kill citizens across the globe. In recent years, the news has been full of these stories. But we know from history that the use of violence and terror to spread the beliefs of fervent religious groups is not new.

Why Religion Goes Bad

Yet if religions across the globe share the Golden or Silver Rules, how can religion be used for killing, torture, and brute oppression? Charles Kimball, noted professor of religion and expert on Christian-Muslim relations, has identified warning signs of when a religion goes to extremes and becomes evil.[10] Citing numerous examples, both ancient and current abuses by religions to justify and perpetrate heinous behaviors, Kimball found that the common aspects of religions gone bad include five characteristics: making the claim for having the one, absolute truth; asking for and getting blind obedience; establishing the "ideal time" for their work; that the ends justify any means used to bring about their religious truth; and that the imperative to do so is a holy war. All five of these elements were found hundreds of years ago in the Crusades and the Inquisition, and are now found today in ISIS and the ethnic wars between the Serbians, Croatians, and Bosnians. To some extent we can see variations of these elements, some of them in justifications for slavery, apartheid, and rights to land settlements throughout history and all over the globe. Kimball suggests that the problem is the nature of a religion and whether it is *exclusive* or *inclusive* in terms of the ways to believe. Exclusive religions hold that they and only they have the truth, while inclusive religions acknowledge that while their beliefs may be primary to their followers, other religions may have valid belief systems too. This analysis suggests that the problem is rigidity, in believing that there is only one right religion and that yours is that right religion. This rigidity lacks perspective-taking, which would help people to acknowledge that there is a legitimate worldview of other religions.

Coming at this discussion from the angle of exclusiveness, Sam Harris writes in his book *The End of Faith: Religion, Terror, and the Future of Reason* that fundamentalism is the problem.[11] Harris is skeptical of all religion-based faith because it is not based on evidence but instead on dogma, which is blind faith—we are told by religious leaders that this is so. While I think he may throw the baby out with the bathwater (religion has also contributed to positive social movements such as civil rights, antiwar, and support for the poor), he echoes Kimball's five warning signs of when religion becomes evil. Harris worries that strong faith does not leave room for other faiths, hence a lack of tolerance for religious diversity.

I think his theory helps to explain the horrors perpetrated under religious fundamentalism and in fact can extend to any totalitarian ideology. The purity of the Aryan race espoused by the Nazis was not a religion per se, but it was a fundamentalist faith, that is, a shared ideology with no room for personal deviation, compromise, or questioning. In fact, Kimball's five warning signs fit the Nazi regime well. Instead of a religion, it was an ideology that had the absolute truth, demanded blind obedience, and established that it was at the ideal time in history to come to power and that the ends justified the means. What runs beneath fundamentalism and totalitarianism is that there is "us," our group, against "them," who are the outside others. This difference provokes the need to have a holy crusade on our side to do away with the nonbelievers who are the others. This is possible because the others are seen as less than human, allowing us, and in some extremist religions *commanding* us, to destroy the others. While this may seem oversimplified, the number of historical examples that fit this logic is extensive and has been repeated over time across multiple groups. We also have ample neurological support (as was discussed in chapter 3) that shows us how feelings of otherness provoke human beings to dehumanize others.

How might we stem the horrors that have come from blind faith and devotion to fundamentalist religions? Kimball calls for critical analysis of our religions. He suggests that questioning and analyzing religious principles can allow for personal interpretation rather than blind loyalty. He believes this is one way to achieve inclusiveness for many different religions. We can be believers and practitioners of our own faith but also recognize the possibility that there are other faiths that are important to others and thus have tolerance for religious diversity. Harris asks us to invoke our better sides, the parts of us that are reasonable, honest, and loving. He calls for recognition that we are all interdependent and that our happiness depends on the happiness of others. Both these suggestions include key aspects of empathy, particularly social empathy. When we take the perspective of others while considering the historical context of their groups and imagine stepping into the life experiences of members of that group, we can gain a deeper understanding of others, which hopefully results in tolerance. Social empathy can help us to view the larger world as an extension of our kin and not pit one group against another.

Context Matters, and So Does History

Perhaps the most important piece in understanding the role religion has played in oppression and terror is analyzing the context of these applications. When groups claim they are killing for the sake of their religion, we need to be very thorough in understanding what is happening before we can take their actions to be true representation of an entire religion. When someone murders a doctor who performs abortions because that doctor is regarded as anti-Christian for doing so, do we call all Christians murderers? When the Ku Klux Klan calls itself a Christian organization that believes in White Supremacy, do we think all Christians are White Supremacists?[12] And if a suicide bomber is Muslim, are all Muslims dangerous?

As Kimball explains, extremist positions are the issue, not religion generally. The historical pattern that chaos and social breakdown of a civilization can create an opening for the emergence of charismatic leaders who promise the glory of a perfect world if we just follow their ideology and rules was discussed in chapter 2. They claim their ideology is the only way to achieve this perfect world, and therefore those who do not believe as they do stand in the way of creating it. Contextual events come together to allow for the emergence of such ideologies. This is extremism. It then follows that part of creating this perfect world includes stopping or eliminating those who do not believe. For some religious leaders, this is taken literally through killing nonbelievers.

Killing nonbelievers is extreme, but there are less violent ways of expressing that the way nonbelievers live is wrong and inadequate to bring about their salvation. For example, missionaries believe they are improving the lives of nonbelievers. They travel the world to convert others to their beliefs. In the process, they assume that any other religions of the nonbelievers are not sufficient to bring about the perfect world, so they do not recognize the nonbelievers' practices as legitimate, instead continuing to advocate for their own religion. This view of one and only one way to live ignores the historical experiences of cultures that may have existed for generations with a set of beliefs that are very important to them.

One group believing it has the ultimate truth to bring about a perfect world and trying to eliminate those who disagree is difficult unless there is an absence or a hiatus of empathy. How do we stop violence in the name of religious beliefs? One tool is social empathy. When we are not rigid in our thinking of us versus them and instead see ourselves as similar human beings, it becomes difficult to kill and maim because we would be doing so to our own. When we believe that there are many good ideas and that our religion is not the only way to make the world better, we can accept other groups and work with them to develop shared communities.

More Subtle Uses of Religion Can Validate Ethnocentrist Ways of Governing

Compared to earlier history, today in our country we do not see application of religion to large-scale violence or as legal justification in courtrooms. However, we do see religion infused into discussions of social issues such as abortion, homosexuality, and the death penalty. While many would argue that holding principles that protect human life is moral and represents the good side of religion, when the expression of these beliefs has one group claiming they have the truth and those who do not share their view are demonized as evil and should be imprisoned or even killed, then religion steps over the line from compassion to lack of empathy. Luckily, most situations in this country in which religion is the lens through which people view their world do not lead to violence. But in many cases, there is still an *us versus them* perspective, and as a result there is a lack of empathy.

In the 1990s I attended gay rights marches and saw firsthand the counter-protesters with signs that damned gay people to hell, saying that "God hates fags" and that homosexuality is a sin. These antigay groups identified themselves through their shirts and signs as members of religious groups. I remember them yelling at us marchers that we should die. These protesters' fury against homosexuality was based in biblical quotations that they printed on their signs and in the literature they handed out. One of the key principles of extremist religious views is using texts literally, although often only selectively. There are excellent biblical scholars who have analyzed text and are worth reading if you are interested in more detail than I can provide.[13] In the case of opposition to homosexuality, two passages in the book of Leviticus in the Old Testament are most often cited:

> Thou shalt not lie with mankind, as with womankind; it is an abomination. (Leviticus 18:22)

> If a man also lie with mankind, as he lieth with a woman, both of them have committed an abomination: they shall surely be put to death; their blood shall be upon them. (Leviticus 20:13)

Those are very severe warnings. But so are a lot of admonitions in the Old and New Testaments, which are not taken literally:

> If a man marries a woman and she is found not to be a virgin, she is to be stoned to death. (Deuteronomy 22:13)

> A stubborn or rebellious son shall be brought to the authorities and stoned to death. (Deuteronomy 20:11)

> It is an abomination to trim the hair on one's temples or to trim one's beard. (Leviticus 19:28)

> People who divorce, then remarry, commit adultery. (Matthew 5:3, 19:9 and Mark 10:11)

> If your right hand causes you to sin, cut it off and cast it from you. (Matthew 5:30)

> Women must keep silent in the churches, they are not permitted to speak. (I Corinthians 14:34)

I am not saying that these passages are not worth studying, and they can be a guide to choices we make in life. But to claim that they are the law of the land and the only right or moral way would mean following every commandment, however far it may be from current lifestyles and laws of the land. Selectively picking and choosing passages for justification of one's beliefs often accompanies extremist views that can set a religious group on the path to the dangerous characteristics of religion gone bad that Kimball describes.

Gay rights is not the only issue that religious groups have opposed vehemently. Abortion has also been on their list of atrocities by nonbelievers. The extremist group the Army of God advocated the killing of doctors who performed abortions, and followers were successful in killing several doctors as well as bombing clinics.[14]

Even recent policy issues have seen elected officials base their political positions on their personal religion. At a recent congressional hearing on food assistance, Representative Jodey Arrington (R-Texas) quoted scripture as rationale for cutting the Supplemental Nutrition Assistance Program. He cited 2 Thessalonians 3:10 that states, "If a man will not work, he shall not eat."[15] While policy makers are free to have their ideas about how social programs should be operated, when the justification for policies rests in the religious texts of one particular religion, that brings up other questions: Should public laws be based on religion? Which religion? Which parts? Who gets to decide?

Of course, the majority of people in the United States who identify as a member of a religion do not hold extremists views that drive them to wish death upon nonbelievers. But the possibility of the abuse of religion through government worried the founders of this country. They were very concerned about the power of religion to dictate extremist views and also were worried that if one religion was intertwined with government, as had been the case in England and Europe, there would be no room for religious freedom. The solution they put forth was to address the place of religion in the highest law of the land, the U.S. Constitution.

Separation of Religion and State

One of the things that makes U.S. democracy so special is recognition of the potential misplaced power of religion in government.

Understanding the possibility that religion in government can lead to abuses of power dates back hundreds of years to the writing of the Bill of Rights, amendments made to the U.S. Constitution two years after its adoption. In the first sentence of the First Amendment, separation between religion and government was laid out: "Congress shall make no law respecting an establishment of religion, or prohibiting the free exercise thereof." This short initial part of the First Amendment does two very important things: it prevents the government from setting up one religion as the most important religion, and it guarantees freedom to worship and believe what we want without government interference. Because the First Amendment guarantees that no religion will be given priority or preference, it paves the way for religious tolerance and religious diversity. James Madison, one of the Founding Fathers and the fourth president of the United States, believed that our freedom arises from having numerous equal religions: "Multiplicity of sects, which pervades America . . . is the best and only security for religious liberty in any society. For where there is such a variety of sects, there cannot be a majority of any sect to oppress and persecute the rest."[16]

This is the legal strength in our country that prevents bad tribal behaviors of religious groups. However, even with constitutional backing of the separation between major religious beliefs and public rules, policies and practices can be blurry. We do have an overlap between the dominant religion of Christianity and the larger culture of the nation.

When I was in high school, classmates of mine would gather early in the morning for a Christian Bible study and prayer session. Although it was a public school, they were free to meet before classes started. I was asked to join. My reply was that I was not of their religion and would not be able to say the prayers that they said because those prayers were not part of my tradition and did not reflect my beliefs. It was incomprehensible to my friends that I did not believe in what they thought were prayers anybody could say. They also had no understanding that the New Testament was not part of my religion. They would insist that I participate, not to try and convert me, but simply because they felt that their Bible study would help me and make me feel better, as it did for them. Even as a young teenager, I understood that their Protestant beliefs felt so universal to them that my being Jewish could not possibly matter. There are some very fundamental beliefs that differ between Christianity and Judaism, and the prayers that both religions say have some similarities, but they also diverge greatly. My friends were completely unaware of those differences. I, on the other hand, was acutely aware of those differences.

Why were my friends unaware of what I (and my siblings) were deeply aware of? We came of age in the 1960s and 1970s, and it was often difficult to separate American beliefs from Protestant beliefs, especially in my small town community (when I was growing up it was officially a village; now it has grown and does not at all reflect how it was fifty years ago, so context and history are important). In fact, I can still sing in Latin the Christmas song we sang in the chorale that talked about "our Lord," which I was well aware was not my deity. But it was the norm, it was accepted. We celebrated Christmas in my schools as a national holiday, not a religious day. When I got kicked off the girls' basketball team because I could not come to the practice held on the Jewish holiday of Rosh Hashanah, I did not even tell my parents. What was the point? It was the way things were. I honestly was not angry or bitter. I was disappointed, but it was just the way things were. I have heard similar stories from friends about their being members of a minority religion. It was just the way things were. Actually, I knew from the stories of my parents growing up that it was much better for me than it had been for them. My father had to lie about his religion to get a job as a bus boy cleaning away dirty dishes from lunch tables. I certainly could work at all sorts of menial jobs in our village without worrying that my religion would prevent that, at least if I did not ask too often for special days off or for special treatment. The separation of religion and state has strengthened in practice over the past fifty years.

Thus, while religious teachings such as treating others as we want to be treated ourselves can support empathy, religious organizations and groups have not always been the best guides for empathic behavior. There are teachings that fit well, but the organized execution of religion can miss the mark. For that reason, the separation of religion and state is important. The constitutional mandate that there be a separation between religion and government holds the promise of building social empathy into the governing structures of our modern government. We can be devoutly committed to our own religion and also be tolerant of other religions. We build that tolerance through empathic insight, through walking in the shoes of others, including contextual understanding of how we each got to where we are today. This view allows for a diversity of religions to coexist, and it is backed up by the law of the land.

Not a Lot of Research on Empathy and Religion

Although religion and empathy can be connected, there is minimal research on this relationship. Here is what the research we have suggests. One role of religion is that it may act as a way of extending kinship.[17] Remember the power of kin selection in promoting altruistic behaviors for those we identify as part of our kinship circle? One idea of how empathy gets extended beyond our religious group is that language and images that extend our kinship, such as the concept of "brotherly love" or more recently "the family of humankind," are used by religions to express caring among all people. Maybe one positive function of religion is to extend the boundaries of our image of kin beyond actual physical relationships to ideological relationships. But this is not a given. As the eminent empathy psychologist C. Daniel Batson warns, although religious imagery can extend our thinking in terms of who is part of our family, it can also be narrowed to see those who do not believe in our religion as "heathens" or "infidels" who consequently need to be converted or eliminated. As we know, history has provided ample proof of that.

In specific research on empathy and religion, it seems that the link with empathy is not in religious practice but in how we process religious content.[18] That is, being a religious person by way of membership and practice is not related to empathy, but those who interpret religious content symbolically as opposed to literally do report higher levels of empathy. I would suggest that this research reflects Kimball's suggestion that critical analysis of religion supports tolerance of diverse religions, which can reflect empathic insight. Another study found that the process of spirituality, unrelated to belonging to a religious sect, is closely associated with empathy.[19] That relationship also makes sense. Spirituality involves engaging in self-transcendence or self-development, which involves stepping outside of one's own world to consider the concerns of others. That practice requires the flexibility to take different perspectives and try to understand them.[20] Being spiritual is different from being involved in religious practice and seems more likely to be related to empathy.

In fact, some religious practices can be barriers to empathy. Rituals are set practices that are required of members of religious groups. Religions use these rituals to build group cohesiveness. However, research on rituals finds that they can also serve to separate group members from others who do not belong and do not participate in those rituals. This sense of separation due to performance of rituals can lead to discrimination.[21] In fact, the stricter the rituals are and the more effort it takes to follow them, the greater the sense of otherness and separation.

It would be instructive to consider how the components of social empathy, contextual understanding, and macro perspective-taking relate to religion. There is no research specifically on social empathy and religion, but there is research available on religious identity and taking the perspective of others in the area of race. When it comes to understanding race, those who identify as more orthodox in their religious beliefs view racial inequality as an individual problem rather than due to structural conditions, while those with less orthodox religious beliefs hold the opposite view.[22] This difference makes sense based on the brain science of otherness and race that we reviewed in chapter 3, as well as the characteristics of strong religious identification that we have reviewed in this chapter. Religious orthodoxy instills strong identification with one's own religion and separateness from others, stirring the sense of tribal identification strongly. Inequality due to race would be a problem outside the group and would trigger an us versus them differentiation. That view is compatible with an individualized focus of race. Considering structural reasons for racial inequality would suggest viewing the problem as across groups and built into all of society, making it a shared problem. That does not mean orthodox religious people are not concerned about racial inequality, but that they would be likely to approach it differently than those who see it as a structural problem.

How might these differing views of racial inequality, as either individualistic or structural in origin, affect the ways we might use empathy to approach the problem? If we use empathic insights to understand others who are different by race, those who hold more orthodox religious views would be more likely to engage in interpersonal empathy and less likely to engage in social empathy. So we might ask: What difference is there in approaching the problem of racial inequality with interpersonal empathy but not social empathy? For those with an individualistic view of race in America, the "solution" would be to improve race relations, which would emphasize improving how people of different races interact with each other. For those who are less orthodox in their approach to religion, the "solution" would be to address racism, which would mean confronting the structural systemic factors in our society that contribute to racial inequality.

The example of race helps us to see that people of different religious orientations can be empathic, but the focus in their empathy can differ, and the result is approaching issues from very different perspectives. Working on race relations involves changing individual people's behaviors. Working on structures of inequality between races involves changing access to opportunities such as education and employment, in addition to addressing widely held stereotypes about racial groups. Of course, there is overlap between an interpersonal approach and a structural approach, but emphasis on which approach might be taken seems to be linked to one's own religious orientation. The difference in these approaches is not that we should choose one or the other, they are both important, but that they take very different forms in action. In addition, those very different ways of responding to racial inequality are representative of how our personal belief systems can influence what empathic steps we might choose in response to social issues.

Teachings from Religion that Guide Me to Be Empathic

The Golden Rule, love my neighbor as myself, does not work for me. Over the years I have had many good neighbors, some great neighbors, and some not so good neighbors. I have had neighbors that I have had to call the police on because of violent fights and rowdy drug parties. I have also had neighbors who were incredibly kind and helped me through difficult times. So are we to take "love thy neighbor as thyself" literally? There was no way I was going to love neighbors who were violent and frightening! So what about the meaning of that very famous biblical phrase? Based on some of my experiences, I do not want to love all my neighbors. That is a lot to ask of us with people who are randomly in our proximity. Does that make me unempathic? I don't think so, but it shows me that using the Golden Rule is not the best guide for being empathic. Yet religion can support empathy.

Writing this chapter has helped me to identify how religion has played a part in my own development of empathy. As I look back on what I was taught as part of my religious education, I realize that there were key lessons that probably contributed to my thinking on empathy and development of social empathy. If you are reading this section, then I decided to keep it in the book. I had decided to write it out because it would be helpful for me to see how my thinking grew from a couple of lessons learned in my teenage years. My hesitancy in sharing it is that I am only a case of one. How relevant to others is my experience? But seeds planted early seem to have grown over the years, so I share with you my relationship with religion and discovering some of the building blocks I now use for empathy.

When I was in high school, I attended a youth group retreat that included several study sessions with our rabbi. In our community, this rabbi was considered to be a brilliant intellectual, which was rather intimidating at the age of fourteen. But to his credit, he treated us as adults who could handle sophisticated thinking. He had us read from Martin Buber's book *I and Thou*.[23] What I remember most from those lessons was the concept of two different types of relationships. One is the "I-it" in which we experience others in a way that is an object to be known, utilized, or put to some purpose. It is the kind of relationship that is useful but not engaging in a meaningful way. The other is the "I-thou," which is an encounter with another in which we form a relationship; we participate with the other and share the experience. There is more to Buber's work, but the fact that I remember these two types of relationships and that we were taught how important it is to try and create I-thou relationships and not I-it interactions is for me an important piece of my development to becoming an empathic person.

The other teaching that was significant for me was the Silver Rule as taught through a parable about a rabbi of over two thousand years ago, Hillel.[24] The story goes that a man came to Hillel and asked him if he could be taught the Torah (the first five books of the Old Testament) while standing on one foot. Hillel, although sensing that he was being mocked, replies, "That which is hateful to you, do not do unto others. That is the entire Torah. The rest is commentary—go study." From this parable I was taught that first and foremost, thinking about my actions in relations to others is key. But I was also expected to learn about how to do that; it would not just happen without thinking and learning. Knowing what I now know, the two parts of empathy, the physiological unconscious interaction and the cognitive thinking part that involves perspective-taking, self-other awareness, and contextual understanding, were there in the Silver Rule story.

Of course, there are countless other experiences and encounters within my family and community that contributed to my learning to engage empathically. But my experience is that religion can also play a part and provide opportunities to teach empathy. Given the historical misuse of religion, it is encouraging for me to remember the positive contributions that religion can make to help us engage empathically.

CHAPTER SEVEN

Can We Have Empathy with Technology?

AS SOON AS I write "empathy and technology" it will be outdated. Such is the world of both the new neuroscience of empathy and tracking the evolution of technology. But to not talk about empathy and technology would be to ignore what is a very important relationship. By now, I hope we can agree that empathy is about connections made, or not made, among individuals, groups, and even communities. It is part of how we interpret the behaviors of others and how we act toward them. This interplay among human beings has involved direct face-to-face contact for most of human history. Human beings have been conversant with each other for at least fifty thousand years (of course, records of this are nonexistent, so it is left to biologists, anthropologists, archeologists, linguists, and a host of other scientists to argue this point—some believe humans had language much earlier, while others dispute that idea). For thousands of years before that humans were communicating in ways that were forerunners to developed languages.

Communication is part of the process we go through to understand the behaviors of others, which we also know to be integral to our

survival. Thus, we can assume that some of the components or variations of the components of empathy have been shared among people
for a very long time. Technological communication, on the other
hand, is in its infancy in terms of human history. The first telephone
call was placed in 1876 and the first email was sent in 1971. The first
website went live twenty years later in 1991. Facebook was launched
in 2004. Live distance communication between people is not even 150
years old, and the forms of communication that seem ubiquitous like
smartphones and tablets are a mere fifteen to twenty years old. That
means that the only generation to have grown up with this technology
is today's young adults. We will not know definitively for years to come
what impact, if any, this new way of growing up will have on people.
All forms of technology as a part of human relationships is very new
in the spectrum of human development. We are only in the very early
stages of understanding what the positive and negative consequences
may be of all our forms of electronic communication. In this chapter
I will do my best to share what we know now and how our understanding of brain science and empathy may give us insight into what
technology can offer in terms of building empathy, and how, on the
other hand, it might hinder empathy.

Let me start by saying that I think using the technology we have
today to communicate is not the same as interacting face to face.
"Reading" people's behaviors and emotions and being able to mirror them is best done live and in person. I say that for one primary reason: you can take in the entire context and use all your
senses better than if the person is delivered to you via an electronic
medium. However, I am not, I repeat, *not* against technology. After
my mother died, we decided to move my father to live near one of
his children. At the time I was living in Arizona, so relocating him
to me made a lot of sense, and I was the least likely to move in the
coming years. We were right; it was a wise move. It was also the early
years of cell phones, and that technology made my life as the primary
geographic caretaker inordinately better. I could go out, travel, and
still be reachable in an emergency. I left the theater in the middle of
a movie to rush to the emergency room on the night my father had
a heart attack because the staff with him were able to call me immediately. I was in the emergency room minutes after he arrived, and he
was immediately less agitated when he saw me. Modern technology

made that possible. I could give you a hundred examples in which my family used cell phones to connect in good ways that were life altering. My experience is shared by others, as research has shown that there are positive communication aspects to the rise in use of mobile phones.[1]

I was sitting on a plane reading when I realized I needed to address the topic of empathy and technology in this book. I grabbed my bag and frantically looked for paper and a pen so I could jot the idea down so I would not forget it. I had the pen in hand and was trying to think where I might have a spare piece of paper when I laughed at myself. There in my bag was my ultra-lightweight Surface laptop computer that I bought because it had a great keyboard I could attach or detach and that would allow me to write in ways that were almost like writing on my full keyboard at home. I stashed the pen, grabbed my laptop, and started writing this chapter. Technology had triumphed again, although using it was not my first reaction in that immediate moment of need. I know that for anyone years younger than I am, it would not have occurred to them to dig for paper and pencil, but I was raised in a different era, and so learning technology has all been introduced new at various times in my life. I love word processors and did everything I could to afford the first-generation home desktop computers so I could write my papers in the new way that allowed for any number of rewrites and drafts, all without having to take paper from a tree. Today I would be hard pressed to tell you how many different computers and cell phones I have gone through; in fact, I can't. For me, and I imagine everyone reading this book, technology is a vital part of our lives.

But what about empathy and technology? Is technology helping or hindering empathy? My immediate response to those questions is: we don't know. Things are emerging and changing so fast that only time will tell. However, we can and should consider the question. I have touched on it in other chapters, for example in the idea of using media to connect people to the stories of other people's lives across great distances. As I was writing this on the plane, I wondered if there was enough research out there to write an entire chapter to address this question, or if it would be a collection of questions for the future. I discovered that it is both, but there are a lot more questions than there is research.

What We Know About Empathy and Technology Today

Interest in research on technology and empathy has primarily taken two paths, one to assess the positive aspects of communicating and sharing of ourselves with others via technology and one to assess negative influences, that is, how impersonal and negative communication can become via technology. The positive interest focuses on how technology can extend connections and help us to see through virtual reality what other people's lives are like. The negative concern focuses on the power of disturbing content, such as violent video games, and anonymity as a pathway to less empathy or worse, disregard for others. The overarching question is: Should we be encouraged or concerned about technology and human relations?

Over a thousand people born since 1980 (those considered the internet generation) participated in an online survey that tried to assess whether use of online communication reduces time spent face to face with others and how virtual empathy compares to face-to-face empathy.[2] These are two important questions to ask, and thankfully we have some data to look at. The results of the study showed that going online did not reduce people's face-to-face communication. In fact, communicating online with someone you already know might actually increase the chances that you will connect with that person offline. This suggests that for people with whom we already have a relationship, staying in touch online might actually support and even advance our connections with the person face to face. In terms of the other part of the question, real-world empathy scores were higher than virtual empathy scores, but they were significantly related in a positive direction. That is, the higher the ability for empathy in face-to-face encounters, the higher online as well, but overall, face-to-face empathy is stronger than virtual empathy. This makes sense because of the lack of context and because there are fewer nonverbal cues available through the online medium. The same researchers looked at social support, the feeling of being supported by family, friends, and other significant people in your life, and how that might be conveyed online versus in person. Their analysis revealed that the feeling of being supported was stronger through in-person empathy than through virtual empathy. That is not to say that feeling understood by others through online communication is not helpful, but it is not nearly as strong as getting that empathic understanding in person.

The finding that one's sense of empathy from others exchanged through face-to-face interactions is stronger than from online interactions, while not surprising, does not mean that we should totally write off support that comes from the world of technology. Development of empathy has been found in the online world, particularly with specialized support groups. In research on people involved in patient online communities (online social networks made up of members who come together to gain information, share experiences, and offer emotional support around a common issue), the member experience of such groups can enhance empathy through building trust and sharing information.[3] Furthermore, the higher the levels of empathy built within the online community, the more trusting and supported members feel. These positive feelings are most likely to evolve when members feel a common social identity, the sense that they are part of a community. This online finding reflects what we already know about feeling part of an ingroup or being a member of a tribe. We have stronger empathy with (and from) members of our own group, however that gets defined. Therefore, if we can replicate group cohesiveness online as we do in person, there will be stronger feelings of empathy for those in our groups.

Text messaging is another form of communication that deserves our attention. More and more, the health field is using the text message medium to send updates, reminders, and information to patients about ways to take care of their health. For example, text messages sent to help people with diabetes remember to take their medications[4] and information and positive reinforcement sent via text to patients in weight-loss programs[5] all seemed to help those involved in the programs. In an effort to use the health promotion models of text messaging, a group of researchers employed similar methods to try and increase people's empathy and prosocial behaviors.[6] The researchers sent one set of participants empathy-building messages such as "Think about your last social interaction. What was important to them in the conversation? Can you try to see the world as they do?" and "Smile at the next person you see, no matter who they are." The other group members either received general messages or no messages. When the groups were compared over time as to whether they felt more empathic and actually behaved more empathically, those who received the empathy-building messages showed more empathy, prosocial responses, and behaviors. The one difference that seemed to confound the researchers a bit was that even though the outside indicators of empathy and prosocial behaviors increased for the participants, that is, those who received the empathy-inducing texts actually showed more empathy, the participants themselves did not feel they were more empathic.

When I read that I was reminded of a course I taught on social empathy. I wanted to test out my work in the classroom, so several years ago I developed and taught the course. The first thing I did was have each student take the Social Empathy Index, a survey that my research group had developed to measure interpersonal and social empathy. Fifteen weeks later, at the end of the course, I had them take the survey again and compare the results. I confess I was a little nervous. Could I teach about empathy and in the process help people to be more empathic? Overall, all the students had increases in most of the components, but some did go down. We had a lively discussion afterward. The sense of the group was that before the course started they thought they were more empathic than they assessed themselves to be after learning the details and depth of information on empathy. What they expressed was that because they were social work students, they scored themselves high on the items because, well, that is what social workers are good at. But once they delved deeply into all the dimensions of empathy, they were more aware of what skills and abilities they had and were stricter about how they assessed their own empathy. By the end of the course they felt they had a much better understanding of empathy, but now they also had higher expectations of themselves. That was why they were scoring themselves lower in some places. They did not think they were less empathic, they were just more accurate. I think that is what the researchers with the text messaging program may have found as well. When we teach empathy, we raise people's awareness, and while that can help them to be more empathic, it can also raise their expectations and assessments of where they are in terms of being empathic.

Even I had that experience. Once I learned about all the components of empathy, I realized that I could be much better at taking other people's perspectives and handling situations with more emotion regulation because I understood the concepts more clearly. It reminded me of when I learned to play soccer years after I had been playing recreationally. I thought I was a good soccer player, but when my coach pointed out things that I could do better, my realization was that the way I originally saw myself play was forever changed and my expectations were higher. Ultimately I think it made me a better soccer player, and I think my research on empathy has made me more empathic as well. But in the process it felt like I regressed before I improved. Although that is how it felt, I don't think that is how it actually played out. I didn't get worse, I just raised the bar and expected more of myself.

What About Young People?

Adolescence is a key time for neural development. It has also become recognized as a developmental period with greater use of technology and time spent on computers, smartphones, and video games. Because of the newness of all these forms of technology, it is only people in their twenties and early thirties who have lived their entire lives with such technology surrounding them. This generation will be the first to tell us about the impact of technology and their development. But they will not be the first generation to live through the creation and evolution of a new form of communication.

If we consider the entirety of human development, our species has had to accommodate numerous changes in communication: the introduction and spread of the written word, printing press, telephones, silent and then sound movies, and television. And with each generation, these advances were accommodated and absorbed, although they were often preceded by concern from the previous generations who had not experienced these forms of communication. I had no idea that over two thousand years ago Socrates worried that the invention of the written word would cause people to be forgetful and not use their memories. He considered the characters of letters to be outside people and would lead them away from using their own skills of thinking and using memory.[7]

Today we cannot imagine a world without the written word. As noted in chapter 2, the creation of the printing press allowed for more and more people to read about other people and develop perspective-taking skills. The written word and the ability of the printing press to make those words accessible to the average person helped build empathy across human civilizations. And that positive contribution may also be the case for technology.

What research we have on brain development during adolescence finds no evidence that the use of the internet has any measurable impact on neural development.[8] While there may not be a physiological impact, there may be social impacts. For example, using social networking sites such as Facebook can aid in adolescent development by connecting friends, getting to know people better, and enhancing the quality of relationships. A review of over twenty studies found that adolescents' use of social networking sites is an extension of their offline relationships and in general benefits their sense of self.[9] Groups on the internet can be places for youths to find others who share their interests or their identity. Such connections can aid in adolescent development by providing social support. However, one study that closely tracked the sense of well-being of a group of young adult Facebook users in relation to their use of the site found that Facebook use predicted negative shifts in how they were feeling and how satisfied they were with their lives.[10] The researchers did their best to control for other reasons that may have influenced their feelings, such as simply having a bad day. They also compared how the participants felt interacting in person with people at the same time and found that direct contact made them feel better. Thus, it is unlikely that technological communication can replace or greatly improve the relations young people have in their face-to-face world.

The research that is out there shows us that online communication is not wildly different from face-to-face communication. The more we already know someone and the more we are connected as part of an identity group, the more empathy there will be between us. And the empathic process is stronger in person. However, developing relationships online can still be done with empathy. As in the case of support groups and building connections, finding people who share your interests or concerns, while difficult in limited geographic areas, can be greatly enlarged by using the online world.

Is There a Downside to Technology?

Violent video games, cyberbullying, and internet trolls show us that not all that is online and available through today's technology is a good thing. Indeed there are aspects of new technology that are disturbing and need our attention to assess how people, especially young people, are impacted.

Research has shown that there are changes in brain communication immediately after watching violent media or playing violent video games.[11] Some research suggests that exposure to media violence lessens the brain's activity to regulate emotions, which can lead to impulsive behavior. Other research suggests that there can be positive aspects, such as improved ability to process visual input. But even this positive change comes at a cost, which is that of becoming desensitized to the violence. These studies monitored brain activity in labs while participants used or viewed videos or immediately following. What might be the longer-term impact? Although these neural changes may be problematic, the changes seem to be short term. Recent research has shown that when long-term impact is assessed, there does not seem to be an influence.[12] In fact, the researchers suggest that the use of violent video games may be a symptom and not a cause for aggressiveness or low empathy. That is, those who already have lower levels of empathy or higher levels of aggression may be more inclined to play violent video games, thereby reinforcing their personality, while those who do not share those traits are not affected negatively by playing the games.

Although long term there may not be a lasting effect, the power of violent and sexist video games to reinforce existing stereotypes can be significant. For example, among young men, stronger identification with domineering male characters in such videos was connected to less empathy for female victims of violence.[13] It may be that violent videos do not cause a lack of empathy, but they may serve as reinforcement for existing beliefs.

I would suggest that based on what we know about the neural processing of empathy, for those who are highly empathic and have strong abilities to mirror and take the perspective of others, the violent imagery of video games that immerse players in virtual reality might be exhausting and overwhelming if played for too long. Think about walking out of a theater after watching an intense movie; everyone is talking about the film and sharing an emotional reaction. This initial experience may very well feel powerful and impact how you are thinking, but the impact dissipates fairly quickly. If it did not, there likely would be fewer people going to watch intense movies. After all, imagine being emotionally impacted for weeks by one movie or video. We would be emotionally overwhelmed and we might stop watching. Thus, there may well be a self-selection of who uses violent media (those who are more desensitized to violence or feeling emotions), and as such it is a marker of predisposed personality traits rather than causing changes in one's personality.

Overall, the research we have suggests that for those who have empathy or are in the process of developing it, technology may enhance those abilities, particularly with people we already have a relationship with, and may introduce us to new people with whom we can explore developing connections. But for those who are already struggling with connecting to others, technology may reinforce the distance. That seems to be the case with two areas of concern on the internet: cyberbullying and "trolling," the practice of negating and harassing others online.

Cyberbullying is bullying that occurs online. It is characterized by the same aspects of bullying, which I define as intentional aggressive actions taken against another person who is vulnerable by virtue of characteristics that the bully regards as a weakness. The 24/7 nature of the online world and the option of anonymity make cyberbullying particularly concerning with today's growing reach of technology. That raises the question of whether cyberbullying is a greater problem than face-to-face bullying and therefore a different problem, or if it is another medium for the overall problem of bullying. Data on thousands of school-aged children show that bullying in person is more common, with about one in four young people reporting in-person bullying compared to about one in fourteen experiencing cyberbullying.[14] But there is tremendous overlap, with most youth who are cyberbullied also facing the problem in person. This is another example of the internet serving as an additional outlet for behaviors that occur frequently in person.

In fact, it appears that the characteristics of bullies do carry over to cyberbullies. Low levels of empathy are related to both face-to-face and online bullying.[15] It is interesting to delve more deeply into the studies. There is a difference between the ability of bullies to *experience* the emotions of others compared to *understanding* the emotions of others.[16] For bullies, feeling the emotions of others is low, but understanding their behaviors can still be fine. What this tells us in terms of the components of empathy is that those who bully tend to have low levels of the unconscious affective response part of empathy but higher levels of perspective-taking. They can read other people's behaviors but not feel them. (You may recall from chapter 6 that this same characteristic was found in people diagnosed with psychopathy. While not all bullies are psychopathic, bullying is a behavior common to those with psychopathy.)

Reading other people without feeling what they feel can lead to taking power over others through manipulation and bullying. There may also be another missing piece of empathy for bullies. High impulsivity is related to all forms of bullying. High impulsivity means acting out without much self-control and without thinking about the consequences of those actions. Having difficulty with self-control suggests that bullying is accompanied by low levels of emotion regulation. Thus, by parsing the components of empathy when analyzing bullying we can better understand what might help to change the behavior of bullies. Focusing on perspective-taking—imagine what the other person is thinking—may not help as much as getting a bully to feel what another person is feeling. It may also be important to help curb impulsive behavior, getting those with bullying tendencies to curb their own emotions and to try to think before acting. Of course, these are skills we try to teach all children, and for good reason. It gets harder if those lessons were not learned young and need to be learned later in life. That is a challenge we will talk about in chapter 8.

What we do know is that, as with other behaviors, a person who is not a bully in person will probably not find cyberbullying attractive, while the person who is known to bully others face to face will find online bullying to be another forum for that behavior. If those who bully are reported to have lower levels of empathy, raising the levels of empathy among those who are bullies may help to move them away from such behaviors. Empathy may be a tool to counteract bullying, but only if we can target the underlying missing parts. I would suggest that emotion regulation is key, as well as testing to see if affective response is missing so that we can teach people who lack the ability to feel other people's emotions to either tap into their own emotions or work around that deficit.

In her book *Sticks and Stones: Defeating the Culture of Bullying and Rediscovering the Power of Character and Empathy*, Emily Bazelon looks closely at several cases of cyberbullying, giving us insight into the victims and the bullies themselves.[17] We know bullying is not new, but because technology makes it possible to enter into a person's world 24/7, even while they are in the safety of their own home, cyberbullying is that much more critical to address. After delving deeply into the young people's lives, she also suggests that one approach to decrease bullying is to build empathy. She not only advocates for teaching empathy to keep kids from becoming bullies but also suggests that increasing the empathy of the bystanders, those who either pass along the bully's messages or can choose not to and stop the amplification of the bully's messages, may be more important. When it comes to young people, the support of peers is incredibly important, and to have a peer's support to stop a bully from harassment can be life-saving. Empathy for a victim can be key to becoming a bystander who takes an active stand against bullying. This is especially important because bullies often use othering as a way to cut victims off from any outside support. How many of us can remember what it felt like to be made fun of, and what relief there was when the target of the joke was someone else? That made us feel part of the ingroup, although at the expense of someone who was identified as being an outsider. Empathy can motivate those who are not the targets of bullying to speak up and disrupt the victimization of the bully's target.

Trolling

I would argue that trolling is a specialized form of cyberbullying. While doing research for this chapter I came across an entire book that looked at internet trolling from a scholarly perspective. The book, *This Is Why We Can't Have Nice Things: Mapping the Relationship Between Online Trolling and Mainstream Culture* by Whitney Phillips, is based on her doctoral dissertation that documented years of research on internet trolling.[18] Kudos to Dr. Phillips for tackling this topic and to her committee members for approving it and granting her a degree. While this may be new territory for research, it likely marks the beginning of what will be a cascade of dissertations and scholarly articles on human behavior and the World Wide Web. I had a lot of ideas about the dark side of the web gleaned from media coverage and my limited personal experiences. I was pleased to find a source that actually used rigorous social science research methods to look at the practice of trolling. Trolling is still evolving, but generally it is defined as the online practice of posting or engaging in discussions in order to disrupt and upset as many people as possible. Phillips argues that trolling is an amplification of cultural problems and that it is a symptom and not a cause. It reflects mainstream practices that trolls take to extremes. We have normalized news reports that are sensationalized through attention-grabbing headlines and talk shows that trash people who believe differently. The political mudslinging of election campaigns and the way elected officials are sometimes discussed (for example, as aliens not born here or relatives to accomplices of assassins, all myths but sensationalized in the media nonetheless) are examples of mainstream culture's desensitizing us to issues and depersonalizing those with whom we do not agree. Using anonymity, trolling opens the world of criticism and depersonalization to anyone. Posting anonymously lifts social prohibitions, permitting one to say things that would not be said in person. However, while the troll is typically anonymous, trolling is done to known targets, setting up an imbalance of power. (When I read this, I thought of the Ku Klux Klan terrorizing and lynching and how they hid their identities under hoods while their victims were not masked. They used their anonymity to inflate their power). This is a strong critique of our culture; trolling is a reflection of what we tolerate, and even encourage, in our modern society.

Phillips makes several important points that suggest trolling lacks empathy. Although trolling can be directed at anyone, it is disproportionately directed at people of color, women, and LGBTQ folks; it disparages human attachments by mocking connections, ideology, and sentimentality; and it celebrates anonymity, making personal responsibility nonexistent. Taken together, trolls operate from positions of power and privilege, trampling on ethics of civic and social behavior. "Trolls exercise what can only be described as pure privilege—they refuse to treat others as they insist on being treated. Instead, they do what they want, when they want, to whomever they want, with almost perfect impunity."[19] What is sorely missing is feeling what others are feeling, understanding those feelings by walking in another's shoes, and thinking about context and the historical events that have shaped our world. What is missing is empathy.

This lack of empathy in internet trolling is supported by a recent study that sampled over four hundred people online and compared their levels of psychopathy, sadism, and empathy with their engagement in online trolling.[20] They found that men were more likely to participate in online trolling and that higher levels of psychopathy and sadism predicted this behavior. The researchers also found that the online trolls reflected the same characteristics of in-person psychopathy in relation to empathy—they could recognize the emotional pain of their cyber victims, which helped them to manipulate and play on that pain, but could not feel their victims' emotions.

There are so many examples of trolling and all are disturbing by definition. I debated even citing any examples, as I do not want to be a contributing bystander. But a couple of examples really disturbed me, not so much for the content but for the intrusion into civil and personal life. The first example happened in the summer of 2017 as the political primary period began leading up to the 2018 election.[21] One of the declared challengers, a Democrat for the U.S. Senate, launched her campaign through her Facebook account. Deedra Abboud is an attorney who happens to be Muslim and wears a headscarf. Anyone can see that on her Facebook page. She wrote a post about religious freedom that caught the attention of many critics (which is a kind word for internet trolls—I cannot say for sure whether these were people who identify as such, but their responses fit the definition). People freely posted comments about sending her back (she was born in the United States), used profanities, called her names like "towel-head" and member of a "filthy death cult," and used male-dominated sexual threats. All of these comments are reflective of trolling. She received hate mail, threats, and counter-protests from white suprema-cist groups. All for declaring her intention to run for political office, a democratic right that we all have. So what bothers the trolls? That she is doing so as a member of a nondominant religion, Islam, with an ideological commitment to religious freedom, and as a woman. I admire Deedra Abboud because she did not stop her campaign, and ironically the haters actually brought national attention to it. But the lack of empathy is unmistakable.

The second example was personal. One of my favorite pastimes is following professional baseball. I have loved the sport since I was a child and enjoy watching and reading about my team. I often go to the team's web page, read the news articles, and even read the com-ments section. I had followed the team for years, and one day I decided to join in the online comments. (I confess it was likely motivated by procrastination, keeping me busy on the computer in a much more enjoyable way than work.) My experience entering a chat on a baseball team page was horrible—my first posted opinion got shredded and my intellect was called into question. It took all of two minutes. I never posted again. I love baseball, and that was my favorite team, but the vitriol of fellow fans was just too much for me to accommodate in something that is a hobby and supposed to be fun. I had experienced the trolling goal: they not only disagreed with my comment but also demeaned me personally. It had the powerful effect of shutting me down.

There are countless examples. Just go online and read through the comments posted in response to news articles, editorials, blogs, or even memorials. The vitriol is especially disturbing when the target is a woman. My own experiences helped me to feel how unempathic the world of the internet can be and the power of trolling to shape our technological dialogue.

Twitter

I have no research to report on Twitter and empathy. When I initially researched "Twitter and empathy" on Google Scholar I got six results. I had never seen a Google search result that did not even have a second page. No research, no evidence to support or disclaim a relationship between empathy and Twitter. Although I have no research per se, I do have some thoughts on the medium and how it fits our discussion on empathy and technology. Twitter may be a very popular form of communication, but I would argue it is limited and very narrow, leaving very little room for empathic expression.

One-way announcements of up to 280 characters are not interaction. (And my point is reinforced by the fact that Twitter decided to double the limit from 140 to 280 characters in late 2017.) It provides information that might lead to an empathic thought because it might trigger affective mentalizing, but it involves very little actual personal exchange among people. For example, a person might post a moving comment, and then hundreds of others will retweet it to reinforce the feeling. Some people might post a response, but for the most part there is no dialogue. In fact, one of those six items that came up in my early search for "Twitter and empathy" was a blog written by a young person lamenting the slew of tragic headlines shared on Twitter each morning, having the effect of desensitizing people to human conditions.[22] The writer agreed that being informed instantaneously was helpful but that the slew of information had a numbing effect. We know from brain research that is true.[23] So for that reason I think Twitter has very little to contribute to developing interpersonal and social empathy among people and groups. I suppose saying that will invite trolling, but then that would then prove my point. It is an excellent forum for information exchange, although the veracity and accuracy of that information is minimally controlled. This means that, like so much of technology, the burden of proof is on the user, not the producer of information. This one-way responsibility is not unique to Twitter, but it is more pronounced.

As I write this in the winter of 2018, it would be negligent of me to not address the use of Twitter by the most powerful person in the United States, the president. Donald Trump is not the first president to use Twitter; Barack Obama had (and still has) an official Twitter account. However, Trump is the first president to use it so personally and so often. It has been described by his staff as his official communication, raising Twitter to the place of national policy.[24] Yet the president has mixed in personal comments, put-downs (for example, his comments about the TV news show hosts Mika Brzezinski and Joe Scarborough in his June 29, 2017, tweet: "low I.Q. Crazy Mika, along with Psycho Joe . . . she was bleeding badly from a face-lift"), and misinformation (citing voter fraud when research disputes that, inauguration numbers that defy photographs of the event, etc.), all delivered directly to citizens. From the time he declared candidacy through the first year of his term in office, Trump had insulted 425 people, places, and things through his Twitter posts. How do we know this? Because the *New York Times* keeps a running tally you can view at https://www.nytimes.com/interactive/2016/01/28/upshot/donald-trump-twitter-insults.html.

His use of Twitter is immediate, without much if any editing or staff advice based on the posting time of many (done in the wee hours of the morning) and the spelling and grammatical errors, as well as the corrections or deletions that follow. During the last month of the presidential campaign, candidate Trump averaged seven tweets a day. During the first one hundred days of his presidency, he averaged four per day.[25] In spite of this open and direct form of communication, people may not find it as helpful or as desirable as the president does. After six months of the Trump presidency, polling showed that 68 percent thought his use of Twitter was inappropriate, 65 percent thought it was insulting, 58 percent thought it was not effective, and 73 percent said it was not refreshing.[26] This is encouraging for those of us who would like to see more meaningful communication exchanges modeled in the public domain. If the public continues to find presidential use of Twitter to be ineffective, maybe it will be replaced with more positive interactions that reflect more human interaction and possibly more interpersonal and social empathy.

It is too soon to say what the long-term impact of this style of communication, short bursts of information in 280 characters or less, will be, but it does reflect some key missing components of empathy. The speed of posting often shows minimal emotion regulation, the superficial nature of having only space for a few sentences belies deeper analysis of the world through historical and contextual understanding, and the predominate one-way mode of communication reflects announcing to others instead of engaging in discussion, which minimizes perspective-taking and shows poor self-other awareness. That is not to say that Twitter is not useful; rather, we need to be clear on its shortcomings in terms of facilitating deep connections among people and fostering empathy.

So Is Technology Helpful or Harmful in Terms of Empathy?

Twitter, social media, text messages, use of email—these are all tools. Tools are only as helpful or as harmful as the user. The same hammer can be used to build something or destroy something. I can be mean or nice to people in person or online; that is up to me regardless of the technology. It is important to remember that so we don't argue about whether technology is good or bad without considering the person behind it. Who we are as people influences how we use technology as well as how technology impacts us.

Used well, technology can help us to connect to people far away, share ideas, and tell our stories. It can open the world to people who live in isolation due to physical limitations or geographic distance. Pictures are worth a thousand words, although too many and we may become desensitized. I am a teacher, and through the reach of the internet I have students all over the world. That is an incredible opportunity and responsibility for me and my students. That is what I think sums up technology: it gives us new opportunities to touch the lives of others, but we must remember to do so responsibly and to treat others as we would want to be treated, just like in person. That is how technology can help us to be empathic.

CHAPTER EIGHT

Social Empathy—Making the World a Better Place

WHEN I FIRST presented the title of this chapter as a possible book title, I got polite responses that suggested I was being naïve and over-simplifying how to address real-world problems. The concern was that I made it sound like empathy is the answer to all social ills, which seemed too easy and superficial. Before I make my case that social empathy spread widely can indeed make the world a better place, let me clarify a few things. I think empathy is not easy, and to be empathic we have to work at it every day, even those of us with high levels of both interpersonal and social empathy. Although some components of empathy may come naturally to us, developing the full array of empathy and maintaining it on a daily basis is a very advanced ability. Throughout history, human beings have made progress in becoming more empathic. In the United States we have taken hundreds of years to develop enough social empathy to do away with slavery, forbid public lynchings, outlaw crimes based on hatred of certain groups, and develop greater tolerance of people who are different from original dominant groups. Despite such progress, we still have numerous public laws and rules that do not reflect empathic understanding; we still have intolerance of racial, ethnic, gender, sexual, and physical differences; we still lack empathic insight into the lives of people who are different from ourselves; and we have never made a public reckoning or apology for the cruel displacement of ancestral Native Americans nor for the brutal enslavement of ancestral African Americans. Developing empathy is a process for both individuals and society. Being fully empathic requires success at interpersonal empathy, followed by cognitive training to gain social empathy.

Interpersonal Empathy and Social Empathy Are Linked

Fully engaging in all aspects of empathy requires first enhancing awareness of our surroundings and other people, followed by our willingness to develop a deeper understanding of what it all means. The initial part of that work is to develop one's interpersonal empathy skills. The second part is to build on those skills to become socially empathic. This takes work. It helps to understand how the two forms of empathy fit together.

Let's do a quick review of what we know about empathy. Human beings survive best when they can read other people and other people can read them. Because of our evolutionary imperative to survive, our empathic feelings are strongest for those others who will help us survive and reproduce our species. In early human history, this meant those who were part of our tribe, those who would band with us to improve our chances for survival and reproduction. That meant those who were closest to us because there were no means to travel great distances. And those closest to us were those who most likely looked like us. This tendency, which was very useful in early human history, is likely deeply embedded as a result of passing this ability on genetically and through social learning. However, moving forward in human history, relying *only* on those who physically resembled us and were part of our small tribe constrained human development.

To expand beyond geographic areas in pursuit of resources, sometimes to enhance survival and sometimes to enhance power, required expansion of contact with different groups, cultures, and ideas. Our tribal instinct, which fosters a bias toward greater interpersonal empathy for those who are like us, limits the expansion of societies. Being wary and fearful of people who are different from us may have been helpful for early survival, but today it creates an "us versus them" mentality that is neither helpful nor healthy for a democratic society. There are extremist groups who want to create separate societies by race, but what does that really mean? For example, does such an all-white group plan to not have commerce with people of different races or ethnicities? Do they plan to not buy products made outside of the United States? What about products that are made by people of different races here in this country? Do they choose to live in all-white enclaves? And if they do, do they plan to do all the work involved in keeping up their community, such as farming to feed themselves, sewing their own clothes, and building their own roads? Or by separatism do they mean they are free to live in their all-white enclave but live off the work of others who are of different races and ethnicities? We already had that system; it's called slavery.

The reality of today is that we are a global, multicultural world. We eat food that is grown all over the world, picked and processed by people of different races and ethnicities; we wear clothing made by people from many different countries with fabrics made in other countries; we drive cars that are assembled in one country from parts made in another. We are not a homogenous tribe that keeps to itself. We are members of the largest tribe in the world—the tribe of humanity. (The only way to live as separate tribes is to turn back history like some small groups like the Amish do; in our free society, groups can do that under the mantle of freedom of religion but do so by shunning modernity.) The task of social empathy is to overcome our biases based on small tribalism to embrace the diversity of our large tribalism of the human species. Why? Because that large tribalism allows us to recognize our connection to others, to see that we are part of a larger community. That broader perspective paves the path to economic and social growth.

The research on empathy that I have been involved in over the years has helped me to better understand the connection between interpersonal and social empathy. My research team analyzed responses given on the Social Empathy Index by hundreds of students.[1] We hypothesized that people would fall across a spectrum of low to high interpersonal empathy and low to high social empathy. Furthermore, we suspected that the levels of interpersonal and social empathy would be linked, and that it would be unlikely to have high social empathy without a high level of interpersonal empathy. Our findings supported this relationship. The majority of participants had equal levels, that is, those who were low in interpersonal empathy were also low in social empathy, the same as with those who scored medium and high. A small amount, less than 5 percent, scored high in social empathy but low in interpersonal, and an even smaller number, less than 2 percent, scored high in interpersonal empathy but low in social empathy. The abilities seem to go hand in hand. Almost half the group scored in the medium levels of both interpersonal and social empathy, with one-third reporting low levels and only one out of six scoring high in both. In recent research done with a broader population of people across several states in the United States, my colleagues and I discovered similar findings. The majority of people have the same levels of interpersonal and social empathy, with a smaller number at the high end than in the middle or low ends, and very few scored high in social empathy without also being high in interpersonal empathy.[2]

It is not surprising that interpersonal empathy is linked to social empathy. What makes the link? Attention to context. With interpersonal empathy, we not only mirror and read the behaviors of others but also do it while taking in the context because we are sophisticated cognitive beings. For example, in a brain imaging study people viewed video images of the action of a hand holding a teacup.[3] Although the action never changed, the settings did—one had no background, the second had a beautifully set table suggesting that a tea party was about to take place, and the third had a messy table with the same tea party items, portraying the end of a party. The task of grasping the tea cup was the same in all the videos, but the contexts differed. Brain activity for the grasping action was the same, but the cognitive processing differed across the three contexts and even differed from seeing just the context without the hand holding the teacup. We have the ability to mirror the grasping while at the same time changing our neural processing depending on the context. Consider another example. Again using brain imaging, researchers tested the neural activity of participants viewing pictures of hands being injected by a needle.[4] One group was given no explanation, while the other group was told that they were viewing a biopsy needle being injected into an anesthetized hand so there was no feeling of pain. Both groups had brain activity that showed automatic response to pain (they mirrored the action), but the group with the explanation of what was going on had additional brain activity in the areas of the brain that involve self-other awareness and perspective-taking. The research shows us that we may have an immediate mirroring reaction to what we see, but we take in the context and make meaning of it through our cognitive or thinking abilities. We often do that unconsciously when we interact with another person. Broadening our thinking to include a more developed, and hence conscious, analysis of the context can expand our understanding of others. The social empathy component of contextual understanding is key for us to make meaning out of our empathic feelings in a broader way.

The other component of social empathy, macro perspective-taking (which includes a sense of self-other awareness), builds on our individual ability of stepping into the shoes of another by applying it to other groups. That means not just looking at individuals but also thinking about what it might be like to be part of a different race, culture, gender, or any other group defined by characteristics different from your own. How does macro perspective-taking differ from interpersonal empathy perspective-taking? The difference is that we consider what being part of a different group means across all walks of life. For example, in the summer of 2016 there was a video of a young boy being rescued from a bombed building in Aleppo, Syria. The video of the rescue and the photo of the five-year-old boy, bloodied, covered in dust, and sitting in an ambulance, went viral and was viewed by millions.[5] It definitely sparked strong feelings, as we would expect of other human beings watching the shocking imagery. The first feelings of mirrored pain and fright were our shared affective response. This may have prompted thoughts about what could be done for this little boy, reflecting self-other awareness and perspective-taking. We had engaged in interpersonal empathy. For some, the next step was thinking about what it means to be a child living in a war-torn city, followed by attempts to understand what the political and social reasons for such violence were. It involves stepping into the society and understanding the different groups, who they are, their history, and what they want. This is contextual understanding and macro perspective-taking. The interpersonal empathy level is important; it connects us to another human being, even from thousands of miles away. The social empathy level leads us to understand what motivates groups to behave the way they do and what it means to be a part of that group, not just in that moment, but throughout history. Using social empathy as our viewing lens can move us to understand complicated social and political situations.

Viewing the world with social empathy is a tall order and takes a lot of time and energy, more than we have for every social issue. I am not suggesting that we drop everything and learn about all cultures and groups. What I am advocating is that when we face situations that we want to understand, we need to take the time to be socially empathic by engaging in contextual understanding and macro perspective-taking. A picture may put a face to the war in Syria, prompting news coverage as well as more details about who was fighting and why. The more we contextualize our knowledge and engage in macro perspective-taking, the deeper our understanding.

Increasing empathy may not guarantee action, but as discussed in chapter 2, it is related to prosocial behavior and can be the impetus for taking action such as being altruistic or cooperative. So too with social empathy. With the example of the young boy in Syria, thinking more broadly through social empathy can move us to advocate for bringing more Syrian refugees into this country, sending international aid, helping in the efforts to free Syrian citizens being held as hostages, or pressuring the Syrian government to end hostilities. In addition to motivating us to take broader action, being socially empathic has the benefit of helping us to feel part of the larger society, which is empowering.[6] We feel that we can have an impact on the world outside us, that we matter and make a difference. Taking in the larger context not only informs us about what others do and why but also joins us with those others in meaningful ways.

Social Empathy Is a Way of Thinking

While interpersonal empathy is built on the unconscious mirroring of actions that are then processed in an individual's brain, social empathy is a mindset, a way of seeing the world and framing your thinking. Yes, it involves certain abilities and training and is built on interpersonal empathy, but more than anything it is choosing how we want to view the world. It requires that we step into the shoes of many others, especially people who do not look like us, do not live near us, and may not speak the same language. I use the metaphor of a camera: looking at the world through a close-up lens is interpersonal empathy, while looking at the world through a wide-angle lens is social empathy.

What does it matter if we are interpersonally empathic but do not progress to be socially empathic? In chapter 1 I introduced the interpersonal empathy component of perspective-taking with the example of trying to understand what life might be like living in poverty as a parent with young children receiving public assistance. That is an individual perspective. It is important and helpful in gaining greater awareness into the lives of people who are different. But it does not transfer over to understanding how that person got to where he or she is. This requires a broader empathic view. This requires social empathy. This means considering the social empathy component of placing ourselves as members of other groups, ones that may be outgroups, and doing so while learning about their history and lived experiences. It may require learning new ways to look at social issues, which may mean practicing creating new neural pathways. What does taking a social empathy perspective look like?

The Path to Empathy

There is no one way to get there. It is not a straight line. It is a journey. But the good news is that the more empathic you become, the more others around you will be empathic. Mirroring is powerful. If we behave in positive ways, we can enjoy the return of that positive behavior. Of course, it is not a guarantee that all other people have the ability to mirror and be empathic, so you may not be rewarded with reciprocated empathy all the time. But my experience is that it works a lot more than it doesn't, so practicing empathy regularly pays off.

It's Never Too Late: We Can Learn Empathy

A person can learn to be empathic at any age. Many books and articles provide exercises that can help us to learn how to become more empathic. With seven components of interpersonal and social empathy, there are seven distinct areas of empathy to work on and improve. It would take numerous additional chapters to cover all the ways to teach empathy. Although I have no intention of doing that, in the epilogue I highlight a couple of ways we can teach social empathy, some on the small scale of a classroom and some on the large scale of a community or nation-state. Learning empathy is a life-long process.

Empathy, like learning a foreign language or learning to read, is much easier to learn when you are young. As children, our brains are malleable and can more easily adjust to changes in the way we gather input. This flexibility is called "neuroplasticity," the ability of our brains to change as a result of different experiences we have and to adjust to new ways of thinking.[7] This is the course of human development. The brain grows and develops its neural pathways as children take in new experiences. Although we do not know the exact mechanisms for changing the brain, we can see the results.

Scientists with expertise in neuroplasticity have conducted numerous experiments to test how adaptable our brains are to change. One revealing experiment had all participants learn a five-finger routine played on a keyboard with their right hand.[8] They were then divided into two groups. The first group went on to practice the routine physically, while the other group was tasked with practicing mentally. Brain mapping techniques to view and measure brain activity showed increased cortical output for the trained right hand for both groups, and it increased over time. What was surprising was that after learning the task, not just the actual physical practice but also the mental imaging of the routine increased the brain's activity in the area of the brain where the activity was mastered. This research demonstrated that the brain can be changed by physically experiencing an action as well as by mentally imagining that action. This dual process of learning reminds me of the numerous examples I have seen over the years watching the Olympics. Many of the athletes have talked about taking time to mentally visualize themselves doing their routines. I am sure this is done in part to sharpen their focus before performing, but brain research tells us that this mental imaging of doing a task has a strong impact on increasing one's ability to physically perform the task.

This team of researchers, led by Alvaro Pascual-Leone of the Center for Non-Invasive Brain Stimulation at Harvard Medical School in Boston, has done a great deal of research on neuroplasticity. One interesting area of research focused on sensory deprivation, specifically the loss of sight and hearing, and how the brain compensates for the loss of these inputs over time. The research is conducted at a very sophisticated level of neural analysis. As you know, I am not a neuroscientist, so I apologize if I am oversimplifying this very detailed work. Based on my reading of the research, the human brain is capable of reorganizing neurocircuits. For example, with blindness, a person's sense of where sound is coming from is enhanced, as is verbal memory. In someone who loses hearing, peripheral vision becomes enhanced. The brain seems to compensate for the loss of one input by enhancing others, using those regions of the brain to do different tasks.[9]

The researchers found another interesting characteristic of our brains. Other parts of the brain are recruited to help with the reorganization. The brain uses the area reserved for the lost sense as well as other areas of the brain. The rerouting can be unique to the individual, so the brain patterns might look different for each person. But what is shared is the ability of rerouting. This is good news for learning to be empathic. Our brain is malleable, so we can learn new skills even when we are older or have some neural damage. We have the cognitive abilities to process input to improve our self-other awareness, perspective-taking, emotion regulation, and contextual understanding. These empathic skills use multiple parts of the brain, some overlapping and some different. Even if some parts are not as capable as others, we now know we can tap the brain's ability to reroute our cognitive processes to still learn new skills. It takes practice, but the plasticity of the brain allows for the creation of new neural pathways.

Poverty Tests Our Social Empathy

So what does taking a social empathy perspective look like? I spent twenty years of my career studying the social, economic, and political costs of poverty in the United States. It was trying to explain to students what it means to be poor in the United States that contributed to my thinking about social empathy. I was stumped by those students who seemed very concerned about the well-being of people but who were very hard lined about poverty. They felt welfare was an unearned and undeserved handout and were against it. Over the years I found that teaching about the context of poverty and trying to get students to imagine all the conditions that go along with it helped to generate a better understanding of what it means to be poor in America. This was what set me on the path to conceptualize and articulate social empathy. Thus, as I close this last chapter, I would like to share the analysis of poverty, following up on what I introduced in chapter 1.

As you may recall, studying the changes that were made in 1996 to "end welfare as we know it" was a strong impetus for my research on social empathy. In chapter 1 I discussed the first ten years of the program and how it had gone from a program that covered more than two-thirds of poor families to covering less than half. Being poor had not changed; what had changed was whether the government would help out. That was the first ten years. How about the second ten years? The Department of Health and Human Services reported to Congress on the program in 2016 in its *Eleventh Report*.[10] In 2017 the Congressional Research Service compiled data on TANF (the cash assistance program that was at the heart of ending welfare as we know it) into a report for members of Congress.[11] A look at the data from both these sources told me that I was right: this policy was not about helping people who were poor; it was about getting them off welfare. Before the 1996 legislation was passed, 82 percent of eligible families were in the program. This dropped to 28 percent in 2012. For children, the drop was from 85 percent to 36 percent. What happened? There were more than fifteen million children in poverty in 1995, and that number was the same in 2012. Yet TANF coverage had dropped precipitously. Why were so many eligible poor people not covered by the program, many more than in 1996? If we were changing "welfare as we know it" to help poor people move from government assistance to working and providing their own support, then the numbers in poverty should have been lower with the decrease in TANF coverage and the portion of eligible people covered by the program should have at least stayed the same.

You might be asking if these numbers are from advocacy groups or "political agitators." I purposely chose to use resources from the government designed to inform members of Congress. The Congressional Research Service is nonpartisan; it exists solely to provide information to members of Congress from both parties. The data I used were collected and put into reports expressly for members of Congress making policy decisions. The data show that the "end of welfare as we know it" has been to remove the one and only program that provides cash assistance to poor families from the lives of millions of poor children. Why? Answering this question requires looking at what policy makers say and do. In chapter 1 I cited some of the rhetoric of 1996. Ostensibly, the reason was to promote self-sufficiency, getting people out of poverty by their own efforts. More recent comments help to explain the current state of TANF and public assistance. The sentiment expressed is that we don't want to give "free stuff," the term used by Mitt Romney and Jeb Bush when they were running for president in 2012 and 2016,[12] or transfer money from the "makers to the takers," as House Majority Leader Paul Ryan said about welfare when he was a vice presidential candidate in 2012.[13] (In fairness, in the years since he has apologized for using those terms, but has not led any legislative efforts to change TANF to cover more of those who are eligible.) The purpose had changed. It wasn't about helping people become self-sufficient; instead it was about not giving people aid because it was viewed as "free stuff." (You may be saying that this sentiment was there twenty years ago, which is likely true. But it was not stated openly. The fact that the openly stated reason had changed shows a change in the context.) This is important social empathy contextual information. Those in power were expressing ideas that shed light on why, after twenty years of policy change, people were still poor and worse off in terms of coverage, yet government assistance continued to be cut.

I do understand the reluctance to provide cash assistance. Once people receive the money, we cannot control how they spend it. This irritates people because they feel they work hard and have earned the right to spend their money how they want. Giving government money to people not working feels like a slap in the face. From a mirroring perspective, if I work and you don't, we are different and my connection to you is very weak or even hostile. You do not look at all like me.

I have had many students over the years share this view with me. I remember one young woman in particular. She came up to me after class and told me she was angry at a friend of hers because she got pregnant, had a baby, and now was staying home with the baby collecting government assistance. My student, on the other hand, was working several part-time jobs and going to college, in her view being productive and not living off the government. We chatted some about this unfairness. I asked her: What if I could guarantee she got the same amount of money as her friend but there would be one condition? She laughed and said absolutely she would take the money, so what was the condition? The condition was that she had to have a baby, just like her friend, and she had to care for that baby, just like her friend. She had to accept the life of her friend as her own. I was putting my student in the shoes of her friend. She laughed and said if she had a baby she could not go to school, and if she did not go to school and get a degree she could not get a good job. My point exactly. It is one thing to compare what I have to others, but empathy does not let me pick and choose which parts of my life to compare with the lives of others. That is the important step of self-other awareness and perspective-taking.

What is all this free stuff anyway? The cash assistance provided by the government averages about $375 a month for a family of one adult and two young children, which comes to $4,500 a year. That can only happen for a total of five years over a person's lifetime. On the other hand, the official measure of poverty for that family of three is $20,780.[14] We officially think a family of three is poor if their income falls below $20,780. But we think that giving them cash, $1,500 a year for each person, is too much. Let's add in food support. The average family of three who is eligible for food support gets about $375 a month through the Supplemental Nutrition Assistance Program (SNAP).[15] This is not cash but rather credit to be used to purchase food items. It cannot be used for paper goods, cleaning supplies, diapers, alcohol, cigarettes, or other items that people purchase at grocery stores. It cannot even be used for prepared food from a deli counter, just basic food items. Some poor families, about one out of four, get housing support too. All told, if you add in all that free stuff, there are still 17 percent of children living in poverty.[16] The best we do by giving government assistance drops the poverty rate 4 to 5 percentage points. In terms of real children, that changes the number of children in poverty from fifteen million to twelve million. Even after all the welfare programs give them free stuff, we leave millions of children to grow up poor.

I get all sorts of deductions on my tax return so I don't have to pay as much in taxes, which means real money in my pocket, but that is not free stuff. So what is the difference? A big part of the difference is about us versus them: those who work versus those who don't, those who have higher education versus those who don't, those raising children with a partner versus those raising children alone, those who are middle to upper class and those who are low income to poor, and those who are white versus those who are people of color. These are the differences that are in play when we debate welfare. As I pointed out in chapter 1, those who make the policy decisions do not and have never lived as do most of the recipients of TANF. There is no walking in their shoes.

Looking at the policy changes made to welfare from the perspective of empathy suggests that the issue might have triggered personal concerns but not societal concerns. Those involved in this policy may have had good levels of interpersonal empathy, but I suspect they did not have the mindset of social empathy. They viewed poor people as individuals responsible for their own situations, not as part of our larger shared group of people living in the Unites States of America.

Social Empathy Can Broaden Our Focus

Maybe I have not convinced you that we provide minimal assistance to poor people. Suppose that you are right that we should not give people free stuff. Does it really make sense to cut back on all the programs that give people free stuff like food through SNAP, health care through Medicaid, or education through Pell Grants? Actually, there are a number of self-serving reasons for those of us who do not use these programs to want these programs to continue. If we expand our view of the context and imagine the experiences of other groups, we can see those of us who are poor as well as those of us who are not all in the same picture. First there is the economic connection. My sister works at a county hospital in which three-quarters of its patients are on Medicaid or Medicare. Her job as a nurse is paid for by the money collected by the hospital from the government payments made for the medical treatment given to all those patients. Her family is grateful for her paycheck. I work at a state university. My salary in part comes from direct state support and federal support through all the loans and grants my students use to pay their tuition, and I am very grateful for my paycheck. When a person with SNAP benefits uses them, that person is spending money in the community at a grocery store that employs people locally. These examples support the rationale behind government transfers.

When the government pays for things with resources that get spent right away, there is an economic stimulus effect. I know that most people associate this line of thinking with liberals and Democrats, but that is not always true. Republican president George W. Bush, once in 2001 and again in 2008, pushed for tax rebates, money sent directly to American households with the goal of having them spend the money to stimulate the economy. I remember getting my $300 check. It was not life altering, but I did feel like it was easy to spend because it was unexpected. It may seem silly to expect a check of $300 dollars to make a big difference. In 2008, the program transferred $158 billion across 128 million households.[17] It might not have been huge for each family, but that much money pumped into the economy, most of which was spent quickly and locally, was significant at the time. It was significant because it was money that was used and passed through many sets of hands. However, one-time government transfers such as the Bush tax rebate do not make a big difference in the long term. That is where programs that transfer money on a regular basis like SNAP benefit all of us.

The SNAP program transfers $70 billion a year that can only be spent on food items.[18] The people who qualify for the program are in economic need, so they spend their allotments right away. This has the effect of the government pumping billions of dollars into local grocery stores, which pay the salaries of workers, who then spend their paychecks on rent, cars, clothing, and other consumer products. When the grocery store sells what it stocks on the shelves, it orders more groceries from producers, who then need more supplies to bake bread or grow tomatoes to sell in the grocery aisles. This is called the "multiplier effect," an economic term that describes the phenomenon that for every dollar spent there is more than a dollar in wealth created, which increases the more times that dollar changes hands.

I have seen the mathematical computations that support this concept, all of which are complicated, and I lack the skills to fully explain. In table 8.1 I have put together a very simplified version of this math. Suppose the government gives $1,000 to a person to spend on his or her daily living. Some of that money gets "lost" in the way of taxes or savings, but most of it gets spent. In my simple example, $200 gets lost, but the rest is spent. After the initial spending, there is $800 left to spend by others who were paid from the original $1,000 transfer. Then there is $600, on down to zero. If you total up the column of money available to be spent (the first column on the left), it equals $3,000, which shows a multiplier of three: the initial $1,000 passed hands and was spent by others, creating an economic effect of three times the original amount. This is the multiplier effect.

The effectiveness of government transfers to stimulate the economy has worked. Maybe you think some of that is okay but that if we do too much of it, people will just sit around and not do anything but

TABLE 8.1
The Multiplier Effect

Money Available to Spend	Money "Lost" through Savings, Taxes, Foreign Spending, etc.	Money Spent, Which Moves to Next Row for Others to Spend
$1,000	($200)	$800
$800	($200)	$600
$600	($200)	$400
$400	($200)	$200
$200	($200)	$0

collect their check or food stamps. Would you? Would a check for $1,500 per year and food coupons worth on average $1,500 per year keep you home, doing nothing but "living on the dole"? Imagine yourself getting this level of "free stuff" and think about how much it would change your desire to work, earn more money, and be able to buy things. Still not convinced? Maybe the economic argument is not strong enough to convince you that we should take a socially empathic view of public policy.

What about the moral aspect? Remember that empathy is highly correlated with moral behavior. Morality is something we cherish in the United States; at least all of our religions seem to agree on that. Social inequality and deprivation is a moral issue. Do we want to live in a country in which one out of every five children grows up in poverty? And if that child is black or Hispanic, one out of every three grows up in poverty? We know a lot about the problems with growing up in poverty, including the physical deprivation of unhealthy living quarters, poor nutrition, and family stress. How many of us would choose to live in poverty? Very few because we know it is not a healthy or safe way to live. There are millions of families who are near poor, with income below even double the poverty level, about $40,000 per year for a family of three. One-third of white families and 60 percent of black and Hispanic children are in families with this low level of income. Thus, there are not only very poor children but also more children growing up in struggling low-income families. Why do we want to raise generations of children who live in homes stressed by poverty? Is it too expensive to take care of children?

Poverty can be better understood through social empathy. Poverty is measurable and changeable. We have evidence that raising people's financial means works. Do you know what the most successful government program at fighting poverty is? Social Security. Without the retirement, disability, and survivor benefits of Social Security and health insurance through Medicare, another 22 million people would be in poverty, an increase from 13.5 percent to 20.5 percent.[19] You may be thinking that Social Security is different from welfare. People appreciate Social Security and consider it an earned right because they have paid into it in order to get benefits. That is true today, but the amount received through monthly benefits and health care is more than what people have paid in. A couple retiring today who earned average wages over their lifetime, working from age twenty-two until retirement at age sixty-five, would have paid in about $700,000 in taxes but receive over a million dollars in benefits.[20] Our support of Social Security is so strong and positive that we accept that it is costly to us as a nation.

We make policy decisions that dictate where we spend our money as a nation. We also make policies about how much money people must contribute to be part of society, that is, how much and what gets taxed. One of the arguments for why we do not provide more resources for people who are poor is because we would have to change our budget either by changing our priorities of what we spend money on or by raising more money through taxes. Although neither is politically easy, it is a choice that we as a nation make.

I was trying to figure out where we could find money to help poor people. In my research on the national budget, I found something called "tax expenditures," which is an interesting way of saying tax breaks through special exceptions, deductions, and exemptions. I counted over two hundred tax breaks listed by the Congressional Joint Commission on Taxation for a total of $1.2 trillion dollars that normally would be paid in taxes if it were not for all the exceptions.[21] Some of these tax breaks are common to us, such as the deduction for mortgage interest we pay on our homes and charitable donations. Others benefit corporations, such as depreciations on business properties. Others are more specific like credit for orphan drug research or timber growing. Those of us who benefit from these exceptions don't typically think of them as a break. But each one was a policy decision made as a deliberate choice to forego taxes paid to the government. The point I am trying to make is that using social empathy as the lens through which we view the circumstances of other people's lives and through it imagining what it would be like to be in someone else's shoes, we might consider a particular tax credit not as valuable as raising extra funds to go to the poorest families.

In fact, the tax policy debates in Congress during the fall of 2017 and the actual policy that was passed made that very point—sort of. Congress members advocated for the elimination of some deductions and exemptions to increase government revenue. But that extra revenue was not targeted for poor people or medical care; rather, it was directed to the top earners and corporations (by way of tax breaks for those two groups). The argument made was that extra money in the hands of the top income earners and corporations would encourage them to expand and ultimately create new jobs. That may happen, but it takes time, and it "trickles down." This term reflects the economic theory behind their rationale. Although referred to as "trickle down theory," it is more officially called "supply-side economics," that is, enhancing those at the top who are the suppliers to then pass on the benefits they accrued. If lawmakers wanted to get more jobs and support to those who are in greatest need, they would simply use our current system of getting resources in the hands of those who are most likely to use them and thereby tap the multiplier effect. Instead, they chose the much slower path that might or might not work, given how long it takes and what can happen to the economy in the meantime.

As I tell my students, public policies are choices that are socially constructed. These policies can be changed. History is full of examples like ending slavery; granting all people the right to vote; creating Social Security, Medicare, and Medicaid; and legalizing same-sex marriage, just to name a few. Each of these major policy changes reflected awareness and understanding of the lives of people who benefited from these changes. That is social empathy.

Social Empathy Can Lead to Social Movements

Unfortunately, waiting for policy makers to become socially empathic seems to take forever. Instead, social empathy on the part of citizens can mobilize people to advocate on behalf of themselves or other groups to get policy makers to understand the feelings and needs of others. The civil rights movement of the 1960s is a very strong example of this: those in power were not willing to pass laws to ensure voting rights and civil protections until major social upheaval pushed enough of them to pass civil rights policies. The civil rights movement promoted socially empathic insight to see what life was like for those in powerless oppressed communities.

Today we have seen a great deal of attention on unacceptable behavior by those in power through the MeToo movement, which is centered on the belief that women who have been victimized should be heard and believed. The phrase was already in use beginning in 2006, when Tarana Burke, an advocate for young women of color, created it and used it as part of the organization she started, Just BE Inc. I think the words Tarana posted on the group's website show what empathic insight can do.[22] She recalls her experience with a young girl confiding to her about being sexually abused. Tarana's reaction was to send the young girl to someone else because it was so difficult to hear. As she confides, she could not bring herself to say "me too." Tarana's empathic insight of that moment propelled her to commit her life to doing that. When actress Alyssa Milano tweeted the idea of sharing me too stories after the allegations of sexual victimization by Hollywood producer Harvey Weinstein became public, the response was immediate and widespread. Millions of women shared their stories via Twitter, Facebook, and other means of communication. Men also came forward.

The stories of what happened to so many women are not new, but that we believe them is. It shows not just a respect for their experience but also a feeling of shared emotional experience, that of being victimized. If this expression of empathic insight helps us to understand the experiences of those who work for, or aspire to work for, someone in power, then we expand our understanding from personal stories to shared experiences and become aware of historical context. When those who are powerless are heard and supported, that awareness can also change how those in charge treat those who work for them. It can spread to policy making. When this happens, we see how interpersonal empathy leads to social empathy.

One Last Thing

When I teach, I like to close with the "takeaway" for the day, the point that "if you only remember one thing, this is it." In closing this book, I would like to share the takeaway, the thoughts that more than anything I hope will stay with you.

We are hard wired to share other people's feelings and to mirror their experiences. We can choose to ignore these feelings or we can think about what they mean on a personal and societal level. It takes work to do this thinking. It takes skill to keep straight what feelings are yours and what feelings belong to others. It can be exhilarating and exhausting to walk in the shoes of others and to imagine their lives. We need the strong ability of taking care of our own emotions while doing this. We need to think broadly and to consider what others have experienced over time because of the characteristics that define who they are. History and context matter. Understanding all this and being understood is the full array of empathy; it is what makes human beings unique and brings us together as the tribe of humanity. When we engage empathically, we not only become better companions to our friends and families but also connect with people from all walks of life in ways that protect us from fear and misconceptions about those others.

It may be naïve or simplistic of me to ask us to be more socially empathic in order to create a better world. I willingly accept that critique because if even just a few more of us become a little more empathic, it will impact others. Those who are influenced to be more empathic will in turn influence others. That is the history of empathy. Empathy spreads from one person to another, from one group to another, until differences fade and "they" becomes "us."

Epilogue

Teaching Social Empathy

SOCIAL EMPATHY IS a skill that is learned. Some of us have learned it without realizing it as we have moved through our lives. Others of us have yet to incorporate social empathy in our worldview. For those new to social empathy, as well as those who want to further develop their skills, there are all sorts of exercises and practices that can be used to enhance one's social empathy. We would need another book to do justice to all the ways one can learn social empathy. As a small step toward that, I describe a few ways that have worked for me with a simple model I developed as a framework for learning to become socially empathic.[1] The framework consists of three levels, and each can build on the one before. The goal is to expose ourselves to new people and situations, learn as much as we can about those people and their lived experiences, and, when possible, take the steps to immerse ourselves in different cultures, situations, and locations.

Three-Tiered Framework for Learning Social Empathy

Level 1: EXPOSURE

Meet new people with the goal of having contact with people who
are different from you. Visit new places that reflect cultures that are
new and different to you. Think about and discuss ideas and values
that are new and different to you.

Level 2: EXPLANATION

Learn about what contributes to the differences between you and
others. What happened historically? What is different about your
ancestry and the course of history for your ancestors compared to
members of other groups? Were there opportunities or barriers in
your background that are unique or the same as other groups? How
have other groups experienced opportunity? Be sure to research
credible data that factually support your understanding of opportunities and barriers.

Level 3: EXPERIENCE

Walk in another's shoes—imagine yourself in the life of a person
who is different from you in class, race, culture, gender, sexual identity, age, national origin, or ability. Try to feel that experience as if it
is real for you. Think about what you learned in level 2 that explains
why and how the other person's life may differ from your own or
may be similar. What was it like throughout history to be a member
of that group? What is it like today? How is the current situation a
product of or influenced by history? How would your life today be
different if you were a member of that group instead of your own?
Search out ways that you can actually experience firsthand these differences over a meaningful period of time.

Teaching Social Empathy on a Small Scale

Getting people to understand how other's experiences growing up
differ from their own can be a challenge. We often refer to different
life starting places as differences in privilege. By privilege we mean

that some groups have more access to resources and opportunities than do others. These days, the minute we talk about privilege, people become defensive about their upbringing. The recognition that membership in certain groups can place us "ahead" or "behind" others at the start of life is very disturbing. If you tell me that I was born into a group that had a head start in resources and opportunities, then I have to examine where I am today to assess if I got there through my own efforts or if I glided on the efforts of others who came before. If I was born to a group with barriers to accessing resources and privileges, then what lies before me? Am I destined to always be behind? These are very penetrating questions because they ask us to examine what social and economic class means in America. In the United States we pride ourselves on opportunity for all, so any unfairness in the starting place seems un-American. However, the reality is that we do not all start at the same place. Some of us are born to rich parents; some of us to poor parents; some of us in a neighborhood with public parks, libraries, and good schools; and others of us in neighborhoods that are dangerous and lack public parks, libraries, good schools. By framing our view of the start of life through the lens of social empathy, we take a wide-angle look at what some of us had and some of us did not.

There is an exercise I use in my classroom to make this point. To start with, I give everyone a piece of paper with the picture of a ladder on it. The starting place for the exercise is on the middle rung. I ask questions, and depending on the answer, the students move one step up the ladder or one step down the ladder.

The questions include things like "If you grew up in a neighborhood that felt safe and secure, move up one rung," "If your ancestors were forced to come to this country, move down one rung," "If you were harassed because of your race or ethnicity, move down one rung," and "If you have inherited money or property, move up one rung." You can develop these questions to fit your group. After the questions are asked, the students mark where they ended up on the ladder. Then we discuss what that means. This exercise is based on one that is done physically in a large room with people either taking a step backward or forward.[2] I do not do it that way because of my experience watching people's discomfort moving forward or backward. This is where I used interpersonal empathy to see that the power of visual impressions of people moving to different levels can stereotype people, and it does

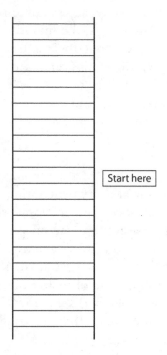

Start here

Figure E.1 The privilege ladder

not protect the privacy of each individual. I prefer to do the exercise on paper in private for each person. The goal is to open the door to a discussion of where we all started off in life and what we had in our childhoods that may have shaped where we are today. It is a beginning for talking about historical and contextual differences in people's lives.

Visit a Museum

I have found that museums are incredibly powerful places to cultivate empathy. Exhibits use images and real artifacts to tell the stories of people who we can never meet. Our minds and bodies can be viscerally moved to learn about what people have gone through, and at the same time all the components of empathy can be stimulated. In her book *Artifacts and Allegiances: How Museums Put the Nation and the World on Display*, sociologist Peggy Levitt explores the roles of museums in our societies and the messages they can share.[3] She identifies one of the perspectives shared by many of the museum professionals she interviewed that "museums can and should encourage empathy, curiosity, tolerance, creativity and critical thinking."[4] I applaud this perspective.

When we think about ways to enhance our skills in the components of interpersonal and social empathy, I can attest to the power of museums to indeed do just that. In chapter 2 I shared the power that the exhibit on lynching had to move me to depths of understanding of a historical time and events that shaped the African American experience in the United States. I know that museums are often thought of as stuffy places for eggheads or showcases for colonial thievery of indigenous artifacts, and I will let Dr. Levitt's book help us to better understand those arguments. Instead, I am going to take a moment to share some of my most moving moments in museums that brought to life the experiences of people of different cultures, races, and time periods in empathic ways.

The horrors of an atomic bomb were made real for me at the Peace Museum in Hiroshima when I saw photos of burned survivors of the atomic bomb dropped there. Spending a few hours in the museum taught me more about the dangers of nuclear war than all that I had read or learned in school or gained from political rallies against nuclear proliferation that I attended. The photographs of American Indian children before and after they were "civilized" by boarding schools that stripped them of every piece of their native lives is a permanent exhibit at the Heard Museum in Phoenix that I take all my visitors to see because it tells a story of oppression that I never learned about in all my years of schooling and explains so much about what it means to be Native American in this country. I have been to Yad Vashem, the Holocaust memorial museum in Jerusalem, and the images there of people in box cars and concentrations camps, faces that look like those in photographs of my relatives, are empathically seared in my memory. There are other museums that have moved me deeply while teaching me about the lives of others: the Civil Rights Museum in Atlanta, the Tolerance Museum in Los Angeles, the murals painted by Diego Rivera in Mexico City, the Apartheid Museum in South Africa, and many, many more.

I include visits to museums because they offer powerful ways to enlighten ourselves about the lives of others. I am especially drawn to the museums that tell the stories of people who were not included in my history schoolbooks. These museums tend to be small and new and use imagery to tell stories in very moving ways. That is a tool for teaching social empathy. Sometimes we can see exhibits in real time, before they are enshrined in a museum. I recall in 1993 when I saw hundreds of panels of the AIDS Quilt spread across the mall in Washington, DC, each panel telling a personal story captured by friends and family members to remember and celebrate the lives of those who had died from AIDS. It was not designed to teach me details or information, but rather to teach me about the deep sense of loss that was spreading across the nation. It made those who died of AIDS real people, helping to change the face of the disease from one of "gay cancer" to a public epidemic we all should be concerned about. These are some of my stories of engaging empathy through the work of museums and exhibits. I know I am not alone in having those experiences. I applaud the school field trips to those museums and am dismayed that they are first to get cut when school budgets are tight.

Read a Book or Go to a Movie

The suggestion to read a book or go to a movie is simple and obvious. The reason is because it works. I am sure you have many books and movies that helped shape your thinking and gave you a window into the lives of people different from you. The list of books and movies that have given us empathic insight would be very long, and new titles can be added every day. I know how powerful books can be because I have never forgotten what I felt and learned by reading the book *Black Like Me* by John Howard Griffin. Here is what I wrote almost ten years ago for a piece on personal reflections about privilege:

Liz remembers:

It was only a book, required reading for an English class when I was 14 years old. The book was *Black Like Me*, the account of John Howard Griffin, a white journalist who darkened his skin and spent 6 weeks traveling through the South as an African American man. Reading that book had the most profound impact on me then, and has stayed etched in my memory for almost 40 years. It was the first time I remember feeling outrage at social injustice because I really felt the agony and fear of hatred and discrimination as if I were there with the author. For the first time that I can recall, I simultaneously felt what another person was feeling and understood the social injustice that was a consequence of the privilege I had, the privilege of being white.

I grew up in middle class America in an almost all white world of home, school, synagogue, and summer camp. My family was active in the Civil Rights movement, I even heard Martin Luther King speak twice, including his famous speech on the Mall in Washington, DC in August of 1963. But until I read *Black Like Me*, I don't think I got it, that I understood racism and white privilege. I have no recollection of any class discussion, activities, or writing that might have gone with the reading assignment. But I do remember vividly the book and its effect on me.[5]

Any book or movie that can leave an indelible mark on our lives for decades is an extremely powerful way to teach us to be socially empathic.

Teaching Social Empathy Writ Large

Storytelling and witnessing are effective ways to share our experiences and hear what others have to say. It can be incredibly powerful when done on a large scale to address injustices. It also needs to be done with sensitivity because telling one's story can also open up old wounds and have the effect of retraumatizing people. For those reasons, great care should be taken when organizing public storytelling or witnessing.

Hearing firsthand from perpetrators and victims not only allows people to have their voices heard, but can also open dialogue and exchange of what it was like to have been on the other side. One of the most potent public efforts to witness and address large-scale actions of social injustice has been truth and reconciliation commissions. There are guidelines from organizations and from those commissions that have been successful in creating a process to allow victims and perpetrators to effectively share their stories.[6] Although now closed, the first truth and reconciliation process held in the United States took place in Greensboro, North Carolina. In 1979, five anti-Klan demonstrators were killed by Klan members who claimed self-defense. The court cases that followed did not help to give a sense of justice to the community, nor was a full investigation of the event conducted. Community members organized the commission and held hearings in 2005 with a final report released in 2006. It is an incredibly inspiring example of how a community transformed the consequences of a painful and unjust event into an opportunity for public expression and reconciliation. The commission members are very candid about what worked and what did not, so their experience can be replicated by other communities. The executive summary of the report can be found at http://www.greensborotrc.org/exec_summary.pdf.

Witnessing and storytelling can also be powerful tools in making people's experiences known to those in power and in positions to influence public policy making. There is a great deal of information on how to testify before elected officials and how to get people's stories heard by those in power. One of the most recent resources is from a group of former congressional staffers who developed the *Indivisible Guide*, available at https://www.indivisibleguide.com.

These are just a handful of actions that can be used to build exposure, explanation, and experience to the lived realities of others. As a result of taking those steps, we become better practitioners of social empathy. If you would like more information on social empathy and how we might build a more socially empathic world, please visit the Social Empathy Center at http://www.socialempathy.org.

Notes

1. What Is Empathy?

1. Batson, C. D. (2011). These things called empathy: Eight related but distinct phenomena. In J. Decety and W. Ickes (Eds.), *The social neuroscience of empathy*, pp. 3–15. Cambridge, MA: MIT Press.

2. Coplan, A. (2011). Understanding empathy: Its features and effects. In A. Coplan and P. Goldie (Eds.), *Empathy: Philosophical and psychological perspectives*, pp. 3–18. New York: Oxford University Press.

3. Singer, T., and Decety, J. (2011). Social neuroscience of empathy. In J. Decety and J. T. Cacioppo (Eds.), *The Oxford handbook of social neuroscience*, pp. 551–64. New York: Oxford University Press.

The literature on the neuroscience of empathy, while relatively new, is developing rapidly. I have tried to include as much of that research throughout the book as possible. A sample of additional sources that outline the emerging neuroscience linked to identifying empathy includes: Decety, J., and Jackson, P. L. (2004). The functional architecture of human empathy. *Behavioral and Cognitive Neuroscience Reviews* 3, 71–100; Decety, J., and Lamm C. (2006). Human empathy through the lens of social neuroscience. *The Scientific World Journal* 6, 1146–63; Decety, J. (2015). The neural pathways, development and functions of empathy. *Current Opinion in Behavioral Science* 3, 1–6; Singer and Decety 2011, pp. 551–64; Singer, T., and Lamm, C. (2009). The social neuroscience of empathy. *The Year in Cognitive Neuroscience 2009: Annals of the New York Academy of Science* 1156, 81–96.

4. A history of the development of the term *empathy* can be found in Davis, M. H. (1996). *Empathy: A social psychological approach*. Boulder, CO: Westview Press.

5. Hackney, H. (1978). The evolution of empathy. *Personnel and Guidance Journal* 57 (1), 35–38.

6. An excellent source that traces the history of violence throughout human development and across civilizations worldwide is Steven Pinker's *The Better Angels of Our Nature: Why Violence Has Declined* (New York: Viking, 2011). Pinker documents the extent of violence throughout history and what events and structures incubate or suppress violence.

7. de Waal, F. B. M. (2009). *The age of empathy: Nature's lessons for a kinder society*. New York: Random House.

8. de Waal 2009, p. 67.

9. Darwin, C. (1981). *The descent of man and selection in relation to sex*. Princeton, NJ: Princeton University Press.

10. Shermer, M. (2006). *Why Darwin matters: The case against intelligent design*. New York: Henry Holt. See particularly pp. 130–32.

11. Shermer 2006, p. 72.

12. Of course, I am referring to all of humanity with all its forms of gender expression and sexual identity. But to preserve the accuracy of the words of Darwin, I have left his use of narrow gender terms, such as here where he uses the word *man* to refer to all human beings. Consider this an example of how we have changed language empathically by refusing to use a narrow term like man to assume the meaning of all of humanity.

13. Shermer 2006, p. 106.

14. A comprehensive source on mirroring is Marco Iacoboni's *Mirroring people: The new science of how we connect with others* (New York: Farrar, Straus and Giroux, 2008). Foundational work on mirroring was done by the Italian neuroscientist Giacomo Rizzolatti. Some sources for his work include: Rizzolatti, G., Fabbri-Destro, M., and Cattaneo, L. (2009). Mirror neurons and their clinical relevance. *Nature Clinical Practice Neurology* 5 (1), 24–34; Rizzolatti, G., and Craighero, L. (2004). The mirror neuron system. *Annual Review of Neuroscience* 27, 169–92.

15. Müller, B. C. N., Maaskant, A. J., van Baaren, R. B., and Dijksterhuis, A. (2012). Prosocial consequences of imitation. *Psychological Reports* 110 (3), 891–98.

16. van Baaren, R., Holland, R. W., Kawakami, K., and van Knippenberg, A. (2004). Mimicry and prosocial behavior. *Psychological Science* 15 (1), 71–74.

17. Bowlby, J. (1969). *Attachment and loss*, Volume 1: *Attachment*. New York: Basic Books.

18. Mukulincer, M., and Shaver, P. R. (2015). An attachment perspective on prosocial attitudes and behavior. In D. A. Schroeder and W. G. Graziano (Eds.), *The Oxford handbook of prosocial behavior*, pp. 209–30. New York: Oxford University Press.

19. A more detailed discussion of the brain biology behind empathy can be found in chapter 2 of *Assessing Empathy*, which reflects the work of my research team as we developed instruments to measure interpersonal

and social empathy. Segal, E. A., Gerdes, K. E., Lietz, C. A., Wagaman, M. A., and Geiger, J. M. (2017). *Assessing empathy*. New York: Columbia University Press. For general background on the neuroscience aspects of empathy, see Kilroy, E., and Aziz-Zadeh, L. (2017). Neuroimaging research on empathy and shared neural networks. In M. Kondo (Ed.), *Empathy: An evidence-based interdisciplinary perspective*, pp. 25–41. London: InTech Open Publishers.

20. For more on affective response, see Decety, J., and Skelly, L. R. (2014). The neural underpinnings of the experience of empathy: Lessons for psychopathy. In K. N. Ochsner and S. M. Kosslyn (Eds.), *The Oxford handbook of cognitive neuroscience*, Volume 2: *The cutting edges*, pp. 228–43. New York: Oxford University Press; Fonagy, P., Gergely, G., Jurist, E., and Target, M. (2004). *Affect regulation, mentalization, and the development of the self*. New York: Other Press.

21. For more on affective mentalizing, see Schnell, K., Bluschke, S., Konradt, B., and Walter, H. (2011). Functional relations of empathy and mentalizing: An fMRI study on the neural basis of cognitive empathy. *NeuroImage* 54, 1743–54.

22. For more on self-other awareness, see Decety, J., and Sommerville, J. A. (2003). Shared representations between self and other: A social cognitive neuroscience view. *Trends in Cognitive Sciences* 7 (12), 527–33; Moran, J. M., Kelley, W. M., and Heatherton, T. F. (2014). Self-knowledge. In *The Oxford handbook of cognitive neuroscience*, Volume 2: *The cutting edges*, 135–47.

23. For more on emotional contagion and the difference with empathy, see Hatfield, E., Rapson, R. L., and Le, Y-C. L. (2011). Emotional contagion and empathy. In *The social neuroscience of empathy*, pp. 19–30; McCall, C., and Singer, T. (2013). Empathy and the brain. In S. Baron-Cohen, H. Tager-Flusberg, and M. V. Lombardo (Eds.), *Understanding other minds: Perspectives from developmental social neuroscience*, pp. 195–213. New York: Oxford University Press.

24. For more on perspective taking, see Decety, J. (2005). Perspective taking as the royal avenue to empathy. In B. F. Malle and S. D. Hodges (Eds.), *Other minds: How humans bridge the divide between self and others*, pp. 143–57. New York: Guilford Press. Coplan 2011 gives an excellent explanation of the difference between self-focused and other-focused perspective taking.

25. I use the term *welfare* here because that is what is typically used in common speech and is the term that my students usually come into the classroom using. But the term I prefer to use as a public policy researcher is *public assistance*, which is the accurate term and does not bring up all sorts of biases and negative associations.

26. For more on emotion regulation, see Eisenberg, N., Smith, C. L., Sadovsky, A., and Spinrad, T. L. (2004). Effortful control: Relations with emotion regulation, adjustment, and socialization in childhood. In R. F. Baumeister and K. D. Vohs (Eds.), *Handbook of self-regulation: Research, theory, and applications,* pp. 259–82. New York: Guilford Press.

27. Zaki, J., and Ochsner, K. (2012). The neuroscience of empathy: Progress, pitfalls and promise. *Nature Neuroscience* 15 (5), 675–80.

28. Galinsky, A. D., Ku, G., and Wang, C. S. (2005). Perspective-taking and self-other overlap: Fostering social bonds and facilitating social coordination. *Group Processes and Intergroup Relations* 8 (2), 109–24.

29. Roan, L., Strong, B., Foss, P., Yager, M., Gelbach, H., and Metcalf, K. A. (2009). *Social perspective taking.* Technical Report 1259. Arlington, VA: U.S. Army Research Institute for the Behavioral Social Sciences.

30. The data on public assistance can be found in the Ninth and Tenth Reports to Congress on the Temporary Assistance for Needy Families Program, available through the U.S. Department of Health and Human Services Administration for Children and Families Office of Family Assistance, http://www.acf.hhs.gov/programs/ofa/resource-library/search?area[2377] =2377&type[3085]=3085.

31. Segal, E. A. (2006). Welfare as we *should* know it: Social empathy and welfare reform. In K. M. Kilty and E. A. Segal (Eds.), *The promise of welfare reform: Political rhetoric and the reality of poverty in the twenty-first century,* pp. 265–74. New York: Haworth Press.

32. Segal, E. A., and Kilty, K. M. (2003). Political promises for welfare reform. *Journal of Poverty* 7 (1–2), 51–67.

33. These quotes come directly from the *Congressional Record* 1996 (142 [115], H9493–9415) on the day the legislation was passed, July 31, 1996. Journalist Jason DeParle wrote a compelling book that gives a detailed look at what went on politically over welfare reform while looking at the lives of three families and how those changes directly affected them: DeParle, J. (2004). *American dream: Three women, ten kids, and a nation's drive to end welfare.* New York: Penguin. This is an example of social empathy in action.

34. Eisenberg, N. (2002). Distinctions among various modes of empathy-related reactions: A matter of importance in humans. *Behavioral and Brain Sciences* 25 (1), 33–34.

35. Davis, M. H. (1980). A multidimensional approach to individual differences in empathy. *JSAS Catalog of Selected Documents in Psychology* 10, 85; Davis, M. H. (1983). Measuring individual differences in empathy: Evidence for a multidimensional approach. *Journal of Personality and Social Psychology* 44 (1), 113–26.

36. Decety, J., and Lamm C. (2011). Empathy versus personal distress: Recent evidence from social neuroscience. In *The social neuroscience of empathy,* pp. 199-214.

37. At the time, this gaffe made by the former First Lady got a lot of mention, but was dropped rather quickly, likely as a courtesy to a woman who was no longer technically in the public realm (although her son was the sitting president and was criticized for problems with the federal government's response to Hurricane Katrina). The original story can be found at "Barbara Bush: Things working out 'very well' for poor evacuees from New Orleans," *Editor and Publisher*, September 5, 2005, http://www.editorandpublisher .com/news/barbara-bush-things-working-out-very-well-for-poor-evacuees -from-new-orleans. A follow up to that story can be found at "One year ago today: Barbara Bush's infamous remarks about Hurricane Katrina evacuees," *Editor and Publisher*, September 5, 2006, and can be found at http://www .editorandpublisher.com/news/one-year-ago-today-barbara-bush-s -infamous-remarks-about-hurricane-katrina-evacuees.

38. Selk, A. (February 4, 2018). "Paul Ryan celebrated the tax cut with a tweet about a secretary saving $1.50 a week," *Washington Post*. https://www .washingtonpost.com/news/the-fix/wp/2018/02/03/paul-ryan -celebrated-the-tax-cut-with-a-tweet-about-a-secretary-saving-1-50-a-week; Cochrane, E. (February 3, 2018). "Paul Ryan deletes tweet lauding a $1.50 benefit from the new tax law," *New York Times*. https://www.nytimes.com /2018/02/03/us/politics/paul-ryan-tweet.html.

39. Goetz, J. I., Keltner, D., and Simon-Thomas, E. (2010). Compassion: An evolutionary analysis and empirical review. *Psychological Bulletin* 136 (3), 351–74.

40. Singer and Lamm 2009, p. 84.

41. Bloom, P. (2016). *Against empathy: The case for rational compassion*. New York: HarperCollins.

42. Bloom 2016, p. 16.

43. Bloom 2016, p. 5.

2. Why Do We Need Empathy?

1. John Bowlby is considered the originator of attachment theory. A great deal of research has followed and a comprehensive examination can be found in the *Handbook of Attachment: Theory, Research, and Clinical Applications*, third edition, edited by J. Cassidy and P. R. Shaver (New York: Guilford Press, 2016). The chapter titled "A lifespan perspective on attachment and care for others" is particularly helpful in explaining how empathy is related.

2. Mukulincer, M., and Shaver, P. R. (2015). An attachment perspective on prosocial attitudes and behavior. In D. A. Schroeder and W. G. Graziano (Eds.), *The Oxford handbook of prosocial behavior*, pp. 209–30. New York: Oxford University Press.

3. Decety, J., and Meyer, M. (2008). From emotion resonance to empathic understanding: A social developmental neuroscience account. *Development and Psychopathology* 20, 1053–80.

4. Nelson, C. A., Fox, N. A., and Zeanah, C. H. (2014). *Romania's abandoned children: Deprivation, brain development and the struggle for recovery.* Cambridge, MA: Harvard University Press.

5. Kim, S., and Kochanska, G. (2017). Relational antecedents and social implications of the emotion of empathy: Evidence from three studies. *Emotion* 17 (6), 981–92.

6. Batson, C. D., and Shaw, L. L. (1991). Evidence for altruism: Toward a pluralism of prosocial motives. *Psychological Inquiry* 2 (2), 107–22.

7. Hamilton, W. D. (1964). The genetic evolution of social behavior. *Journal of Theoretical Biology* 7 (parts 1 and 2), 1–52.

8. de Waal, F. B. M. (2008). Putting the altruism back into altruism: The evolution of empathy. *Annual Review of Psychology* 59, 279–300.

9. de Waal, F. B. M. (2012). The antiquity of empathy. *Science* 336, 874–76.

10. See chapter 3 for a detailed discussion of otherness and what it means.

11. Stone, B. L. (2008). The evolution of culture and sociology. *American Sociologist* 39 (1), 68–85.

12. Rumble, A. C., Van Lange, P. A. M., and Parks, C. (2010). The benefits of empathy: When empathy may sustain cooperation in social dilemmas. *European Journal of Social Psychology* 40, 856–66.

13. Young, L., and Waytz, A. (2013). Mind attribution is for morality. In S. Baron-Cohen, H. Tager-Flusberg, and M. V. Lombardo (Eds.), *Understanding other minds*, pp. 93–103. New York: Oxford University Press.

14. Hoffman, M. L. (2000). *Empathy and moral development: Implications for caring and justice.* Cambridge, UK: Cambridge University Press (multiple empathizing can be found on page 24); Hoffman, M. L. (2011). Empathy, justice, and the law. In A. Coplan and P. Goldie (Eds.), *Empathy: Philosophical and psychological perspectives*, pp. 230–54. New York: Oxford University Press.

15. For an account of this painful breakdown in morality and empathy, see Ortiz, E., and Lubell, B. (May 9, 2017). "Penn State fraternity death." *NBC News.* http://www.nbcnews.com/news/us-news/penn-state-fraternity -death-why-did-no-one-call-911-n756951. The full story is also recounted in Flanagan, C. (2017). A death at Penn State. *The Atlantic*, 320 (4), 92–105.

16. These are just a few of the stories I found: Boroff, D. (April 21, 2014). "Texas boy used money he raised for PS4 to buy 100 smoke detectors." *New York Daily News.* http://www.nydailynews.com/news/national/boy -money-raised-ps4-buy-smoke-detectors-article-1.1763469; World Bank. (November 11, 2014). "Children helping other children." https://www .youtube.com/watch?v=Z5p5mHB3dy8; ABC News. (November 27, 2014). "Disney's CitizenKid highlights children doing good." https://www.youtube .com/watch?v=lcYvVgcWINw.

17. Hauser, D. J., Preston, S. D., and Stansfield, R. B. (2013). Altruism in the wild: When affiliative motives to help positive people overtake empathic motives to help the distressed. *Journal of Experimental Psychology* 143 (3), 1295–1305.

18. Aknin, L. B., Hamlin, J. K., and Dunn, E. W. (2012). Giving leads to happiness in young children. *PLos ONE* 7 (6), e39211, 1–4. Earlier research indicates that prosocial helping behavior begins early in life. See Warneken, F., and Tomasello, M. (2007). Helping and cooperation at 14 months of age. *Infancy* 11, 271–94.

19. Ali, R. M., and Bozorgi, Z. C. (2016). The relationship of altruistic behavior, empathetic sense, and social responsibility with happiness among university students. *Practice in Clinical Psychology* 4 (1), 51–56.

20. Helliwell, J., Layard, R., and Sachs, J. (2017). *World happiness report 2017.* New York: Sustainable Development Solutions Network.

21. Hampton, K. N. (2016). Why is helping behavior declining in the United States but not in Canada?: Ethnic diversity, new technologies, and other explanation. *City and Community* 15 (4), 380–99.

22. van der Meer, T., and Tolsma, J. (2014). Ethnic diversity and its effects on social cohesion. *Annual Review of Sociology* 40, 459–78.

23. van der Meer and Tolsma's (2014) research included Western European countries. They found that attitudes toward immigrants in those countries looked more like Canada's than the United States' and thus reinforced their conclusion of the influence of the uniqueness of U.S. history and the legacy of slavery. Since the studies they reviewed, Western Europe has been targeted by terrorists, many of who are immigrants or one generation removed from immigration. We might see a change in attitudes toward multiculturalism and diversity in future research as a consequence of these terror events.

24. Rifkin, J. (2009). *The empathic civilization: The race to global consciousness in a world in crisis.* New York: Penguin.

25. Rifkin 2009, p. 197.

26. Pinker, S. (2011). *The better angels of our nature: Why violence has declined.* New York: Viking.

27. Equal Justice Initiative. (2015). *Lynching in America: Confronting the legacy of racial terror*, 2nd ed. Montgomery, AL: Author.

28. Read Taylor Dumpson's letter here: http://www.ausg.org/ausg_president _taylor_dumpson_statement_racist_incident.

29. As cited in Takaki, R. (2008). *A different mirror: A history of multicultural America*, rev. ed. New York: Back Bay Books/Little, Brown, p. 82.

30. See the Library of Congress site for the actual legislation and accompanying justifications by Congress and President Jackson at https://www.loc .gov/rr/program/bib/ourdocs/Indian.html.

31. Lim, D., and DeSteno, D. (2016). Suffering and compassion: The links among adverse life experiences, empathy, compassion, and prosocial behavior. *Emotion* 16 (2), 175–82.

32. Benard, B. (2004). *Resiliency: What we have learned*. San Francisco, CA: WestEd.

33. Lietz, C. A. (2011). Empathic action and family resilience: A narrative examination of the benefits of helping others. *Journal of Social Service Research* 37 (3), 254–65.

34. Righetti, F., Gere, J., Hofmann, W., Visserman, M. L., and Van Lange, P. A. M. (2016). The burden of empathy: Partners' responses to divergence of interests in daily life. *Emotion* 16 (5), 684–90.

35. Manczak, E. M., DeLongis, A., and Chen, E. (2016). Does empathy have a cost? Diverging psychological and physiological effects within families. *Health Psychology* 35 (3), 211–18.

36. Covell, C. N., Huss, M. T., and Langhinrichsen-Rohling, J. (2007). Empathic deficits among male batterers: A multidimensional approach. *Journal of Family Violence* 22 (3), 165–74.

37. Gini, G., Albiero, P., Benelli, B., and Altoe, G. (2008). Determinants of adolescents' active defending and passive bystanding behavior in bullying. *Journal of Adolescence* 31, 93–105.

38. Elsegood, K. J., and Duff, S. C. (2010). Theory of mind in men who have sexually offended against children. *Sexual Abuse: A Journal of Research and Treatment* 22 (1), 112–31.

39. Baron-Cohen, S. (2011). *The science of evil: On empathy and the origins of cruelty*. New York: Basic Books.

40. Glick, P. (2008). When neighbors blame neighbors: Scapegoating and the breakdown of ethnic relations. In V. M. Esses and R. A. Vernon (Eds.), *Explaining the breakdown of ethnic relations*, pp. 123–46. Malden, MA: Blackwell.

41. Almeida, P. R., Seixas, M. J., Ferreira-Santos, F., Vieira, J. B., Paiva, T. O., Moreira, P. S., and Costa, P. (2015). Empathic, moral and antisocial outcomes associated with distinct components of psychopathy in healthy individuals: A triarchic model approach. *Personality and Individual Differences* 85, 205–11.

3. If It's So Important, Why Is Empathy So Hard?

1. Lamm, C., Meltzoff, A. N., and Decety, J. (2009). How do we empathize with someone who is not like us? A functional magnetic resonance study. *Journal of Cognitive Neuroscience* 22 (2), 362–76.

2. Recall the discussion of kin selection in chapter 2.

3. Tajfel, H. (1970). Experiments in intergroup discrimination. *Scientific American* 223 (5), 96–102; Tajfel, H., Billig, M., Bundy, R., and Flament, C. (1971). Social categorization and intergroup behavior. *European Journal of*

Social Psychology 1 (2), 149–78; Billig, M., and Tajfel, H. (1973). Social categorization and similarity in intergroup behavior. *European Journal of Social Psychology* 3 (1), 27–52.

4. Brewer, M. B. (1979). In-group bias in the minimal intergroup situation: A cognitive motivational analysis. *Psychological Bulletin* 86 (2), 307–24.

5. Brown, L. M., Bradley, M. M., and Lang, P. J. (2006). Affective reactions to pictures of ingroup and outgroup members. *Biological Psychology* 71, 303–11; Gutsell, J. N., and Inzlicht, M. (2012). Intergroup differences in the sharing of emotive states: Neural evidence of an empathy gap. *Social Cognitive and Affective Neuroscience* 7, 596–603; Mathur, V. A., Harada, T., Lipke, T., and Chiao, J. Y. (2010). Neural basis of extraordinary empathy and altruistic motivation. *Neuroimage* 51, 1468–75; O'Brien, E., and Ellsworth, P. C. (2012). More than skin deep: Visceral states are not projected onto dissimilar others. *Psychological Science* 23 (4), 391–96; Molenberghs, P. (2013). The neuroscience of in-group-bias. *Neuroscience and Biobehavioral Reviews* 37, 1530–36; Molenberghs, P., and Morrison, S. (2014). The role of the medial prefrontal cortex in social categorization. *Social Cognitive and Affective Neuroscience* 9, 292–96.

6. Cikara, M., and Van Bavel, J. J. (2014). The neuroscience of intergroup relations: An integrative review. *Perspectives on Psychological Science* 9 (3), 245–74.

7. Eres, R., and Molenberghs, P. (2013). The influence of group membership on the neural correlates involved in empathy. *Frontiers in Human Neuroscience* 7 (article 176), 1–6; Meyer, M. L., Masten, C. L., Ma, Y., Wang, C., Shi, Z., Eisenberger, N. I., and Han, S. (2013). Empathy for the social suffering of friends and strangers recruits distinct patterns of brain activation. *Social Cognitive and Affective Neuroscience* 8 (4), 446–54.

8. Swann, W. B., Jetten, J., Gómez, Á., Whitehouse, H., and Bastian, B. (2012). When group membership gets personal: A theory of identity fusion. *Psychological Review* 119 (3), 441–56.

9. Pew Research Center. (2016). "Sharp differences over who is hurt, helped by their race." http://www.pewresearch.org/fact-tank/2016/07/18/sharp-differences-over-who-is-hurt-helped-by-their-race.

10. LeBron James's NBA press conference—first question asked—at the 2:30 minute mark at https://www.youtube.com/watch?v=ogUhRjYYAJs.

11. Alexander, M. (2012). *The new Jim Crow: Mass incarceration in the age of colorblindness.* New York: New Press.

12. Alexander 2012, pp. 243–44.

13. Eres, R., and Molenberghs, P. (2013). The influence of group membership on the neural correlates involved in empathy. *Frontiers in Human Neuroscience* 7 (article 176), 1–6.

14. Avenanti, A., Sirigu, A., and Aglioti, S. M. (2010). Racial bias reduces empathic sensorimotor resonance with other-race pain. *Current Biology* 20, 1018–22.

15. Gutsell, J. N., and Inzlicht, M. (2012). Intergroup differences in the sharing of emotive states: Neural evidence of an empathy gap. *Social Cognitive and Affective Neuroscience* 7, 596–603.

16. Chiao, J. Y., and Mathur, V. A. (2010). Intergroup empathy: How does race affect empathic neural responses? *Current Biology* 20, R478–R80.

17. Tajfel, H. (1970). Experiments in intergroup discrimination. *Scientific American* 223 (5), 96–102; Cikara, M., and Van Bavel, J. J. (2014). The neuroscience of intergroup relations: An integrative review. *Perspectives on Psychological Science* 9 (3), 245–74.

18. Kurzban, R., Tooby, J., and Cosmides, L. (2001). Can race be erased? Coalitional computation and social categorization. *Proceedings of the National Academy of Sciences* 98 (26), 15387–92; Van Bavel, J. J., and Cunningham, W. A. (2009). Self-categorization with a novel mixed-race group moderates automatic social and racial biases. *Personality and Social Psychology Bulletin* 35 (3), 321–35.

19. Decety, J., Echols, S., and Correll, J. (2009). The blame game: The effect of responsibility and social stigma on empathy for pain. *Journal of Cognitive Neuroscience* 22 (5), 985–97.

20. For a full history of AIDS and the public policies that were debated during the 1980s and 1990s, see Shilts, R. (1987). *And the Band Played On.* New York: Penguin. It was also made into an HBO movie.

21. Hobson, N. M., and Inzlicht, M. (2016). The mere presence of an outgroup member disrupts the brain's feedback-monitoring system. *Social Cognitive and Affective Neuroscience* 11 (11), 1698–1706.

22. Lotz-Schmitt, K., Siem, B., and Stürmer, S. (2015). Empathy as a motivator of dyadic helping across group boundaries: The dis-inhibiting effect of the recipient's perceived benevolence. *Group Processes and Intergroup Relations* 20 (2), 1–27.

23. Pinker, S. (2011). *The better angels of our nature: Why violence has declined.* New York: Viking.

24. Harris, L. T., and Fiske, S. T. (2006). Dehumanizing the lowest of the low: Neuroimaging responses to extreme out-groups. *Psychological Science* 17 (10), 847–53.

25. Glick, P. (2005). Choice of scapegoats. In J. F. Dovidio, P. Glick, and L. A. Rudman (Eds.), *On the nature of prejudice: 50 years after Allport,* pp. 244–61. Malden, MA: Blackwell; Glick, P. (2008). When neighbors blame neighbors: Scapegoating and the breakdown of ethnic relations. In V. M. Esses and R. A. Vernon (Eds.), *Explaining the breakdown of ethnic relations,* pp. 123–46. Malden, MA: Blackwell; Glick, P., and Paluck, E. L. (2013).

The aftermath of genocide: History as a proximal cause. *Journal of Social Issues* 69 (1), 200–208.

26. Staub, E. (2015). The roots of helping, heroic rescue and resistance to and the prevention of mass violence: Active bystandership in extreme times and in building peaceful societies. In D. A. Schroeder and W. G. Graziano (Eds.), *The Oxford handbook of prosocial behavior*, pp. 693–717. New York: Oxford University Press.

27. Cikara, M., Bruneau, E., Van Bavel, J. J., and Saxe, R. (2014). Their pain gives us pleasure: How intergroup dynamics shape empathic failures and counter-empathic responses. *Journal of Experimental Social Psychology* 55, 110–25.

28. Fox, G. R., Sobhani, M., and Aziz-Zadeh, L. (2013). Witnessing hateful people in pain modulates brain activity in regions associated with physical pain and reward. *Frontiers in Psychology* 4 (article 772), 1–13.

29. The studies are discussed fully in Baumeister, R. F. (1997). *Evil inside human violence and cruelty*. New York: Holt Paperbacks.

30. See Baumeister 1997, pp. 211–12.

31. Grossman, D. (2009). *On killing: The psychological cost of learning to kill in war and society*, rev. ed. New York: Little, Brown.

32. Grossman 2009, p. 161.

33. Saguy, T., Szekeres, H., Nouri, R., Goldenberg, A., Doron, G., Dovidio, J. F., Yunger, C., and Halperin, E. (2015). Awareness of intergroup help can rehumanize the out-group. *Social Psychological and Personality Science* 6 (5), 551–58.

34. Jones, R. P. (2015). *The end of white Christian America*. New York: Simon & Schuster.

35. Shretha, L. B., and Heisler, E. J. (2011). *The changing demographic profile of the United States*. Washington, DC: Congressional Research Service.

36. In polling done in 2017, the Pew Research Center found that 62 percent of Americans support same-sex marriage, compared to a low of 31 percent in 2004. Pew Research Center. (June 26, 2017). "Support for same-sex marriage grows, even among groups that had been skeptical." http://www.people-press.org/2017/06/26/support-for-same-sex-marriage -grows-even-among-groups-that-had-been-skeptical.

37. Public Religion Research Institute. (April 20, 2015). "Attitudes on same-sex marriage in every state." http://www.prri.org/spotlight/map-every -states-opinion-on-same-sex-marriage.

38. For state voting in the 2012 presidential election, see http:// www.270towin.com.

39. U.S. Bureau of Labor Statistics. (2014). BLS Report No. 1052. *Women in the labor force: A databook.*

40. Newport, F. (December 23, 2016). "Five key findings on religion in the U.S." http://news.gallup.com/poll/200186/five-key-findings-religion .aspx.

41. Pew Research Center. (August 18, 2016). "Clinton, Trump supporters have starkly different views of a changing nation." http://www.people-press .org/2016/08/18/clinton-trump-supporters-have-starkly-different-views-of -a-changing-nation.

42. Kraus, M. W., Côté, S., and Keltner, D. (2010). Social class, contextualism, and empathic accuracy. *Psychological Science* 21 (11), 1716–23; DeTurk, S. (2001). Intercultural empathy: Myth, competency, or possibility for alliance building? *Communication Education* 50, 374–84.

43. Daily Kos. (n.d.). "2012 election results." http://images.dailykos.com /images/146419/lightbox/Intro2.png?1433260066

44. Stephan, W. G. (2014). Intergroup anxiety: Theory, research, and practice. *Personality and Social Psychology Review* 18 (3), 239–55.

45. Turner, R. N., Hewstone, M., Voci, A., Paolini, S., and Christ, O. (2007). Reducing prejudice via direct and extended cross-group friendship. *European Review of Social Psychology* 18, 212–55.

46. Vezzali, L., Hewstone, M., Capozza, D., Trifiletti, E., and Di Bernardo, G. A. (2017). Improving intergroup relations with extended contact among young children: Mediation by intergroup empathy and moderation by direct intergroup contact. *Journal of Community and Applied Social Psychology* 27, 35–49.

47. For a full account of the events that happened in Charlottesville, Virginia, on August 11–12, 2017, see Heim, J. (August 14, 2017). "Recounting a day of rage, hate, violence, and death." *Washington Post.* https://www.washingtonpost .com/graphics/2017/local/charlottesville-timeline/?utm.

48. For a brief history, see United States Holocaust Memorial Museum. (n.d.). "Kristallnacht." https://www.ushmm.org/wlc/en/article.php?ModuleId =10005201.

4. Are Power and Politics Barriers to Empathy?

1. Fiske, S. T. (1993). Controlling other people: The impact of power on stereotyping. *American Psychologist* 48, 621–28.

2. Sturm, R. E., and Antonakis, J. (2015). Interpersonal power: A review, critique, and research agenda. *Journal of Management* 41 (1), 136–63.

3. Cited in Corn, D. (October 19, 2016). "Donald Trump is completely obsessed with revenge." *Mother Jones.* http://www.motherjones.com/politics /2016/10/donald-trump-obsessed-with-revenge.

4. Conover, C. (April 1, 2014). "Senate passes latest version of budget, veto threats arise." *Arizona Public Media.* https://news.azpm.org/s/17941-senate -passes-budget-again.

5. Obama, B. (May 1, 2009). "White House press conference." http:// www.whitehouse.gov/the-press-office/press-briefing-press-secretary -robert-gibbs-5-1-09.

6. Christophersen, J. (April 9, 2013). "Obama's empathy rule: Alive and well in the second term." *National Review.* http://www.nationalreview .com/bench-memos/345108/obamas-empathy-rule-alive-and-well-second -term-james-christophersen.

7. Pew Research Center. (September 18, 2014). *Teaching the children: Sharp ideological differences, some common ground.*

8. Dodd, M. D., Hibbing, J. R., and Smith, K. B. (2011). The politics of attention: Gaze-cuing effects are moderated by political temperament. *Attention, Perception, and Psychophysics* 73 (1), 24–29.

9. Amodio, D. M., Jost, J. T., Master, S. L., and Yee, C. M. (2007). Neurocognitive correlates of liberalism and conservatism. *Nature Neuroscience* 10, 1246–47.

10. Alford, J. R., Funk, C. L., and Hibbing, J. R. (2005). Are political orientations genetically transmitted? *American Political Science Review* 99 (2), 153–67.

11. Block, J., and Block, J. H. (2006). Nursery school personality and political orientation two decades later. *Journal of Research in Personality* 40, 734–49.

12. Jost, H. T., Glaser, J., Kruglanski, A. W., and Sulloway, F. J. (2003). Political conservatism as motivated social cognition. *Psychological Bulletin* 129 (3), 339–75.

13. Napier, J. L., Huang, J., Vonasch, A. J., and Bargh, J. A. (2018). Superheroes for change: Physical safety promotes socially (but not economically) progressive attitudes among conservatives. *European Journal of Social Psychology* 48 (2), 187–95.

14. Chiao, J. Y., Mathur, V. A., Harada, T., and Lipke, T. (2009). Neural basis of preference for human social hierarchy versus egalitarianism. *Annals of the New York Academy of Sciences* 1167, 174–81.

15. Sherman, G. D., Lerner, J. S., Renshon, J., Ma-Kellams, C., and Joel, S. (2015). Perceiving others' feelings: The importance of personality and social structure. *Social Psychological and Personality Science* 6 (5), 559–69.

16. Sidanius, J., Kteily, N., Sheehy-Skeffington, J., Ho, A. K., Sibley, C., and Duriez, B. (2013). You're inferior and not worth our concern: The interface between empathy and social dominance orientation. *Journal of Personality* 81 (3), 313–23.

17. Chen, S., Lee-Chai, A. Y., and Bargh, J. A. (2001). Relationship orientation as a moderator of the effects of social power. *Journal of Personality and Social Psychology* 80 (2), 173–87.

18. Fiske, S. T. (1993). Controlling other people: The impact of power on stereotyping. *American Psychologist* 48, 621–28, p. 624.

19. Hogeveen, J., Inzlicht, M., and Obhi, S. S. (2014). Power changes how the brain responds to others. *Journal of Experimental Psychology* 143 (2), 755–62.

20. van Kleef, G. A., Oveis, C., van der Löwe, I., LuoKogan, A., Goetz, J., and Keltner, D. (2008). Power, distress, and compassion: Turning a blind eye to the suffering of others. *Psychological Science* 19 (12), 1315–22.

21. Guinote, A. (2007a). Power affects basic cognition: Increased attentional inhibition and flexibility. *Journal of Experimental Social Psychology* 43, 685–97 (use of the term *peripheral information* can be found on p. 694); Guinote, A. (2007b). Power and goal pursuit. *Personality and Social Psychology Bulletin* 33, 1076–87.

22. Smith, P. K., and Trope, Y. (2006). You focus on the forest when you're in charge of the trees: Power priming and abstract information processing. *Journal of Personality and Social Psychology* 90, 578–96; Smith, P. K., Jostmann, N. B., Galinsky, A. D., and van Dijk, W. W. (2008). Lacking power impairs executive functions. *Psychological Science* 19, 441–47.

23. Galinsky, A. D., Magee, J. C., Inesi, M. E., and Gruenfeld, D. H. (2006). Power and perspectives not taken. *Psychological Science* 17 (12), 1068–74.

24. Lammers, J., Galinsky, A. D., Dubois, D., and Rucker, D. D. (2015). Power and morality. *Current Opinion in Psychology* 6, 15–19.

25. Galinsky, A. D., Gruenfeld, D. H., Magee, J. C. (2003). From power to action. *Journal of Personality and Social Psychology* 85 (3), 453–66.

26. Lammers, J., Stoker, J. I., Jordan, J., Pollmann, M., and Stapel, A. (2011). Power increases infidelity among men and women. *Psychological Science* 22 (9), 1191–97.

27. Piff, P. K., Stancato, D. M., Côté, S., Mendoza-Denton, R., and Keltner, D. (2012). Higher social class predicts increased unethical behavior. *Proceedings of the National Academy of Sciences* 109 (11), 4086–91.

28. Van Kleef, G. A., Oveis, C., Homan, A. C., van der Löwe, I., and Keltner, D. (2015). Power gets you high: The powerful are more inspired by themselves than by others. *Social Psychological and Personality Science* 6 (4), 472–80, p. 478.

29. Boksem, M. A. S., Smolders, R., and De Cremer, D. (2012). Social power and approach-related neural activity. *Social Cognitive and Affective Neuroscience* 7 (5), 516–20.

30. Dubois, D., Rucker, D. D., and Galinsky, A. D. (2015). Social class, power, and selfishness: When and why upper and lower class individuals behave unethically. *Journal of Personality and Social Psychology* 108 (3), 436–49.

31. Guinote 2007b.

32. Obama, B. (2006). *The audacity of hope.* New York: Random House, p. 66.

33. Cited in Hoffman, M. L. (2011). Empathy, justice, and the law. In A. Coplan and P. Goldie (Eds.), *Empathy: Philosophical and psychological perspectives,* pp. 231–54. New York: Oxford University Press. See p. 239.

34. Segal, E. A. (1995). Frances Perkins. In F. N. Magill (Ed.), *Great lives from history: American women,* pp. 1438–42. Pasadena, CA: Salem Press.

35. Leuchtenburg, W. E. (1963). *Franklin D. Roosevelt and the New Deal.* New York: Harper & Row, p. 131.

36. An excellent source for learning more about the history of the civil rights movement and the life of Martin Luther King Jr. is a trilogy of books written by Taylor Branch. The first book gives the background and chronicles the events that led up to the March on Washington. Branch, T. (1988). *Parting the waters: America in the King years, 1954–1963.* New York: Simon & Schuster; Branch, T. (1998). *Pillar of fire: America in the King years, 1963–1965.* New York: Simon & Schuster; Branch, T. (2006). *At Canaan's edge: America in the King years, 1965–1968.* New York: Simon & Schuster.

37. Martin Luther King Jr.'s famous "I have a dream" speech is still compelling today. If you have not seen it, I highly recommend taking fifteen minutes to watch it. See it on YouTube at https://www.youtube.com/watch?v =smEqnnklfYs&feature=youtu.be and read the text at https://www.archives .gov/files/press/exhibits/dream-speech.pdf.

38. Mills, N. (2006). Hurricane Katrina and Robert Kennedy. *Dissent Magazine* 53 (2), 5–6.

39. Schmid Mast, M., and Darioly, A. (2014). Emotion recognition accuracy in hierarchical relationships. *Swiss Journal of Psychology* 73 (2), 69–75.

40. Lerer, L. (December 28, 2016). "Trump adopting same behavior he criticized Clinton for." *Chicago Tribune.* http://www.chicagotribune.com /news/nationworld/ct-trump-campaign-promises-20161225-story.html.

41. Lammers, J., and Stapel, D. A. (2011). Power increases dehumanization. *Group Processes and Intergroup Relations* 14 (1), 113–26, p. 113.

42. Lammers and Stapel 2011.

43. Gwinn, J. D., Judd, C. M., and Park, B. (2013). Less power = less human? Effects of power differentials on dehumanization. *Journal of Experimental Social Psychology* 49, 464–70.

44. Segal, E. A., and Wagaman, M. A. (2017). Social empathy as a framework for teaching social justice. *Journal of Social Work Education* 53 (2), 201–11.

45. This definition can be found at http://www.learnersdictionary.com /definition/politically%20correct. Additional interesting takes on political correctness can be found in Safire, W. (2008). *Safire's political dictionary.* Rev. ed. New York: Oxford University Press; Hess, A. (July 19, 2016). How "political correctness" went from punch line to panic. *New York Times Magazine*; and Robbins, S. P. (2016). From the editor—Sticks and stones: Trigger warnings, macroaggressions, and political correctness. *Journal of Social Work Education* 52 (1), 1–5.

46. Direct quotes from the debate can be found at http://www.nytimes .com/live/republican-debate-election-2016-cleveland/trump-on-political -correctness.

47. For an example of this sentiment that political correctness is no longer necessary, see Taranto, J. (November 15, 2016). "Trump vs. political correctness: Some early encouraging signs." *Wall Street Journal.* https://www.wsj .com/articles/trump-vs-political-correctness-1479233123.

48. Côté, S., Kraus, M. W., Cheng, B. H., Oveis, C., van der Löwe, I., Lian, H., and Keltner, D. (2011). Social power facilitates the effect of prosocial orientation on empathic accuracy. *Journal of Personality and Social Psychology* 101 (2), 217–32.

49. Hu, M., Rucker, D. D., Galinsky, A. D. (2016). From the immoral to the incorruptible: How prescriptive expectations turn the powerful into paragons of virtue. *Personality and Social Psychology Bulletin* 42 (6), 826–37.

50. Schmid Mast, M., Jonas, K., and Hall, J. A. (2009). Give a person power and he or she will show interpersonal sensitivity: The phenomenon and its why and when. *Journal of Personality and Social Psychology* 97 (5), 835–50.

51. Blader, S. L., Shirako, A., and Chen, Y.-R. (2016). Looking out from the top: Differential effects of status and power on perspective taking. *Personality and Social Psychology Bulletin* 42 (6), 723–37, p. 731.

52. Kennedy, J. F. (1963). "Of those to whom much is given, much is required." Remarks in Nashville at the 90th Anniversary Convocation of Vanderbilt University, May 18, 1963. Public Papers of the Presidents: John F. Kennedy. https://www.jfklibrary.org/Research/Research-Aids/Ready -Reference/JFK-Quotations.aspx#F. President Kennedy was quoting from the Bible, specifically Luke 12:48.

5. What If Stress, Depression, and Other Health Factors Block Empathy?

1. Rizzolatti, G., and Craighero, L. (2004). The mirror neuron system. *Annual Review of Neuroscience* 27, 169–92.

2. A great source on mirror neurons is Iacoboni, M. (2008). *Mirroring people: The new science of how we connect with others.* New York: Farrar, Straus and Giroux.

3. Hickok, G. (2008). Eight problems for the mirror neuron theory of action understanding in monkeys and humans. *Journal of Cognitive Neuroscience* 21 (7), 1229–43.

4. Iacoboni, M. (2009). Imitation, empathy, and mirror neurons. *Annual Review of Psychology* 60, 653–70.

5. Eagleman, D. (2015). *The brain.* New York: Pantheon Books, p. 181.

6. For more detail, including a plot of the regions within the brain, and the full list of sources, see Segal, E. A., Gerdes, K. E., Lietz, C. A., Wagaman, M. A., and Geiger, J. M. (2017). *Assessing empathy.* New York: Columbia University Press, pp. 36 and 37.

7. Hillis, A. E. (2014). Inability to empathize: Brain lesions that disrupt sharing and understanding another's emotions. *Brain: A Journal of Neurology* 137, 981–97.

8. Yeh, Z.-T., and Tsai, C.-F. (2014). Impairment on theory of mind and empathy in patients with stroke. *Psychiatry and Clinical Neurosciences* 68, 612–20.

9. Herbert, G., Lafargue, G., Bonnetblanc, F., Moritz-Gasser, S., and Duffau, H. (2013). Is the right frontal cortex really crucial in the mentalizing network? A longitudinal study in patients with a slow-growing lesion. *Cortex* 49, 2711–27; Herbert, G., Lafargue, G., Moritz-Gasser, S., de Champfleur, N. M., Costi, E., Bonnetblanc, F., and Duffau, H. (2015). A disconnection account of subjective empathy impairments in diffuse low-grade glioma patients. *Neuropsychologia* 70, 165–76.

10. Sapolsky, R. M. (2004). *Why zebras don't get ulcers: The acclaimed guide to stress, stress-related diseases, and coping.* Third edition. New York: St. Martin's Griffin.

11. Sapolsky 2004, pp. 13–14.

12. National Scientific Council on the Developing Child. (2014). *Excessive stress disrupts the architecture of the developing brain: Working Paper 3.* Cambridge, MA: Harvard University Center on the Developing Child.

13. Arnsten, A. F. T. (2009). Stress signaling pathways that impair prefrontal cortex structure and function. *Nature* 10, 410–22; Lupien, S. J., McEwen, B. S., Gunnar, M. R., and Heim, C. (2009). Effects of stress

throughout the lifespan on the brain, behavior and cognition. *Nature* 10, 434–45; Hanson, J. L., Naceqicz, B. M., Sutterer, M. J., Cayo, A. A., Schaefer, S. M., Rudolph, K. D., Shirtcliff, E. A., Pollak, S. D., and Davidson, R. J. (2015). Behavioral problems after early life stress: Contributions of the hippocampus and amygdala. *Biological Psychology* 77 (4), 314–23.

14. Taylor, S. E. (2010). Mechanisms linking early life stress to adult health outcomes. *Proceedings of the National Academy of Science* 107 (19), 8507–12.

15. Buruck, G., Wendsche, J., Melzer, M., Strobel, A., and Dörfel, D. (2014). Acute psychosocial stress and emotion regulation skills modulate empathic reactions to pain in others. *Frontiers in Psychology* 5, Article 517, 1–16.

16. Tomovo, L., von Dawans, B., Heinrichs, M., Silani, G., and Lamm, C. (2014). Is stress affecting our ability to tune into others? Evidence for gender differences in the effects of stress on self-other distinction. *Psychoneuroendocrinology* 43, 95–104.

17. Wolf, O. T., Schulte, J. M., Drimalla, H., Hamacher-Dang, T. C., Knoch, D., and Dziobek, I. (2015). Enhanced emotional empathy after psychosocial stress in young healthy men. *Stress* 18 (6), 631–37.

18. Evans, G. W., and Fuller-Rowell, E. (2013). Childhood poverty, chronic stress, and young adult working memory: The protective role of self-regulatory capacity. *Developmental Science* 16 (5), 688–96; Chen, E. (2012). Protective factors for health among low-socioeconomic-status individuals. *Current Directions in Psychological Science* 21 (3), 189–93.

19. National Institute of Mental Health. (n.d.). "Post-traumatic stress disorder research." http://www.wellnessproposals.com/mental-health/handouts/nimh/post-traumatic-stress-disorder-research-fact-sheet.pdf.

20. Mazza, M., Tempesta, D., Pino, M. C., Nigri, A., Catalucci, A., Guadagni, V., Gallucci, M., Iaria, G., and Ferrara, M. (2015). Neural activity related to cognitive and emotional empathy in post-traumatic stress disorder. *Behavioural Brain Research* 282 (1), 37–45; Nietlisbach, G., Maercker, A., Rössler, W., and Haker, H. (2010). Are empathic abilities impaired in post-traumatic stress disorder? *Psychological Reports* 106 (3), 832–44.

21. National Center for PTSD. (2015). "Relationships and PTSD." https://www.ptsd.va.gov/public/family/ptsd-and-relationships.asp.

22. Proctor, B. D., Semega, J. L., and Kollar, M. A. (2016). *Income and poverty in the United States: 2015.* Washington, DC: U.S. Census Bureau.

23. Sapolsky 2004, p. 366.

24. Mackey, A. P., Finn, A. S., Leonard, J. A., Jacoby-Senghor, D. S., West, M. R., Gabrieli, C. F. O., and Gabrieli, J. D. E. (2015). Neuroanatomical correlates of the income-achievement gap. *Psychological Science* 26 (6), 925–33; Hair, N. L., Hanson, J. L., Wolfe, B. L., and Pollak, S. D. (2015).

Association of child poverty, brain development, and academic achievement. *JAMA Pediatrics* 169 (9), 822–29.

25. Lawson, G. M., Duda, J. T., Avants, B. B., Wu, J., and Farah, M. J. (2013). Association between children's socioeconomic status and prefrontal cortical thickness. *Developmental Science* 16 (5), 641–52; Gianaros, P. J., Manuck, S. B., Sheu, L. K., Kuan, D. C. H., Votruba-Drzal, E., Craig, A. E., and Hariri, A. R. (2011). Parental education predicts corticostriatal functionality in adulthood. *Cerebral Cortex* 21, 896–910.

26. Kraus, M. W., Piff, P. K., and Keltner, D. (2011). Social class as culture: The convergence of resources and rank in the social realm. *Current Directions in Psychological Science* 20 (4), 246–50.

27. Pietz, P., and Knowles, E. D. (2016). Social class and the motivational relevance of other human beings: Evidence from visual attention. *Psychological Science* 27 (11), 1517–27; Varnum, M. E. W., Blais, C., and Brewer, G. A. (2016). Social class affects Mu-suppression during action observation. *Social Neuroscience* 11 (4), 449–54.

28. Kraus, M. W., Côté, S., and Keltner, D. (2010). Social class, contextualism, and empathic accuracy. *Psychological Science* 21 (11), 1716–23.

29. Office of the Administration for Children and Families, U.S. Department of Health and Human Services. (2018). "Child maltreatment 2016." https://www.acf.hhs.gov/cb/resource/child-maltreatment-2016.

30. Fawley-King, K., and Merz, E. C. (2014). Effects of child maltreatment on brain development. In H. C. Matto, J. Strolin-Goltzman, and M. S. Ballan (Eds.), *Neuroscience for social work: Current research and practice*, pp. 111–39. New York: Springer.

31. National Scientific Council on the Developing Child. (2012). *The science of neglect: The persistent absence of responsive care disrupts the developing brain: Working Paper 12.* Cambridge, MA: Center on the Developing Child at Harvard University.

32. Kim, J., and Cicchetti, D. (2010). Longitudinal pathways linking child maltreatment, emotion regulation, peer relations, and psychopathology. *Journal of Child Psychology and Psychiatry* 51 (6), 706–16.

33. Tupler, L. A., and De Bellis, M. D. (2006). Segmented hippocampal volume in children and adolescents with posttraumatic stress disorder. *Biological Psychiatry* 59 (6), 523–29.

34. Gunnar, M. R., Frenn, K., Wewerka, S. S., and Van Ryzin, M. J. (2009). Moderate versus severe early life stress: Associations with stress reactivity and regulation in 10–12 year old children. *Psychoneuroendocrinology* 34 (1), 62–75.

35. Perez, H. C. S., Ikram, M. A., Direk, N., Prigerson, H. G., Freak-Poli, R., Verhaaren, B. F. J., Hofman, A., Vernooij, M., and Tiemeier, H. (2015). Cognition, structural brain changes and complicated grief. A population-based Study. *Psychological Medicine* 45 (7), 1389–99.

36. Bühler, M., and Mann, K. (2011). Alcohol and the human brain: A systematic review of different neuroimaging methods. *Alcoholism: Clinical and Experimental Research* 35 (10), 1771–93.

37. Welch, K. A., Carson, A., and Lawrie, S. M. (2013). Brain structure in adolescents and young adults with alcohol problems: Systematic review of imaging studies. *Alcohol and Alcoholism* 48 (4), 433–44.

38. Schmidt, T., Roser, P., Ze, O., Juckel, G., Suchan, B., and Thoma, P. (2017). Cortical thickness and trait empathy in patients and people at high risk for alcohol use disorders. *Psychopharmacology* 234, 3521–33.

39. Mischkowski, D., Crocker, J., and Way, B. M. (2016). From painkiller to empathy killer: Acetaminophen (paracetamol) reduces empathy for pain. *Social Cognitive and Affective Neuroscience* 11 (9), 1345–53.

40. Tully, J., and Petrinovic, M. M. (2017). Acetaminophen study yields new insights into neurobiological underpinnings of empathy. *Journal of Neurophysiology* 117 (5), 1844–46.

41. De Dreu, C. W. K., and Kret, M. E. (2016). Oxytocin conditions intergroup relations through upregulated in-group empathy, cooperation, conformity, and defense. *Biological Psychiatry* 79 (3), 165–73; Heinrichs, M., Chen, F. S., and Domes, G. (2013). Social neuropeptides in the human brain: Oxytocin and social behavior. In S. Baron-Cohen, H. Tager-Flusberg, and M. V. Lombardo (Eds.), *Understanding other minds*, pp. 291–307. New York: Oxford University Press.

42. Uzefovsky, F., Shaleve, I., Israel, S., Edelman, S., Raz, Y., Mankuta, D., Knafo-Noam, A., and Ebstein, R. P. (2015). Oxytocin receptor and vasopressin receptor 1a genes are respectively associated with emotional and cognitive empathy. *Hormones and Behavior* 67, 60–65.

43. Palgi, S., Klein, E., and Shamay-Tsoory, S. (2016). The role of oxytocin in empathy PTSD. *Psychological Trauma: Theory, Research, Practice, and Policy* 1, 70–75.

44. Almeida, P. R., Seixas, M. J., Ferreira-Santos, F., Vieira, J. B., Paiva, T. O., Moreira, P. S., and Costa, P. (2015). Empathic, moral, and antisocial outcomes associated with distinct components of psychopathy in healthy individuals: A Triarchic model approach. *Personality and Individual Differences* 85, 205–11.

45. Decety, J., Chen, C., Harenski, C., and Keihl, K. A. (2013). An fMRI study of affective perspective taking in individuals with psychopathy: Imagining another in pain does not evoke empathy. *Frontiers in Human Neuroscience* 7, Article 489, 1–12.

46. Blair, R. J. R. (2007). The amygdala and ventromedial prefrontal cortex in morality and psychopathy. *Trends in Cognitive Sciences* 11 (9), 387–92; Blair, R. J. R. (2010). Psychopathy, frustration, and reactive aggression: The role of ventromedial prefrontal cortex. *British Journal of Psychology* 101, 383–99.

47. Marsh, A. A., Finger, E. C., Fowler, K. A., Jurkowitz, I. T. N., Schechter, J. C., Yu, H. H., Pine, D. S., and Blair, R. J. R. (2011). Reduced amygdala-orbitofrontal connectivity during moral judgments in youths with disruptive behavior disorders and psychopathic traits. *Psychiatry Research: Neuroimaging* 194, 279–86.

48. Luckhurst, C., Hatfiled, E., and Gelvin-Smith, C. (2017). Capacity for empathy and emotional contagion in those with psychopathic personalities. *Interpersona* 11 (1), 70–91.

6. Where Is Religion in Empathy?

1. See Zinn, H. (2003). *A people's history of the United States 1492–present*. New York: HarperCollins Publishers, p. 14.

2. Schiff, S. (September 7, 2015). "The witches of Salem." *The New Yorker*. http://www.newyorker.com/magazine/2015/09/07/the-witches-of-salem.

3. See issue 33 of *Christian History* (1992). "Christianity and the Civil War." http://www.christianitytoday.com/history/issues/issue-33; see also Morrison, L. R. (1980). The religious defense of American slavery before 1830. *Journal of Religious Thought* 37, 16–29.

4. Meager, D. (2007). "Slavery—The abolitionist movement." *Cross Way* (105). http://archive.churchsociety.org/crossway/documents/Cway_105_Slavery Abolitionism.pdf.

5. Peter Nabokov's book *Native American Testimony* (New York: Penguin, 1991) provides moving first-person accounts by American Indians that cover five hundred years of history in the United States country.

6. Pinker, S. (2011). *The better angels of our nature: Why violence has declined*. New York: Viking.

7. Daalder, I. H. (December 1, 1998). "Decision to intervene: How the war in Bosnia ended." https://www.brookings.edu/articles/decision-to-intervene -how-the-war-in-bosnia-ended; Borger, J. (April 4, 2012). "Bosnian war 20 years on: Peace holds but conflict continues to haunt." *The Guardian*. https:// www.theguardian.com/world/2012/apr/04/bosnian-war-20-years-on.

8. Conaway, C. (2016). Shadows in the golden land. *Moment Magazine* 41 (5), 47–55.

9. Jeong, M. (2017). Strangers in their own land. *Moment Magazine* 42 (5), 37–43.

10. Kimball, C. (2008). *When religion becomes evil*. New York: Harper.

11. Harris, S. (2005). *The end of faith: Religion, terror, and the future of reason*. New York: W. W. Norton.

12. WWBT NBC12. (March 31, 2014). "KKK leader: We don't hate people because of their race." http://www.nbc12.com/story/25034656/kkk -leader-we-dont-hate-people-because-of-their-race.

13. Creech, J. (n.d.). "What Does the Bible Say About Homosexuality?" https://www.hrc.org/resources/what-does-the-bible-say-about-homo sexuality; The organization Soulforce (http://www.soulforce.org) has a great deal of information as well.

14. Hutcherson, K. (December 1, 2015). "A brief history of anti-abortion violence." *CNN*. http://www.cnn.com/2015/11/30/us/anti-abortion-violence /index.html.

15. Dewey, C. (March 31, 2017). "GOP lawmaker: The Bible says 'if a man will not work, he shall not eat.'" *Washington Post*. https://washingtonpost .com/news/wonk.wp/2017/03/31/gop-lawmaker-the-bible-says-the -unemployed-shall-not-eat/?utm_term=.53e61939b00.

16. The Founders' Constitution. (2000). "Amendment I (Religion)." http://press-pubs.uchicago.edu/founders/documents/amendI_religions49. html.

17. Batson, C. D. (1983). Sociobiology and the role of religion in promot- ing prosocial behavior: An alternative view. *Journal of Personality and Social Psychology* 45 (6), 1380–85.

18. Duriez, B. (2004). Are religious people nicer people? Taking a closer look at the religion-empathy relationship. *Mental Health, Religion, and Culture* 7 (3), 249–54.

19. Huber, J. T., and MacDonald, D. A. (2012). An investigation of the relations between altruism, empathy, and spirituality. *Journal of Humanistic Psychology* 52 (2), 206–21.

20. Alma, H. A. (2008). Self-development as a spiritual process: The role of empathy and imagination in finding spiritual orientation. *Pastoral Psychology* 57, 59–63.

21. Hobson, N. M., and Inzlicht, M. (2016). Recognizing religion's dark side: Religious ritual increases antisociality and hinders self-control. *Behavioral and Brain Sciences* 39, 30–31; Hobson, N. M., Gino, F., Norton, M. I., and Inzlicht, M. (2017). When novel rituals impact intergroup bias: Evidence from economic games and neurophysiology. *Psychological Science*. https:// doi.org/10.17605/OSF.IO/NXAB7.

22. Brown, R. K., Kaiser, A., and Jackson, J. S. (2014). Worship discourse and white race-based policy attitudes. *Review of Religious Research* 56, 291– 312; Edgell, P., and Tranby, E. (2007). Religion influences on understand- ings of racial inequality in the United States. *Social Problems* 54 (2), 263–88; Hinojosa, V. J., and Park, J. Z. (2004). Religion and the paradox of racial inequality attitudes. *Journal for the Scientific Study of Religion* 42, 229–38.

23. Buber, M. (2010, originally published in English in 1937). *I and thou*. Mansfield Centre, CT: Martino Publishing.

24. The parable can be found in the Talmud, the record of Rabbinic teach- ings (Talmud Shabbat 31a).

7. Can We Have Empathy with Technology?

1. Campbell, S. W., and Park, Y. J. (2008). Social implications of mobile telephony: The rise of personal communication society. *Sociology Compass* 2 (2), 371–87; Ling, R. (2010). *New tech, new ties: How mobile communication is reshaping social cohesion.* Cambridge, MA: MIT Press.

2. Carrier, L. M., Spradlin, A., Bunce, J. P., and Rosen, L. D. (2015). Virtual empathy: Positive and negative impacts of going online upon empathy in young adults. *Computers in Human Behavior* 52, 39–48.

3. Zhao, J., Abrahamson, K., Anderson, J. G., Ha, S., and Widdows, R. (2013). Trust, empathy, social identity, and contribution of knowledge within patient online communities. *Behaviour & Information Technology* 32 (10), 1041–48.

4. Vervloet, M., van Dijk, L., Santen-Reestman, J., van Vlijmen, B., van Wingerden, P., Bouvy, M. L., and de Bakker, D. H. (2012). SMS reminders improve adherence to oral medication in type 2 diabetes patients who are real time electronically monitored. *International Journal of Medical Informatics* 81 (9), 594–604.

5. Patrick, K., Raab, F., Adams, M. A., Dillon, L., Zabinski, M., Rock, C. L., Griswold, W. G., and Norman, G. J. (2009). A text-massage-based intervention for weight loss: Randomized controlled trial. *Journal of Medical Internet Research* 11 (1), e1.

6. Konrath, S., Falk, E., Fuhrel-Forbis, A., Liu, M., Swain, J., Tolman, R., Cunningham, R., and Walton, M. (2015). Can text messages increase empathy and prosocial behavior? The development and initial validation of text to Connect. *PLoS ONE* 10 (9), e0137585.

7. Mills, K. L. (2014). Effects of internet use on the adolescent brain: Despite popular claims, experimental evidence remains scarce. *Science and Society* 18 (8), 385–87. Specifically, see p. 385 and Box 1 for the story on Socrates.

8. Mills 2014.

9. Spies Shapiro, L. A., and Margolin, G. (2014). Growing up wired: Social networking sites and adolescent psychosocial development. *Clinical Child and Family Psychology Review* 17 (1), 1–18.

10. Kross, E., Verduyn, P., Demiralp, E., Park, J., Lee, D. S., Lin, N., Shablack, H., Jonides, J., and Ybarra, O. (2013). Facebook use predicts declines in subjective well-being in young adults. *PLoS ONE* 8 (8), e69841.

11. Kelly, C. R., Grinband, J., and Hirsch, J. (2007). Repeated exposure to media violence is associated with diminished response in an inhibitory frontolimbic network. *PLoS ONE* 12, e1268; Gentile, D. A., Swing, E. L., Anderson, C. A., Rinker, D., and Thomas, K. M. (2016). Differential neural recruitment during violent video game play in violent- and nonviolent-game players. *Psychology of Popular Media Culture* 5 (1), 39–51.

12. Szycik, G. R., Mohammadi, B., Münte, T. F., and te Wildt, B. T. (2017). Lack of evidence that neural empathic responses are blunted in excessive users of violent video games: An fMRI study. *Frontiers in Psychology.* https://doi.org/10.3389/fpsyg.2017.00174

13. Gabbiadini, A., Riva, P., Andrighetto, L., Volpato, C., and Bushman, B. J. (2016). Acting like a tough guy: Violent-sexist video games, identification with game characters, masculine beliefs, and empathy for female violence victims. *PLoS ONE* 11 (4), 1–14.

14. U.S. Department of Education. (2015). *Student reports of bullying and cyber-bullying: Results from the 2013 school crime supplement to the national crime victimization survey.* Washington, DC: National Center for Education Statistics.

15. Joliffe, D., and Farrington, D. P. (2006). Examining the relationship between low empathy and bullying. *Aggressive Behavior* 32, 540–50; Ang, R. P., and Goh, D. H. (2010). Cyberbullying among adolescents: The role of affective and cognitive empathy, and gender. *Child Psychiatry and Human Development* 41, 387–97; Renati, R., Berrone, C., and Zanetti, M. A. (2012). Morally disengaged and unempathic: Do cyberbullies fit these definitions? An exploratory study. *Cyberpsychology, Behavior, and Social Networking* 15 (8), 1–8; Del Rey, R., Lazuras, L., Casas, J. A., Barkoukis, V., Ortega-Ruiz, R., and Tsorbatzoudis, H. (2016). Does empathy predict (cyber)bullying perpetration, and how do age, gender and nationality affect this relationship? *Learning and Individual Differences* 45, 275–81.

16. Joliffe, D., and Farrington, D. P. (2011). Is low empathy related to bullying after controlling for individual and social background variables? *Journal of Adolescence* 34, 59–71.

17. Bazelon, E. (2013). *Sticks and stones: Defeating the culture of bullying and rediscovering the power of character and empathy.* New York: Random House.

18. Phillips, W. (2015). *This is why we can't have nice things: Mapping the relationship between online trolling and mainstream culture.* Cambridge, MA: MIT Press.

19. See Phillips 2015, p. 26.

20. Sest, N., and March, E. (2017). Constructing the cyber-troll: Psychopathy, sadism and empathy. *Personality and Individual Differences* 119, 69–72.

21. Hauslohner, A. (July 20, 2017). "Muslim running for U.S. Senate praised the Founding Fathers. Then the diatribes began." *Washington Post.* https://www.washingtonpost.com/news/post-nation/wp/2017/07/20/muslim-running-for-u-s-senate-praised-the-founding-fathers-then-the-diatribes-began. For a local view of this, see Roberts, L. (July 18, 2017). "AZ Senate candidate under attack for being a Muslim." *Arizona Republic,* Section SR, p. Z8.

22. Cook, B. (March 4, 2014). "The toll of Twitter." *The Shakerite.* https://shakerite.com/opinion/2014/03/04/twitter-and-empathy.

23. The research in Gentile et al. 2016 supports this point. In addition, there are books that draw on the scientific evidence that our brains are not made to deeply process multiple inputs of information at the same time. Several books that cover this are Medina, J. (2008). *Brain rules.* Seattle, WA: Pear Press; Klingberg, T. (2009). *The overflowing brain: Information overload and the limits of working memory.* New York: Oxford University Press; Levitin, D. J. (2014). *The organized mind: Thinking straight in the age of information overload.* New York: Penguin Random House. The Levitin book offers a lot of suggestions on how to deal with today's information overload.

24. Sean Spicer, who at the time held the position of White House press secretary, confirmed that the president's Tweets were official policy at a press conference on June 6, 2017. Jenkins, A. (June 6, 2017). "Sean Spicer says President Trump considers his tweets 'official' White House statements." *Time.* http://time.com/4808270/sean-spicer-donald-trump-twitter -statements.

25. Scott, P. (May 2, 2017). "Donald Trump's Twitter habit tells us a lot about his first 100 days as a president." *The Telegraph.* http://www.telegraph .co.uk/news/2017/04/27/donald-trumps-twitter-habits-tell-us-lot-first -100-days-president.

26. Langer, G. (July 17, 2017). "Public to Trump: Lay off the Twitter (poll)." *ABC News.* http://abcnews.go.com/Politics/public-trump-lay-off-twitter-poll /story?id=48641500.

8. Social Empathy—Making the World a Better Place

1. Segal, E. A., Gerdes, K. E., Lietz, C. A., Wagaman, M. A., and Geiger, J. M. (2017). *Assessing empathy.* New York: Columbia University Press.

2. This is from early analysis of data collected under a National Science Foundation grant (no. 1530847), *Promoting empathy and collaborative decision making for natural resource management using a computer-mediated scenario.*

3. Iacoboni, M., Molnar-Szakacs, I., Gallese, V., Buccino, G., Mazziotta, J. C., and Rizzolatti, G. (2005). Grasping the intentions of others with one's own mirror neuron system. *PLoS Biology* 3 (3), 529–35.

4. Lamm, C., Nusbaum, H. C., Meltzoff, A. N., and Decety, J. (2007). What are you feeling? Using functional magnetic resonance imaging to assess the modulation of sensory and affective responses during empathy for pain. *PLoS ONE* 12 (e1292), 1–16.

5. The image and story of the child in Aleppo, Syria, can be found in Larimer, S., and Bever, L. (August 18, 2016). "The stunned, bloodied face of 5-year-old Omran Daqneesh sums up the horror of Aleppo." *Washington Post*. https://www.washingtonpost.com/news/worldviews/wp/2016/08/17/the-stunned-bloodied-face-of-a-child-survivor-sums-up-the-horror-of-aleppo.

6. Wagaman, M. A. (2011). Social empathy as a framework for adolescent empowerment. *Journal of Social Service Research* 37, 278–93.

7. Davidson, R. J., and Begley, S. (2012). *The emotional life of your brain*. New York: Hudson Street Press; Eagleman, D. (2015). *The brain: The story of you*. New York: Pantheon Books.

8. Pascual-Leone, A., Amedi, A., Fregni, F., and Merabet, L. B. (2005). The plastic human brain cortex. *Annual Review of Neuroscience* 28, 377–401.

9. Merabet, L. B., and Pascual-Leone, A. (2010). Neural reorganization following sensory loss: The opportunity of change. *National Review of Neuroscience* 11 (1), 44–52; Ortiz-Terán, L., Ortiz, T., Perez, D. L., Aragón, J. I., Diez, I., Pascual-Leone, A., and Sepulcre, J. (2016). Brain plasticity in blind subjects centralizes beyond the modal cortices. *Frontiers in Systems Neuroscience*. https://doi.org/10.3389/fnsys.2016.00061; Ortiz-Terán, L., Diez, I., Ortiz, T., Perez, D. L., Aragón, J. I., Costumero, V., Pascual-Leone, A., El Fakhri, G., and Sepulcre, J. (2017). Brain circuit-gene expression relationships and neuroplasticity of multisensory cortices in blind children. *Proceedings of the National Academy of Sciences* 114 (26), 6830–35.

10. Department of Health and Human Services. (2016). *Temporary Assistance for Needy Families program: Eleventh report to Congress*. Washington, DC: Author.

11. Congressional Research Service. (2017). *Temporary Assistance for Needy Families (TANF): Size of the population eligible for receiving cash assistance*. Washington, DC: Author.

12. On Jeb Bush echoing Mitt Romney about government support for the poor as "free stuff," see Sullivan, S. (September 24, 2015). "Jeb Bush: Win black voters with aspirations, not 'free stuff.' " *Washington Post*. https://www.washingtonpost.com/news/post-politics/wp/2015/09/24/jeb-bush-win-black-voters-with-aspiration-not-free-stuff; Benen, S. (September 25, 2015). "Echoing Romney, Jeb reflects on black voters, 'free stuff.' " *MSNBC*. http://www.msnbc.com/rachel-maddow-show/echoing-romney-jeb-reflects-black-voters-free-stuff.

13. To read the text of Paul Ryan explaining his mistake in using terms "makers and takers," see Ryan, P. (March 23, 2016). "Full text: Speaker Ryan on the state of American politics." http://www.speaker.gov/press-release/full-text-speaker-ryan-state-american-politics.

14. U.S. Department of Health and Human Services. (January 18, 2018). "U.S. federal poverty guidelines used to determine financial eligibility for certain federal programs." https://aspe.hhs.gov/poverty-guidelines.

15. SNAP data are available at https://www.fns.usda.gov/pd/supplemental-nutrition-assistance-program-snap.

16. Child Trends. (2016). *Children in poverty: Indicators of child and youth well-being*. Bethesda, MD: Author.

17. White House. (2008). *Fact sheet: Bipartisan growth package will help protect our nation's economic health*. Washington, DC: Office of the President of the United States.

18. SNAP data are available at https://www.fns.usda.gov/pd/supplemental-nutrition-assistance-program-snap.

19. Romig, K., and Sherman, A. (2016). *Social Security keeps 22 million Americans out of poverty*. Washington, DC: Center on Budget and Policy Priorities.

20. Steuerle, C. E., and Quakenbush, C. (2015). *Social Security and Medicare lifetime benefits and taxes*. Washington, DC: Urban Institute.

21. Congressional Joint Commission on Taxation. (January 30, 2017). *Estimates of federal tax expenditures for fiscal years 2016–2020*. Washington, DC: Author.

22. You can read Tarana Burke's explanation of the Me Too movement on her organization's website at http://justbeinc.wixsite.com/justbeinc/the-me-too-movement-cmml.

Epilogue

1. I have been working on this three-tiered model for years. For earlier versions, see Segal, E. A. (2011). Social empathy: A model built on empathy, contextual understanding, and social responsibility that promotes social justice. *Journal of Social Service Research* 37 (3), 266–277; Segal, E. A. (2007). Social empathy: A new paradigm to address poverty. *Journal of Poverty* 11 (3), 65–81.

2. Peace Learner. (March 14, 2016). "Privilege walk lesson plan." https://peacelearner.org/2016/03/14/privilege-walk-lesson-plan.

3. Levitt, P. (2015). *Artifacts and allegiances: How museums put the nation and world on display*. Oakland: University of California Press.

4. Levitt 2015, p. 8.

5. Segal, E. A., Gerdes, K. E., Stromwall, L., and Napoli, M. (2010). Privilege through the lens of empathy. *Reflections: Narratives of Professional Helping* 16 (1), 79–87; 79–80.

6. The Institute for Justice and Reconciliation was developed following the work of the South African Truth and Reconciliation Commission (http://www.justice.gov.za/trc/index.html) to promote such human-centered ways to bring about socioeconomic justice. More information on the institute can be found at http://www.ijr.org.za/about-us. Another source is the International Justice Resource Center (http://www.ijrcenter.org/cases-before -national-courts/truth-and-reconciliation-commissions).

Index